Best Practices For Managing BPI Projects

Six Steps To Success

Gina Abudi • Yusuf Abudi

J.ROSS

PUBLISHING

ISBN-13: 978-1-60427-096-9

Printed and bound in the U.S.A. Printed on acid-free paper.

10 9 8 7 6 5 4 3 2 1

Library of Congress Cataloging-in-Publication Data

Abudi, Gina.
　　Best practices for managing BPI projects : six steps to success / by Gina
Abudi and Yusuf Abudi.
　　　　pages cm
　　　　Includes index.
　　　　ISBN 978-1-60427-096-9 (hardcover : alk. paper) 1. Reengineering
(Management) 2. Organizational effectiveness. 3. Business planning. 4. Project
management. I. Abudi, Yusuf, 1964- II. Title.
　　　　HD58.87.A28 2015
　　　　658.4'063—dc23
　　　　　　　　　　　　2014047498

Direct all inquiries to J. Ross Publishing, Inc., 300 S. Pine Island Rd., Suite 305, Plantation, FL 33324.

Phone: (954) 727-9333
Fax: (561) 892-0700
Web: www.jrosspub.com

ACKNOWLEDGMENTS

I would like to thank my mother, Fay Rusch Schmidt, who has supported me through the writing of this book and in my endeavors as an independent consultant. She has always been there for me and I can't imagine that I would be where I am without her. Her undying support, love, and encouragement has pushed me through many challenges. I'd also like to thank another important person in my life, my husband and co-author, Yusuf Abudi. He has supported me in more ways than he can know.

Thank you also to Mike Goehring who shared a few stories with us for this book. He is a colleague and a dear friend.

Additionally, a big thanks to Drew Gierman, our publisher, without whom this book would not have been possible. And last, but certainly not least, a thank you to all the editors and others at J. Ross Publishing who helped to get this book out the door.

Gina

I would like to thank my parents, Khalil Abudi and Clotilde Abudi, who have always supported me in my efforts. They pushed me to be all I can be and encouraged me every step of the way. My father, Khalil Abudi, was of great assistance in taking a preliminary review of the book for us. Thank you to my wife and co-author, Gina Abudi. She supports me in my efforts and is my biggest fan. Also, thank you to my daughter, Nadia Abudi. I am and will remain proud of who she is and what she has become.

Furthermore, I second Gina's thank you to Drew Gierman, all the editors, and others at J. Ross Publishing who have helped us get this book published.

Yusuf

TABLE OF CONTENTS

FOREWORD

This is a comprehensive and straightforward book on managing business process improvement (BPI) projects. But why a book on managing a BPI project? What makes this type of project so different from any other type of project?

Perhaps the most significant difference between a traditional project and a BPI project is that BPI projects typically cross every boundary within the organization—vertically down through the organizational management structure from the Chairman and CEO to the part-time staff employee, horizontally across all departments from purchasing and product development, to sales and marketing and customer service, and beyond the internal organizational boundaries to stakeholders, such as customers and vendors.

The second most significant difference is that BPI projects are generally in the "spotlight" and are highly visible to management and senior executives. If the project is unsuccessful (fails to deliver the anticipated results), the damage to the business can be significant and the responsibility for the damage can fall on the project manager.

A third important difference is that, by definition, a BPI project involves change of some kind, and most all employees resist change in the way they work, fearing that they will be unable to adapt to the change, or in the worst case, they will find themselves replaced by an automated process or an employee with better or different skills.

A fourth difference is that, while most projects have a well-defined beginning and end, process improvement projects are monitored, measured, and continuously improved on an ongoing basis, requiring the ongoing involvement of the project manager and the continuous improvement team.

In addition to the skills required to manage a traditional project management project, including planning, scheduling, and budgeting, the challenges of managing BPI projects require a general understanding of what is involved in a BPI project and very strong leadership and communications skills. The complexity of BPI projects, the need to socialize the project to get buy-in from a broad range of stakeholders with disparate and often conflicting interests, and the need to facilitate collaboration across cultural interests and concerns, differentiates BPI projects from most other projects. In addition to the basic skills required to manage a traditional project, BPI project managers will need to (1) understand and apply the basic principles of BPI, (2) understand and apply the principles of change management, (3) know how to build and present a business case for the BPI project, (4) facilitate and manage a stakeholder analysis, (5) scope the boundaries of the project, and (6) manage conflict resolution.

The authors, Gina and Yusuf Abudi, two well-known experts in this field, have created a must-read book for any project manager interested in, or already involved in, managing a BPI project. It builds on the principles of traditional project management and extends and applies those principles to a BPI project in a simple step-by-step manner, providing the rationale, tools, and techniques required to manage a BPI project.

Celia Wolf
Founder/CEO/Publisher, BPTrends
Founder/Managing Director, BPTrends Associates
Newton, MA

PREFACE

While there are a number of project management books on the market and a number of books on business processes, there is no guide for best practices on managing business process improvement (BPI) projects—and certainly not with such a focus on the people-side of such initiatives. BPI projects are some of the most challenging projects undertaken by project managers. This book will provide the reader with a six-step approach to managing challenging BPI projects to enable increased success.

Consider this book a project manager's or project team leader's step-by-step guide to effectively and successfully managing BPI projects. This book is not meant to be a review of the Project Management Institute *Project Management Body of Knowledge (PMBOK®) Guide*, nor is it a study guide for the Project Management Professional (PMP®) certification exam. The reader does not have to be a PMP® to utilize this book. It assumes the reader is already managing projects at some level and would like to improve their skills and learn a few tricks and tips to make managing BPI projects a smoother and less stressful process. Some information included—such as information about project charters and scope statements—may seem unnecessary for individuals who are regularly managing projects, but a refresher may provide some new ideas for readers.

This book provides best practices and processes for:

- Socializing the project to get buy-in and support
- Engaging stakeholders throughout the BPI project
- Documenting current (*as-is*) processes, evaluating *could-be* options, and designing *to-be* processes

- Evaluating success against set metrics while capturing and utilizing lessons learned

Additionally, it provides a focus on the people skills needed in order to keep stakeholders and the team engaged, even in the face of adversity and challenges.

When the project manager, in collaboration with the project sponsor, takes the time to effectively plan for BPI projects early on and to regularly communicate with and engage stakeholders throughout the project initiative, chances of BPI project success increases overall. And, after all, isn't success the goal of *every* project manager? I want to emphasize that working in collaboration with the sponsor in planning BPI projects from the beginning is crucial because that level of leadership support is essential. There are organizations that believe unless you are actually *working* on the tasks of the project, nothing is being accomplished. For these organizations, early planning is akin to doing nothing. The authors can tell you that they have invested significant time with a number of clients to discuss the benefit of planning early on, before the team actually begins to work on tasks associated with the project.

Through our work with a variety of clients, we have found that BPI projects often fail when the client neglects to get stakeholders involved as soon as possible and does not keep them engaged and involved throughout the BPI project. Even if a project manager gets a BPI project complete on time and within a set budget, the project is *not* successful if the stakeholders are not happy with the end result. No project team can redesign a process, or develop a new process, in isolation, or with just a few individuals from within the organization. It is essential for the project team to get a variety of individuals involved from *all* levels of the organization that will be impacted by the BPI project—not solely at the management level.

This book will focus more on the critical, or soft, skills side of managing BPI projects, while touching on the technical aspects of the job. Those project managers with strong *people skills* will find that they are better able to engage and involve key stakeholders in BPI projects because they have developed strong relationships. The most successful project managers have the ability to influence and effectively communicate throughout the organization—at all levels. They understand the challenges others face in getting the work done and are able to align their BPI projects to those challenges. Truly, we have seen some great project managers whose people skills are far better than their technical project management skills. These project managers know how to guide and influence others to accomplish the technical aspects of the project while they focus on engaging the people.

AUDIENCE

This book is intended for project and program managers, process improvement specialists, business analysts, business line managers, and business unit managers. Manufacturing specialists and Six Sigma professionals will also find value in this book, as they are often tasked with improving processes within the organization. Students of project management and process improvement will find this book a great resource while in the classroom and outside of the classroom. Individual contributors tasked with leading process improvement initiatives in smaller organizations or in their own work areas will obtain value from the book—helping them to manage such initiatives effectively. Additionally, executives and other leaders within global or national organizations will find this book of value to understand and communicate the importance of facilitating regular evaluation of processes within the organization to ensure continued success in a competitive and global marketplace. Often when executives and other leaders understand the complexity of managing BPI projects, they are better able to support BPI project teams. This support is essential to BPI project team success.

Each chapter shares a variety of stories of both successes and challenges with BPI projects. Upon finishing this book, the reader will have increased confidence and comfort, along with a reduction in stress and frustration in managing BPI projects, regardless of the complexity of the project.

CHAPTER OVERVIEW

The chapters in this book build upon each other. The first few chapters are overview chapters that set the stage for diving into the details of the six phases that are discussed in Chapters 4 through 9. The chapters should be read in order. Chapter 10 provides information on how to ensure continued evaluation of processes within the organization and Chapters 11 and 12 cover essential additional people skills necessary for project managers when leading BPI projects.

Chapter 1: Introduction to Managing Business Process Improvement Projects

Chapter 1 will provide an introduction to BPI projects—focusing on understanding the challenges involved in such initiatives and how to ensure alignment with everything else that may be occurring within the organization. In Chapter 1 we'll also explore how past experiences with BPI projects will impact the current BPI project and how the project manager will need to manage those past experiences.

Chapter 2: Developing Your Initial Plan to Get Started

Chapter 2 will focus on how to develop a high-level project plan to get started on the BPI project and the components involved in such a plan. Of importance to the project manager in these early stages is partnering with the sponsor(s) of the project. Building strong working relationships is essential. Tips and best practices on how to build and maintain working relationships will be shared in Chapter 2 and throughout the book.

Chapter 3: Taking a Project Management Approach to BPI Projects

Chapter 3 will take an overview look at a six-phase approach to managing BPI projects. Along with looking at various components of the project plan, the focus in this chapter will be on working with stakeholders, getting the project team motivated and engaged, and developing the change management framework. Chapter 3 will also discuss the importance of using technology in order to effectively manage complex BPI projects and to more efficiently manage interactions and communications with stakeholders.

Chapter 4: Understanding and Socializing the BPI Project

Chapter 4 will focus on the importance of socializing BPI projects. From a variety of options for socializing the project, to how to ensure regular and consistent communications that work for the stakeholders, the reader will learn how to keep individuals within the organization engaged and committed to the project throughout the project life cycle.

Chapter 5: Analyzing Current Business Processes

Chapter 5 will cover best practices for gathering data, analyzing, and validating current business processes. The value of *quick wins* to keep stakeholders engaged and encouraged, along with how to present BPI project findings to the sponsor will be reviewed.

Chapter 6: Redesigning Business Processes

Redesigning business processes, discussed in Chapter 6, requires input from a variety of individuals to ensure that the best *could-be* processes are developed. A variety of ways for ensuring effective, redesigned processes will be shared along with how to effectively facilitate process mapping workshops. The reader will be presented with a variety of ways to narrow down *could-be* options to develop viable alternatives for refined or new processes for review by key stakeholders, along with best practices for developing and finalizing the *to-be* process.

Chapter 7: Implementing Redesigned Business Processes

Chapter 7 will focus on addressing the challenges and risks associated with implementing redesigned business processes. Effective use of pilot groups to test the redesigned process will be discussed in detail along with how to use sub-teams to ensure pilot groups have the support they need to be successful during implementation.

Chapter 8: Rolling Out the Redesigned Process Organization-wide

Once the project manager is ready to lead the roll out of the finalized process organization-wide, it is essential to have a change management plan in place, based on the complexity of the process being rolled out. In addition to change management planning, communications around the new process, along with the importance of training, will be covered in Chapter 8.

Chapter 9: Evaluating the Success of the BPI Project

Chapter 9 will focus on evaluating the success of the BPI project and, specifically, if the launch of the new process achieved the goals it was set out to accomplish. Chapter 9 will provide best practices to evaluate BPI projects against set metrics and stakeholder expectations in much more detail than simply checking in with the stakeholders using the newly implemented process.

Chapter 10: Continued Evaluation Best Practices

The best organizations continuously evaluate their business processes. Chapter 10 will provide the reader with an understanding of the value and benefit in establishing and promoting a continuous improvement culture within the organization, as well as how to establish and effectively engage cross-functional teams in such efforts.

Chapter 11: The People-side of Change Management

Often project managers will plan for how to manage changes that occur to the project, but neglect considering the people-side of change. Chapter 11 will provide best practices for managing the people-side of change. This includes understanding the personal and workplace-related impacts that affect how individuals will perceive and react to change. In Chapter 11, best practices will be shared for engaging stakeholders throughout the organization in supporting change.

Chapter 12: Managing a Virtual and Diverse Process Improvement Project Team

In today's world, most project managers will work on and/or lead virtual or remote project teams. This adds additional complexity to already challenging BPI projects. Chapter 12 will focus on appreciating diversity on the project team and best practices for ensuring effectiveness of the team when the members are not co-located.

In summary, this book will remain a valuable resource to the reader for years to come. Project managers and others will increase their knowledge, comfort, confidence, and expertise in managing BPI projects regardless of the size and complexity of the initiative.

Happy Reading!

ABOUT THE AUTHORS

 **Gina Abudi**, MBA, has over 20 years of consulting experience in helping businesses develop and implement strategies around projects, processes, and people. She is President of Abudi Consulting Group, LLC, and has led a number of projects including process improvement projects, change management initiatives, facilitation of team meetings and executive strategy sessions, and development and evaluation of PMOs and Centers of Excellence. Gina works closely with a variety of clients to develop and deliver customized workshops, seminars, and training programs to meet long term strategic needs. She is an adjunct faculty member at Granite State College (NH), teaching in the masters of project management and masters of leadership graduate degree programs. Gina is a professional speaker and keynote at a variety of conferences, forums, and corporate and industry events on a variety of management, leadership, and project management topics. She is a professional member of the National Speakers Association (NSA). She is co-author of *The Complete Idiot's Guide to Best Practices for Small Business* (Alpha Books, 2011) and contributing author of *Project Pain Reliever: A Just-In-Time Handbook for Anyone Managing Projects* (J. Ross Publishing, 2011), edited by Dave Garrett, CEO, http://www.projectmanagment.com and http://www.projects atwork.com.

Gina serves as President of the PMI® Massachusetts Bay Chapter Board of Directors; prior to that she served on the Project Management Institute's Global Corporate Council as Chair of the Leadership Team. Gina has been honored as one of the Power 50 from PMI®—one of the 50 most influential executives in project management, working to move the profession forward. Gina received her MBA from Simmons Graduate School of Management.

Yusuf Abudi, Founder and CEO of Abudi Consulting Group, LLC, has over 20 years' experience in process management, IT strategy, and business intelligence. He works with a variety of organizations in evaluating processes and developing processes where none exist. By helping organizations understand their current processes, redesigning, or developing to fill gaps, increases in efficiencies have been realized. He has developed Intranet portals for a variety of organizations to help them better share information on processes and best practices used throughout the organization. Through the use of technology, Yusuf works with clients to more easily respond to changes in the business and in their industries through effective reporting. Additionally, Yusuf has created a number of business applications to enable both universities and pharmaceutical companies to better manage their initiatives and business. Prior to founding the Abudi Consulting Group, Yusuf was Director of Application Development and IT Services at Boston University. Yusuf is also chief photographer for Abudi Photography, LLC, focusing on fine arts photography in architecture, nature, and wildlife.

 Web Added Value™

This book has free material available for download from the
Web Added Value™ resource center at *www.jrosspub.com*

At J. Ross Publishing we are committed to providing today's professional with practical, hands-on tools that enhance the learning experience and give readers an opportunity to apply what they have learned. That is why we offer free ancillary materials available for download on this book and all participating Web Added Value™ publications. These online resources may include interactive versions of material that appears in the book or supplemental templates, worksheets, models, plans, case studies, proposals, spreadsheets and assessment tools, among other things. Whenever you see the WAV™ symbol in any of our publications, it means bonus materials accompany the book and are available from the Web Added Value Download Resource Center at www.jrosspub.com.

Downloads for *Best Practices for Managing BPI Projects: Six Steps to Success* include a variety of relevant questionnaires, surveys, and templates, as well as a threaded case study showing the concepts applied to a real-life project.

INTRODUCTION TO MANAGING BUSINESS PROCESS IMPROVEMENT PROJECTS

We often hear from clients that they are challenged with effectively managing business process improvement (BPI) initiatives. It isn't even the size of the initiative that troubles and worries project managers, but simply the fact that a BPI project will likely be quite visible and a bit contentious within the organization is worrisome for project managers, and will likely entail many challenges. As one client, a senior project manager in his organization with 30 years of experience told us, "I cringe each time I am assigned a BPI project! I just know I am going to have a difficult time dealing with the stakeholders and keeping the team engaged." And yet another client noted that, "The most difficult project I have ever managed was a business process improvement project—and I only had to work across two divisions in the organization! I felt as if all my experience in managing projects just didn't prepare me well enough to manage a business process improvement project."

The goal of this book is to prepare project managers, at all skill levels, to manage BPI projects more effectively and efficiently and with less frustration and stress. This book is not intended to be about the details of process notation and diagramming processes or other technical aspects of business process management; rather, it is intended to help project managers who are already managing projects to learn best practices for managing BPI projects. BPI project teams will always include experts in process notations and the fine details of diagramming

1

processes. This book is to support project managers who need some best practices and want to generally improve in how to effectively manage and oversee BPI projects.

Follow the best practice steps provided throughout this book—from socializing the BPI initiative prior to getting started, through evaluating and measuring the success of the BPI project after implementation—in order to increase the success of BPI projects overall. This book will also provide information on the value and benefit from focusing on the people-side of change management, and engaging and motivating diverse project teams. A project manager's ability to manage the people-side of projects—whether that entails helping stakeholders embrace change, or getting a virtual or remote project team engaged and motivated to contribute to the project goals—is absolutely essential to the success of a BPI project. Most good project managers know how to technically manage their projects. Frankly, that is the easier part of the project manager's role. Likely the challenge project managers face in leading successful BPI projects is in influencing those around them to help achieve that success. Given that, this book will focus on the processes and procedures and important leadership skills needed in order to increase the chances of BPI project success. This book is chock full of best practices necessary to enable project managers to increase their comfort level and confidence in managing such challenging projects.

Let's define two terms that will be utilized throughout this book:

Project: A project has a defined start date and a defined end date. It is undertaken to accomplish something—whether to create a new product or service or improve a process within the organization. A project may also be launched in order to hold an annual customer appreciation event.

Process: A process is an ongoing operation or work effort with no end period. Processes have the following characteristics:
- A starting point of the process and an end point
- Defined users of the process
- Business rules that govern the process
- A link to other processes within the business

Let's look at an example of how a process becomes a project.

An ongoing process for the Human Resource (HR) department is the processing of external training invoices prior to sending them to Accounts Payable. Human Resource's simplified process in place to validate invoices might include:

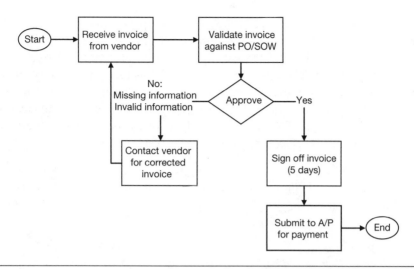

Figure 1.1   Invoice against purchase order validation process

As can be seen in Figure 1.1, when an invoice is received from a vendor, HR's task is to validate that invoice against the Purchase Order or Statement of Work. This validation includes confirming the invoice amount and other relevant information, such as dates of service and items purchased. If all checks out accurately, the invoice is approved and HR signs off on it and submits it to Accounts Payable for processing. This ends the process.

However, if the invoice is inaccurate, the process does not end. HR contacts the vendor for a corrected invoice. A corrected invoice is sent to HR by the vendor, HR validates the invoice and, if now accurate, signs off on it and sends it to Accounts Payable for processing. This is a process as defined earlier.

Now, let's assume that Human Resources wants to change how they process invoices for payment. They would start a BPI project to analyze the current process to improve upon/redefine and implement a new process. The project objective would be to implement a new procedure for processing and validating invoices from contractor trainers for payment. In this example, the goal is to reduce the time to submit to Accounts Payable from five days to three days of receipt from vendor.

Once Human Resources accomplishes this project, the project terminates and an ongoing work effort—a new procedure for processing invoices from vendors—takes over.

Many project managers often assume that if a high-level project sponsor initiates a BPI project, it will be successful. If only that held true 100% of the time!

While certainly executive or senior leadership support is essential for any BPI project; this support alone does not suffice. BPI projects can get total support at the executive level; but if the employees (non-leader stakeholders) do not support the effort, it is destined to fail. After all, it is these employees who are most likely impacted by the BPI project and must work with whatever is implemented. Their support is essential. The organization alone cannot initiate, nor successfully conclude, a BPI project; it must rely on the people within the organization in order to accomplish effective and successful BPI projects.

A national manufacturing client launched a second attempt of a BPI project without considering the following two major mistakes made during the first attempt:

- *Lack of engaging those on the manufacturing floor (the stakeholders closest to the process) in the redesign of the process, which caused the process to be redesigned in a way that did not work for those doing the work and, in fact, took longer to complete tasks than under the previous process*
- *Launching the initiative during the "busy season," thereby causing those on the manufacturing floor to miss deadlines*

Additionally, the project manager assigned to the BPI project focused on those stakeholders who were in his location only and did not bother to reach out to stakeholders at the company's other manufacturing sites. Because he did not do so, he neglected to learn that what works at one site does not necessarily work at another.

Attempt two of the project also failed. Attempt three is being planned currently. What a scary endeavor! A new project manager has been assigned and as her first task, before the project is officially launched, she will be reaching out to all stakeholders at all sites to begin to build relationships and smooth the path to a successful BPI project. She knows that unless something different is done, the third attempt cannot possibly be a success. The first step in relationship building will be acknowledging the errors of the past and explaining what will be done differently this time.

THE VALUE OF EVALUATING BUSINESS PROCESSES

Business process management is a focus on improving the performance of the organization by improving how the work is done within the organization. Effectively, it is looking at processes and procedures for accomplishing the day-to-day work of the organization, which enables the organization to meet its goals.

This might include how sales are made to customers, how products are manufactured or sourced, and how clients are invoiced for services provided. Individuals who focus on business process management regularly evaluate how the work is getting accomplished and look for better ways to get the work done—in less time, with fewer resources, more efficiently, and more effectively. They look for ways to enhance processes to improve customer service and satisfaction, increase revenues, improve profitability, and reduce costs.

Too often organizations launch an evaluation of their business processes *after* something has gone wrong in the business. For example, the organization may have lost key customers or are finding that their products and services no longer meet customer needs and they are losing market share. Or maybe no changes have been made as to how products are manufactured, thereby making product lines unprofitable. Not often enough is the culture of continuous evaluation of business processes considered something that must be done. When companies plan for regular evaluation of business processes, it enables stakeholders to more effectively engage and adapt when the organization does launch a formal, complex BPI project. It enables the adoption of a culture of continuous change within the organization. BPI projects are change initiatives that require *not* just the employees to change how they work, but also require the business to change how things get done in support of their clients and how the organization needs to support their employees' efforts. This may entail changes to technology or other systems that are required for running the organization. When BPI projects cross a number of divisions or functions within the organization—especially within merged organizations or organizations with global offices—it likely will necessitate culture change. Culture change is not an easy task, and certainly not one that should be undertaken without considerable planning. For wide-scale BPI projects to be effective over the long term (and have *sticking* power), organizations must consider the organizational culture, and review how that culture might change or adapt to support the BPI project.

Culture change is a necessity, at some point, for every organization. As organizations change—they grow or contract; launch new products or services, or retire others; change leadership or representatives on Boards of Directors; or face new competition in the market—they are forced to change how they work, think, and meet the needs of clients. This can be dramatic for many stakeholders. Managing change on BPI projects does *not* simply mean managing changes that occur on the BPI project, but also entails managing stakeholder expectations around change itself.

Chapter 10 will focus on best practices for developing a culture of continuous improvement through evaluating business processes on a regular basis.

THE IMPACT OF EMPLOYEES' PAST EXPERIENCES WITH BPI PROJECTS

What is important to realize when a BPI project is launched is that the project is not evaluated or considered on its own. It is unlikely the project management is starting with a clean slate. Every stakeholder involved, or impacted by, the BPI project is thinking about past initiatives in which they have been involved—and I guarantee that they were not all successful projects. For those stakeholders and team members involved in unsuccessful BPI initiatives, the project manager will have to manage perceptions of BPI projects that are negative at their worst, and indifferent at their best.

Past experiences on BPI projects impact how we perceive future BPI projects. If we have not had a good experience on a past BPI project, we are not expecting a good experience on the next BPI project. We immediately focus on all the things that could go wrong and how they will impact us personally.

The project manager must understand and manage these perceptions in order to ensure the BPI project is a success.

Within the Organization

Considering past BPI projects that have been launched and implemented *within* the organization should be a first step when undertaking a BPI project. If the organization captures and analyzes lessons learned from past projects, use this information to better prepare for the current BPI project. Consider also talking with stakeholders who have been involved in past BPI projects in order to understand what they believed was successful about the initiative and whether they believe improvements exist for the next BPI project. Undoubtedly they will have information to share. The data gathered should aid in increasing the chances of success of the current initiative, because the project manager becomes aware of how he must move forward with the initiative based on the last BPI project to avoid the same problems and disappointments. Additionally, the project manager will begin to sort out the project champions from those who resist the project, which will lead the way to more effective and accurate development of project communication plans. This knowledge will be essential to the project planning efforts. Review past BPI projects for the following:

- Success in achieving the goals and objectives of the project
- Success in engaging stakeholders throughout the initiative
- Effectiveness and consistency in communications throughout the engagement
- Channels used for communicating with stakeholders
- Follow up after the completion/implementation of the BPI project

Follow up with those stakeholders who have been the most vocal about BPI projects within the organization—whether positive or negative. These stakeholders will be easy to find—especially the negative ones. Those who have had positive experiences will be champions to help promote and push forward the new BPI project. Those who have had negative experiences will need more attention in order for the project manager to understand the root cause of their negativity and to get them acclimated to, and accepting of, the BPI project.

The project manager will learn a significant amount as an end result of reviewing past BPI projects within the organization—both those projects that were successful and those that failed or were ended prior to completion. And as a bonus, the project manager will begin to build relationships and trust with stakeholders. No BPI project should be initiated without understanding how effective past BPI projects have been. Through the research of past BPI projects, the project manager will learn much that will help better promote and get support for the current BPI project.

In Other Organizations

It's more difficult to understand stakeholder's experiences in BPI projects external to the organization. However, these external experiences *will* impact the stakeholders' expectations of BPI projects and determine whether they are champions or resisters to the BPI effort.

If the project manager (or project team members) notice stakeholders who seem distant, or who are vocal about their disapproval of the project, efforts should be made to probe a bit deeper to understand if there are past *external* BPI projects that are impacting their support of the current initiative. Sometimes the direct approach is best. Until it is understood *why* (the root cause) a stakeholder is against the initiative, the project manager cannot begin to convert those stakeholders to champions who support the effort.

I was working with a Chief Technology Officer (CTO) of a consulting firm to help him develop his plan to evaluate processes around making decisions on technology to be used within the firm, including how technology is selected and implemented. He was trying to get the support of the Chief Finance Officer (CFO), as funding was needed for the BPI project he wanted to launch. The CFO was adamantly opposed to the initiative and, rather, felt that the CTO should be focusing on reducing the amount of technology within the organization. Certainly, part of the initiative was to ensure that better decisions would be made on technology in use and the CTO felt this was adequately explained to the CFO, and also in an executive leadership meeting. He didn't understand where the CFO's concern was coming from. In a private conversation over coffee, the CTO learned that the CFO had gone through a similar BPI project in a past company where the outcome was that more technology was needed, not less. Given the company's current financial situation, the CFO wanted to be sure any investment would focus on efficiencies in the use of technology and reducing technology costs overall. The outcome of their meeting over coffee was that the CTO would ensure that the focus was on increased efficiencies and reduction in technology costs, with an eye toward reducing technology tools/systems. Simply meeting with the CFO enabled the CFO to explain his concerns privately and allowed the CTO to address those concerns and ensure that the CFO would be a champion of the project rather than a resister.

WHAT ELSE IS GOING ON IN THE ORGANIZATION?

In addition to experiences on past BPI projects within and external to the organization, other projects being undertaken within the organization will impact whether or not stakeholders support the BPI initiative. When project managers are tasked with launching BPI initiatives, a best practice is to understand what other projects are being undertaken at around the same time as the planned BPI initiative, to determine if those initiatives may impact the BPI project. The proposed impact on the BPI project could be in any number of ways, including not getting sufficient responses to surveys or interviews, not getting support for documenting current processes or designing new processes, being unable to secure sufficient budget monies, and disengaged stakeholders or project team members in the initiative.

A pharmaceutical client was undertaking a process improvement initiative to change how they engaged with partners on drug research projects. The project manager assigned to the initiative launched the project with no knowledge of other initiatives being undertaken by the organization. The information was never provided to her by the project sponsor, and she didn't even think to ask the question. She soon learned that due to other projects in progress, which included merging two departments and the launch of a new product, many of the team members were finding it difficult to engage in this initiative and a number of stakeholders felt overwhelmed by everything going on. Timing was just not good. While this initiative was important to the organization, it was not as strategically important as some of the other initiatives. In order to ensure success of the BPI initiative, the project manager was able to convince the sponsor to hold off on launch until the other projects wrapped up. She spent the time until launch talking with stakeholders about the upcoming initiative so that when it was launched, she had a head start in engaging stakeholders.

The most effective project managers are well aware of other initiatives that are cither in progress or about to be launched within the organization. This impact of other projects (BPI or not) on a BPI project is not simply the ability of team members to commit to working on the initiative or in engaging stakeholders, but may also impact the project plan and the desired end result of the BPI project. In the story above, the merger of two departments would impact the BPI project that was planned since many of the same stakeholders were part of the departments being merged. It certainly did not make sense to move forward with the BPI project until the departments were merged. Any processes to be fine-tuned or changed under the proposed BPI project would certainly have had to be evaluated yet again once the two departments had merged if the project had moved forward.

BENEFITS AND CHALLENGES IN EVALUATING BUSINESS PROCESSES

Throughout this book we'll go into the benefits of launching BPI projects and the challenges associated with doing so, in more depth. The step-by-step approach and best practices discussed in the following chapters will enable project managers tasked with BPI projects to increase the likelihood of success of their initiatives.

First though, let's agree on the term *business processes*. Business processes are those activities or tasks which enable an organization to produce and deliver a product or service for their customer. Business processes enable invoices to be paid, employees to be hired, development of a new service, or delivery of a product to the customer. Business processes allow customer needs to be fulfilled and the goals of the organization to be accomplished.

There are three specific types of business processes as shown in Table 1.1.

Table 1.1   Types of business processes

Process Type	Examples
Management processes	Processes that enable the governing of the organization. These include strategic management of the organization given its industry and marketplace positioning and systems and processes to control and operate the organization, such as Boards of Directors, stakeholder engagement, and ensuring regulatory compliance.
Operational processes	Processes that enable development, selling and delivery of products and services—the core business of the organization. These include processes around how the product is manufactured, how the product is marketed to potential customers, and how sales are made to those customers.
Supporting processes	Processes that support the core business of the organization. This includes how technical support is provided to customers, how employees are hired and onboarded into the organization, and how customers are invoiced for purchases made.

For the purposes of this book, the focus will be on operational and supporting processes, as these are usually the types of BPI projects to which project managers are assigned to lead.

Let's look at Figure 1.2, a sample business process. This figure depicts a process for training seminar registration. It depicts the process from the point in which the individual visits the website looking for seminars to attend, through registering for the seminar and exiting the website. This process depicts validation of user registration and a path for taking corrective action.

Figure 1.3 depicts sample general inputs and outputs of a business process. It also depicts influencers on the business process, such as enablers, as well as rules and guidelines.

What is shown in Figure 1.3 are:

- The inputs, or forms, documents, and approvals, that go into the process (inputs can also be raw materials in some instances—for example, when the process involves manufacturing)
- The policies and procedures that guide how the process is enforced
- The roles, responsibilities, or technology that enables stakeholders to complete the process
- The outputs from the process, such as reports, products, services, and other deliverables

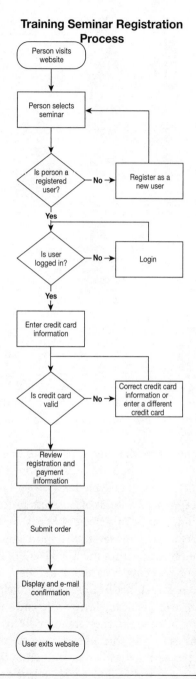

Figure 1.2   Training seminar registration process

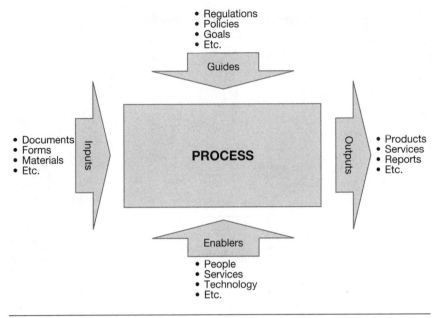

Figure 1.3   Sample general inputs and outputs of a process

The steps of managing a BPI project—from analysis of the current process, to design of initial options or paths that may be taken to improve upon that process, to development of the *to-be* process—will be discussed throughout the remaining chapters of this book.

When an organization takes the time to evaluate their business processes, involving employees from throughout the organization, they move toward realizing the following benefits shown in Table 1.2.

Often, when project managers think of business process projects, the first thing that comes to mind is improving efficiencies within the organization. And yes, BPI projects drive efficiency. However, even more importantly, BPI projects can, and should, drive revenue within the organization. Because the focus on BPI projects is mainly on reducing costs and doing the work in a more efficient and effective manner, we forget that BPI projects can help organizations drive revenue. When project managers can clearly state and show how driving revenue is an end goal of a BPI project, they are more likely to gain commitment for that project. This is especially true when trying to garner commitment at leadership levels. BPI projects that gather support from the lower levels of the organizations first can successfully add leadership levels to that support when those involved in pushing the BPI initiative forward can show how it will drive

Table 1.2   Organizational and individual benefits of evaluating business processes

Organizational Benefits	Individual (Employee) Benefits
• Increased efficiencies overall • Improved customer satisfaction • Increased revenue and profitability • Reduced costs • Improved competition/competitive advantage • Increased market share/market positioning • Faster time-to-market for new products and services • Alignment of roles and responsibilities to meet strategic goals	• Increased employee engagement in the business • Improved skills and knowledge, business acumen • Improved problem solving and decision making • Increased efficiencies in getting work completed • Improved retention of top talent through improved utilization of resources and through enabling for increased opportunities

increased revenue. Remember—nothing engages senior leadership more than a positive impact to the bottom line.

Of course the benefits realized just from evaluating business processes are not sufficient to push an organization forward. Challenges can be numerous, and when an organization is uncertain or not confident about how it might overcome challenges, business processes are left *as is*. Challenges, or fear of potential challenges, must be addressed. Over the long term, fear of launching BPI projects impacts the business when it comes to effectively competing and meeting the needs of customers. There is also an impact on individuals within the organization. Top talent does not stay long in a company that doesn't change and adapt.

ALIGNMENT TO STRATEGIC GOALS

Any BPI project launched within the organization *must* align to strategic goals. Frankly, this holds true for *every* project launched within an organization. The most successful BPI projects launched can be linked back to a long-term strategic goal within the organization. There is often an assumption that BPI projects must be large, transformative business efforts if they are going to be linked to a strategic goal within the organization. This is not necessarily the case. In fact, Gartner notes that, "By 2015, 70% of business process improvement efforts will deliver only incremental improvements rather than transformative business outcomes." Incremental improvements are essential to long-term business success and can more easily garner support from throughout the organization because the BPI effort is being chunked into more easily managed and accepted components. Additionally, if an organization focuses on incremental improvements, they are likely undertaking a review of business processes more frequently overall.

Table 1.3 Examples of launching BPI projects to meet strategic goals

BPI Project Launched	Link to Long-term Strategic Goal(s)
Evaluation of manufacturing processes for a national manufacturer	• Realize efficiencies from new manufacturing equipment installed within facility • Quicker time-to-market of new products to more effectively compete with increased competition • Increased revenue due to shorter time-to-market of new products
Evaluation of processes for how projects are managed within a software development company	• Improve time-to-market of gaming software to improve profitability after two new competitors entered the marketplace • Increased revenue due to shorter time-to-market of software
Refinement/development of processes when two business units merged due to acquisition of a marketing company by a Public Relations firm	• Improved operations and increased efficiencies due to merger in order to support an increased client base • Reduction in headcount where redundancies exist • Reduction in costs due to reduced headcount
Evaluation of HR processes and procedures in onboarding new employees, development of new onboarding programs	• Reduction in turnover rate of new hires; retention of top talent • Increase productivity of new hires (decrease time to be effective in new role)
Review of A/R procedures by Finance	• Reduce time in collecting on client invoices • Improve cash flow

Table 1.4 Example BPI project launched and link to strategic goal and measurement

BPI Project Launched	Link to Long-term Strategic Goal(s)	Measurement Goal
Evaluation of HR processes and procedures in onboarding new employees, development of new onboarding programs	• Reduction in turnover rate of new hires; retention of top talent • Increase productivity of new hires	• Reduce turnover rate from 30% annually of new hires with 1–2 years of service to 10% within the first year. • Increase productivity from 45 to 30 days to become effective and efficient in role.

Table 1.3 provides a few examples from a variety of industries of BPI projects launched, and why they were launched within the organization (specifically their link to long-term strategic goals).

Each of these examples in Table 1.3 is linked to one or more strategic goals within the organization. In Table 1.4, let's look at one of these examples further.

In Table 1.4, it can be assumed that increased productivity for new hires will ultimately increase revenue and profitability, as new hires will be able to contribute to the organization much sooner. Over time, the organization will be able to evaluate the success, or return on investment, of this effort. When there is a metric to measure against, project sponsors and project managers are better able to ensure the BPI projects they launch involve the right people, are planned to ensure meeting the goal set, and have a return on investment component to the project to enable measurement of success.

COMPARING AND CONTRASTING BPI AND OTHER PROJECTS

The following are common for BPI projects, and not necessarily the case for other projects launched within the organization:

- BPI projects always involve some level of change
- BPI projects require extensive participation from within the organization
- Strong project management leadership, specifically in the areas of change management, facilitation, and the ability to develop strong relationships is essential to BPI project success

BPI projects are the most challenging for project managers, and are often the projects that cause the most anxiety and frustration for them. While every project can certainly present challenges to the project manager charged with leading it; BPI projects, because they tend to have a trickle effect throughout the organization, can present the most challenges. These are the projects that are often in the spotlight and for which there is frequently little support initially from throughout the organization.

While every project the project manager leads should be socialized at the onset, much more time must be spent socializing BPI projects. This is because these types of projects involve change, and change is difficult for individuals to adapt to and accept. Socializing, or getting buy-in and support for the BPI project, is not an easy task and, for many organizations, socializing an initiative is akin to doing nothing. Many executives do not believe the project has started until they see people actually producing something. This book will explore, in detail, how to effectively socialize a BPI project. The ability to socialize a BPI project in a variety of ways that works for the individual stakeholders is an essential skill for any project manager leading BPI efforts.

An Introduction to Steering Committees

Steering committees are an advisory group to the BPI project manager and are an important component in getting commitment for BPI projects. Steering committees provide guidance when it comes to securing resources and budget monies; assist with decision making and resolving conflicts between business units; and ensure alignment of the project to company procedures, policies, and long-term organizational goals. A variety of personnel from throughout the organization should serve on steering committees, including:

- The project sponsor
- Executives within the organization
- Senior line of business managers from business units impacted by the BPI project
- Technology support personnel

Consider the steering committee as an extension of the project sponsor for the BPI project. Best practices for forming and utilizing steering committees will be discussed in Chapter 2.

BPI projects have specific steps, or components, that must be completed as part of the project in order to increase the success of the project and to ensure it *sticks* when it is launched. Throughout this book we'll review, in detail, each of these six steps shown in Figure 1.4.

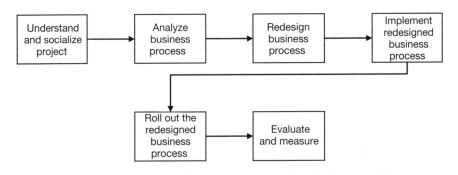

Figure 1.4   Six-step process to managing BPI projects

Understanding Perceptions of Change

Chapter 11 will go into detail on the people-side of change management. Briefly, it is essential to understand that BPI projects involve change for individuals within the organization. While it may appear to be a minor change—such as simply electronically filling out one form instead of another—it may *not* be considered a minor change for the individual involved. People's perceptions of change are impacted by what is going on in the workplace *and* what is going on in their personal lives.

A human resources director was leading an initiative to change the processes and procedures around biannual performance reviews. She reached out to three business unit managers who, for the last year, have been asking for changes to be made to how biannual performance reviews are completed within the organization. Two of the managers were thrilled the project was being launched. The third, however, who was key to the initiative since he had the most staff within the organization, told the human resources director that he did not support the project and would let the executives know that he did not. The human resources director was shocked! This was a key stakeholder who had been, frankly, nagging her for a while about making changes to the performance review process. Further discussions revealed that there was much going on personally for the manager and he just wasn't prepared to have one more change thrust at him. The HR director needed to work closely with this stakeholder to get him on board with the BPI project.

The project manager will not always hear of personal matters that will impact employees' perceptions of change, but it is important to keep in mind that anything happening outside of the workplace will impact how, if, and when change is accepted.

I was working with a project manager of a mid-sized service organization who was responsible for leading an initiative that entailed changing how individuals within the data entry department were inputting customer information. There were eight people in the department and they had, together, 10+ years of experience performing the job. As the current process was defined, it took 12 minutes per customer to input data into the system. The BPI project was to reduce that time from 12 minutes per customer to 8 minutes per customer. This would enable the data entry group to increase their productivity. No one would lose their job with this increased efficiency; rather, they were going to be assigned additional responsibilities. My responsibility was to help the project manager get the BPI initiative off the ground successfully. From the leadership perspective, this was a "no brainer" as the job was improving for the people involved because the time to complete the task was being reduced. How could anyone be unhappy about that? From the perspective of the eight people (the stakeholders) this was a scary endeavor! Would some of them lose their jobs? Would they be able to learn the new process? Would they get training? What happens if they make a mistake? A meeting with the eight stakeholders appeared to calm them down. They were told that they would be involved in the redesign of the process to reduce the time involved and that training would be provided. And, more importantly, no employees would lose their jobs. Jump to mid-project. All seemed to be going well, until suddenly, one of the eight stakeholders seemed disengaged and, even worse, appeared to be trying to convert other stakeholders to her point of view that this project was going to fail and they would likely lose their jobs. Because the project manager had spent time with the stakeholders and developed a strong relationship with each of them, he saw this change early. A one-on-one conversation helped the project manager to understand that, due to current personal difficulties, the stakeholder was feeling insecure about this initiative. A few conversations with the stakeholder enabled her to become the champion for the initiative, as she was initially.

Additionally, as noted earlier, keep in mind that more complex BPI projects will require culture change. For example, if two organizations are merging and there is a need to evaluate and make changes to processes in place in the two organizations to reduce redundancies, the project will require one or both organizations to change the very fabric (culture) of the organization. Given that culture change needs time to take hold, consider how the BPI project might help in beginning to change the culture. When initially thinking about the BPI project about to be launched, consider the following questions about those stakeholders who will have to be engaged in the initiative:

- Who are the key people in the organization outside of a formal leadership role?

In many organizations there are individuals with informal power. These are the individuals others call upon when there is a problem to be solved, a task that requires specific expertise, or input is desired in order for a decision to be made.

These key individuals with informal power have the ability to influence those around them. Ideally, these individuals will be champions of the BPI project, as they will be able to influence others around them to support the project. A survey conducted with 907 human resource, organizational development, and workplace learning professionals and leaders in the United States by People NRG, Inc. in 2011, showed that over 80% of employees accept change when that change is supported by influential non-leaders (key individuals *outside* of a formal leadership role) within the organization. Imagine the benefits to BPI projects if the project manager can convince those influential non-leaders within the organization to support the project efforts?

- What business rules (policies and decision procedures) exist within the organization and (possibly even more important for ensuring buy-in and understanding) what *unspoken* rules exist within the organization?

Those same individuals with informal power within the organization may be able to assist the project manager to understand the unspoken rules that exist. Let's look at this further. Let's assume that there are policies and decision procedures in place for when a customer is given a discount. However, exceptions are sometimes made for a variety of valid reasons. These are not necessarily documented rules and are not part of the formal process, but need to be discovered and considered when analyzing a current process.

- How does the organization communicate: Within departments; department to department; to external clients; from the leadership team down; and from the individual contributors up to leadership?

While there are likely formal communication channels in place, it is also highly likely that there are informal communication channels in place that are absolutely essential to getting stakeholders engaged in BPI projects. These informal channels are often more influential and prolific within the organization than the formal channels. In addition to the formal communication channels, utilize these *informal* channels.

These three questions to be considered provide the project manager with a better understanding of the true culture of the organization. Along with a number of other components, organizational culture is comprised of both formal and informal processes and procedures that allow work to get done, communications to be delivered, problems to be solved, and decisions to be made. An understanding of these components of organizational culture enable the project manager to better engage stakeholders in the initiative and ensure the BPI project truly does meet the needs of the stakeholders. When documenting current processes, the project manager must ensure that both formal and informal processes and procedures are captured for an accurate and true picture of the process being evaluated within the organization. On a side note, understanding the informal processes often helps the project manager to understand how new processes must be developed to ensure support and buy-in from stakeholders.

Challenges in Managing BPI Projects

The majority of challenges around evaluating business processes are in the communication and leadership of such efforts. Communication includes socializing the BPI project *prior* to the actual launch of the initiative. Given how essential communications, from the beginning and throughout the BPI project, is to the success of the initiative, there will be significant focus throughout the chapters of this book on effective communications. Ineffective communication only serves to delay or reduce buy-in for the BPI project, which ultimately leads to BPI project failure.

> *A healthcare insurance organization was evaluating business processes across the organization with an eye toward improvement in how new products and services are developed, marketed, and sold to customers. This BPI initiative was being launched because the organization had gotten to the point where many of their new products and services were launched late and, when launched, did not have the financial impact expected. There was limited communication at the very beginning about the BPI project. In talking with a number of employees throughout the organization, it was believed that this BPI project was being launched to reduce headcount. In reality, this was not the case. The primary goal of the initiative was to improve the process for developing, marketing, and selling new products within the organization so that the organization could more effectively work with the current employees to support customer needs. This simple lapse in communication caused a slowdown in work for three days because employees' conversations focused on who would lose their job and when!*

Challenges also appear when an organization does not educate employees in business process evaluation and the reason (benefits) behind such initiatives. It cannot be expected that employees will be engaged and motivated to contribute to seek efficiencies in business processes when they:

- Do not know why the initiative is being undertaken
- Are unsure of the impact of any BPI initiatives on their own role and responsibilities

- Are not trained in how to effectively participate in such initiatives
- Are not given the time needed to effectively participate in such initiatives
- Do not believe the suggestions and recommendations they make will be considered

When processes are evaluated as part of an annual strategic planning process with employee involvement, it becomes part of the cultural norm and, therefore, reduces the challenges involved in such initiatives. In Chapter 10, we will discuss further how to develop a culture of continuous improvement so that such initiatives become the norm within the organization.

Lack of executive sponsorship is another challenge often faced by those leading BPI initiatives. We may see the desire for a BPI project to be launched from the ground level without sufficient support from the top of the organization. These projects often come about due to the need for those doing the work of the business to find a more efficient way to meet goals and get things accomplished. Often, this is seen in organizations that have reduced headcount where those employees who remain after layoffs are taking on additional responsibilities to keep the business going. It may not garner executive level support due to any number of reasons, with the most common being that the executive team just does not see the need for change, as they do not see a problem. If those who remain after layoffs continue to get the work done, often with heroic efforts, all appears fine at the leadership level. However, without a clear mandate and support from the top for BPI initiatives of any complexity, a number of problems may occur, including the inability to engage key leader stakeholders in the initiative and lack of necessary funding for the project. To engage executives in the need to launch a BPI project, the focus must be on the bottom line. What is the business impact to the organization if the BPI project is launched? For example, will the BPI project when complete:

- Reduce the time to manufacture new products from 18 weeks to 12 weeks?
- Enable an increase in revenue by 10% within one year?
- Increase the client base from 10 key clients to 15 within 6 months?
- Enable reduction in expenses by 25% within two years?

If the business case is made as to why a BPI project should be launched when it doesn't initiate from the top down, the chances of executive support increase significantly. This often requires spending time early on to sell (socialize) the initiative with executives. Consider this time well spent in educating the leadership team in the value of launching the BPI project, focusing on their *hot spots*. These hot spots may be increased revenue, reduced expenses, increased profitability, growth potential, or any other key business drivers that impact the organization at a monetary level.

What's In It for Me?

For the organization, focusing on the bottom line is not *all* that is required to achieve successful BPI projects. In order to effectively engage individual contributors and other nonmanagement employees in BPI projects, shift the focus from the bottom line to benefits for the individuals—or, *what's in it for me*. While everyone in the organization can understand those efforts that are good for the organization's health, at the individual level there is also concern about what is good for the individual—align the BPI project to the benefits for the individual. Table 1.5 provides some examples of individual benefits of BPI projects.

Additionally, when the project manager of a BPI project knows that individuals within a particular department have specific goals to be met and/or are faced with challenges in performing their roles, the project manager might attempt to align the BPI project toward helping to reach those goals or solve those challenges. Nothing increases buy-in and support for an initiative more than when the project manager can help individual contributors see how the BPI project outcome will specifically help them in their individual roles. We'll discuss more about this in Chapter 2 when we discuss building relationships throughout the organization—a key skill for project managers leading BPI projects.

Table 1.5   Examples of individual benefits of BPI projects

Potential Individual Benefits Realized from BPI Projects	
Ability or potential to...	
Learn new skills and increase knowledge; increase business acumen	Participate in reshaping the organization
Have input into designing processes and procedures for workflow; have input into how to complete tasks more effectively and efficiently	Have increased visibility within the organization by participating on the BPI project team
Create additional opportunities that may enable for professional and personal growth	Participate in organization-wide efforts that impact long-term strategy

Web
Added
Value™

This book has free material available for download from the
Web Added Value™ resource center at *www.jrosspub.com*

DEVELOPING YOUR INITIAL PLAN TO GET STARTED

All too frequently, insufficient time is spent on the initial planning stages of business process improvement (BPI) projects. Often project managers move forward with starting the BPI project with no real plan in place stating how or where to begin. Other times project managers are forced to move forward because there is tremendous pressure from upper management to get started. Sufficient planning must be done in order to increase the chances of overall project success. More time spent in these early stages will reduce the chances of major problems occurring on the BPI project.

One client we were working with asked us to lead a BPI project within their organization that impacted all of their business units and would change dramatically how work got done within the organization. We began to discuss early planning with the Chief Executive Officer (CEO). He immediately stopped us and noted that it sounded like we wanted to spend too much time "thinking" about the project and not getting to work on it. From his perspective, planning was synonymous with doing nothing. It took some explaining to help the CEO understand the risks of moving forward without spending time up front planning for the initiative and, specifically, engaging the business units to obtain and understand their thoughts on the BPI project.

While there is no magic formula for determining how much time to spend in the initial planning of the BPI project, consider the following information in

Table 2.1 to help guide project managers in determining how much time is sufficient to increase the success of the project.

Initial planning may or may not be done with the benefit of a project team involved. If a project team has not been assigned to the project in the early stages, consider reaching out to colleagues within the organization to gather their input for the project. This provides diversity in the project manager's planning efforts but, additionally, begins to socialize the BPI project with those who may be impacted by it.

Allison was assigned a BPI project that would impact one business unit within the organization. The team was not expected to be assigned until early planning was complete, as it was uncertain who needed to be involved. However, Allison knew, based on past experiences, that she needed input from others to begin early planning of the project—if she worked alone, she would undoubtedly miss something. (She wasn't the expert on everything!) Allison reached out to a few other project managers within the organization, and to those individuals she knew would be impacted by the project. She asked for their thoughts on the project, specifically focusing on potential issues and risks to the project. This enabled her to more effectively prepare her initial project plan documentation—considering how she would address challenges, risks, and other issues brought to her attention.

DEVELOPING YOUR PRELIMINARY HIGH-LEVEL PROJECT PLAN COMPONENTS

At a minimum, ensure the preliminary project plan includes the following components:

- Project charter and business case
- Scope statement
- Preliminary high-level budget
- Preliminary schedule for the project
- Initial identification of risks

This is the time for the project manager to ensure that he or she has a thorough understanding of the *why* of the project. Why is this BPI project being launched? What goals or objectives are the BPI project expected to satisfy? Does the project manager understand how it is aligned to the long-term strategy of

Table 2.1 Considerations for amount of time to spend in initial planning of the BPI project

Complexity of the BPI project	The complexity of the BPI project will determine the amount of time to be spent up front in initial planning. If the project will impact most all business functions, the project manager will want to spend more time in planning than for a BPI project that will impact only one business function. Project complexity will be discussed further in Chapter 3.
Number of stakeholders and their location	The larger the pool of stakeholders impacted by the BPI project, the more time the project manager will need to spend in reaching out to stakeholders. If stakeholders are not co-located, additional investment should be made in ensuring an understanding of each stakeholder group at remote locations.
Location of BPI project team members	Are the project team members co-located or remotely located? If remote, the project manager will need to spend more time up front in enabling them to develop stronger relationships and getting to know each other so they can work effectively together as a team. Ideally, the project manager will be able to make the case to get a remote team together face-to-face for an initial project kick-off meeting.
Success of last BPI project launched within the organization	How successful was the last BPI project launched within the organization? Were stakeholders engaged? Did stakeholders feel as if their ideas, thoughts, and suggestions were listened to and taken into consideration? Did the implementation of the last BPI project "stick" or did those impacted go back to the old way of working? If there were issues with the last BPI project, the project manager will want to explore further what those issue were to ensure he is prepared to address the issues should they occur again.
Other projects in progress within the organization	What other projects are currently in progress within the organization that will impact the BPI project either in resources, budget monies, or the ability to get commitment from stakeholders?
Support for the BPI initiative from the executive level	Are the executives behind this initiative? Do they support it and are they vocal about that support? The more support from the executive level, the more likely the necessary investment in resources and budget monies for the project. If the project manager does not have executive support, it will be difficult, if not impossible, to be successful with the BPI project.
Risk involved in the BPI project	How much risk is involved in the BPI project? If the project manager is leading a complex BPI project with significant stakeholder involvement required, he will need to spend more time up front in risk management planning activities.

the organization? Does the project manager understand the vision for the project? Without sufficient information about the project, the project manager will be unable to sell it to stakeholders and will be unable to effectively plan for the project's success. The project manager will need to take time ensuring his or her own understanding of the project before socializing it with others. Inevitably a number of questions and concerns will be raised in initial project discussions. The project manager will want to be able to address as many of those questions and concerns as possible. For those questions the project manager cannot address, there needs to be a list of who the *go-to* folks are in the organization for those answers.

As part of preliminary high-level project planning, the project manager should develop an initial description of the BPI project—focusing on the problem to be solved or the challenge to be addressed. Remember, *every* BPI project is launched because a change has to happen. This might be the challenge of a new competitor entering the market that requires an organization to launch products to the market more rapidly or a merger of two organizations that has caused redundancies in business processes that must be resolved to ensure efficiency in operations. We will discuss more about understanding the project need in Chapter 3. Suffice it to say that at this point, in the early planning stages, the project manager needs to spend some time with the project sponsor to develop a complete understanding of the project at hand.

PARTNERING WITH THE SPONSOR

Let us first define *project sponsor* so that we are working with a common definition. Project sponsors are the individuals who provide executive level support for the project. They enable financing, clear barriers, ensure sufficient resources are allocated, and otherwise champion the project. It is essential early on in BPI project planning to partner with the project sponsor to ensure the project manager has a clear understanding of the sponsor's needs as it relates to the project; and that the sponsor understands how to support the project management role (understands the project manager's needs). Don't make the assumption that the project sponsor fully understands what it means to be a sponsor for a BPI project.

A project manager in a university was working with the Dean of Housing to lead an effort to change processes concerning how students are assigned to dorm rooms. The Dean handed the project manager the charter and proceeded to leave for a two-month sabbatical! The project manager was left holding a project charter with no support for securing resources to assist with the project, nor anyone to approach with questions he had about the project! And, he realized that the stakeholders had limited knowledge that the project was approved and was moving forward! In fact, many of the stakeholders had no idea why the process should change—from their perspective, all was working well. To further complicate the matter, the project manager was having difficulty getting stakeholders to help in documenting current processes for assigning dorm rooms, with many of them telling him that "it just happens."

In the initial conversations between the project manager and the sponsor concerning the BPI project, the project manager should inform the sponsor what is needed in order to achieve success in leading the project to a successful conclusion. This might include, for example, asking the project sponsor to:

- Participate in the initial project kick-off meeting to share the sponsor's vision for the BPI project
- Allocate sufficient funding and resources for the project
- Clear any barriers that may arise as the project progresses—for instance, providing assistance in solving complex problems or getting approval for contracts

Project managers should use this time with the project sponsor to ensure an understanding of the sponsor's vision for the project. Figure 2.1 displays a checklist that the project manager might use to acquire the information needed from the project sponsor in order to effectively and successfully manage the project.

This checklist in Figure 2.1 includes questions that should be asked of the project sponsor in order to understand the sponsor's vision for the project and what the sponsor considers to be a successful outcome. These questions also enable the project manager to understand the project in-depth from the sponsor's point of view as it relates to challenges and potential risks. The more the project manager knows about the project, the better he can manage it and the more information he will have to share with the project team and stakeholders in order to engage them in the BPI project. Additionally, this information facilitates more effective initial project planning.

The best and most effective project sponsors have reach throughout the organization, usually coming from a leadership role, though not necessarily an executive or senior leader within the organization. The best and most effective sponsors have strong relationships with senior leaders and executives and are able to support the project manager through these connections. These

☐	Why is the BPI project being launched?
☐	Who are the key stakeholders – individuals vested in the project's end result? (Who needs to be kept happy?)
☐	How is the project aligned to the organization's long-term strategic goals?
☐	What is the sponsor's and other leaders' view of success for this project?
☐	What challenges does the sponsor think might occur on this project and why?
☐	What risks does the sponsor envision for the project and why?
☐	Fast forward to the end of this BPI project, what have you heard from your peers that indicates to you that they believe this project was a success?
☐	Who else should the project manager reach out to on the executive or senior leadership team to learn more about the project?

Figure 2.1   Checklist: questions to ask the project sponsor

connections are essential in helping to secure buy-in to commit funds and human resources to the project, as well as resolving conflicts that may arise between key stakeholders. It is unlikely that the project manager, especially in a larger organization, will have a direct connection into the C-suite, but he will have that connection through other leaders, such as the project manager's direct boss or his boss' boss.

Keep in mind that not *every* project sponsor is an executive or senior leader within the organization.

Samantha was surprised to learn that the sponsor for the department-level BPI project she was assigned to was the department manager. This was the first time she would be working with a sponsor at a middle-management level. Samantha certainly wanted to be respectful of the sponsor and his role, but was concerned that if major issues arose, the sponsor may have limited ability to intervene and assist because there were three layers of leadership between the sponsor and the executive in charge of the department. Samantha expressed to her colleague that she was concerned about major issues because she knew the department was not on-board with the BPI project and, while Samantha realized she needed to work to get them to support it, she was unsure how much support she could expect from the department manager—especially since rumor had it that the department manager's boss was not quite keen about the project.

If the project sponsor does not have reach at the higher levels, the project manager should find ways to engage leaders who are superior to the project's sponsor in order to obtain higher level support for the project. Of course this must be done carefully, so as not to cause issues between the project sponsor and the project manager. The last question posed in Figure 2.1—*Who else should the project manager reach out to on the executive or senior leadership team to learn more about the project?*—enables the project manager to work with the project sponsor in order to proactively reach out to others for information about the project.

In partnering successfully with the project sponsor, the project manager needs to keep the sponsor engaged in the BPI project, just as the project manager would any other stakeholder of the project or the project team members. Certainly the first step in ensuring the involvement of the sponsor is through building a strong working relationship with the sponsor. The sample questions provided in Figure 2.1 are certainly a start in this regard, as they initiate opening up a dialogue with the project sponsor. The project manager should try these best practices to keep sponsors engaged in the project:

- Asking the sponsor to help kick off the BPI project by talking about it from a leadership perspective and specifically focusing on its link to the organizational strategy.
- Inviting the sponsor to key project team meetings, such as when milestones have been met or when a particular problem is being discussed.
- Being a strong project manager who projects confidence in his or her own ability to lead the project team and to successfully conclude the BPI project. This includes bringing not just problems or issues to the project sponsor when leadership support is needed, but rather bringing potential solutions to the table.
- Being honest and upfront when problems arise so that the sponsor is not blindsided.
- Ensuring understanding of the sponsor's expectations and perspectives of the project.
- Regularly reporting on project status and checking in with the sponsor; providing updates and information that needs to be communicated to colleagues about the project's progress.
- Sharing successes with the sponsor and providing a *heads up* when problems do arise so that the sponsor is not caught off guard.

The stronger the partnership with the sponsor, the stronger the increased commitment and support for the BPI project that will be provided to the project team overall.

Steering Committee Formation

Recall the members who comprise the steering committee along with their purpose, discussed in Chapter 1. Here, let's talk further about the steering committee. The steering committee should be formed early on in the project, in conjunction with the project sponsor. The sponsor will provide suggestions and recommendations for steering committee members to the project manager. In some organizations steering committees are utilized to determine the need for a BPI project, and are the individuals who serve as the *sponsor group* for the project.

At a client retail organization, a steering committee is created each year comprised of members of the executive leadership team and division management. Members are rotated on an annual basis. The goal of the steering committee is to select projects to be completed for the year based on prioritization and selection factors tied to organizational long-term strategic needs.

The steering committee provides the project manager details about the BPI project, such as specific goals to be accomplished, along with ensuring alignment to the organization's strategy. The steering committee is not involved in the project planning details, but rather looks at the project from a higher level perspective. The steering committee is responsible for ensuring that the right business units are involved in the project and that each business unit has high-level leadership support for the BPI project. Given that any business units impacted by the BPI project will need to own the deliverables of that project, it is essential that they are involved in the project from the beginning. The steering committee supports the project manager by ensuring that connections are made to the right individuals to help drive project success.

OVERCOMING CHALLENGES AND GETTING LEADERSHIP SUPPORT

While, certainly, challenges will pop up throughout the BPI project implementation, there are some challenges the project manager will likely need to overcome *prior* to project start. Chapter 1 briefly discussed one particular, and definitely key, challenge—executive support for the BPI initiative. This is the first challenge to be overcome in planning the BPI project. Executive support certainly starts with the project sponsor; but let's not assume that because the sponsor supports the project, other executives within the organization also support it.

And, as noted earlier, if the sponsor is *not* an executive within the organization, the project manager will need to find a way to ensure support at the executive level while still keeping the project sponsor engaged.

Let's assume your sponsor is the head of operations in a company that provides training programs to corporations. She is interested in launching a BPI project to improve the processes involved in scheduling training programs at a client site. Specifically, she wants to be sure that all training programs sold to clients have a lead time of three and a half weeks prior to scheduling. This is necessary to reduce costs in securing instructors and in printing of training materials. Currently, 90% of the time, courses are scheduled within one and a half weeks after the signing of contracts. The Chief Finance Officer (CFO) is thrilled that this project has been launched, as he wants to see a reduction in costs. You, as the project manager, believe you have all the support you need. However, when you begin to interview the head of sales to gather information about the project, you learn that he is not supporting the project. He tells you that if this project is launched and a new process is implemented, he will lose 25% of his clients and not make revenue goals. He intends to make the case to the executive team that this project should not go forward. He also tells you the CEO is on his side, as revenue goals are high this year and the CEO won't tolerate any threat to that goal. Your problem? You don't have the support you will need to be successful in this BPI initiative unless you can get the head of sales on board.

As a best practice, the project manager should specifically ask the project sponsor—as part of the initial discussions about the project—who supports the initiative at the executive and senior leadership level and who does not. If the project sponsor is unsure, or cannot answer that there is total support at the executive level, you should probe further with the following questions:

- Why would a leader not support this initiative?
- What is the impact on each leader if this BPI project moves forward? Is it positive or negative? If negative, what does the sponsor believe is the issue that concerns the leader?
- Will this BPI project help or hinder any of the leaders to address a particular challenge they may be having?
- Are there any short- or long-term goals of a particular division that this project may help achieve?

This is not always an easy conversation to have with a sponsor, as it may appear that the project manager is poking into information that he should not be privy to or that is sensitive among the leadership team. However, this information is essential toward understanding how to engage leaders in the BPI project. Leadership support is necessary to overcome any additional number of challenges that the project manager might encounter on the BPI project, including:

- Lack of commitment for resources from business line managers
- Insufficient time allocated to communicate and convey project information to stakeholders
- Lack of budget monies required to implement the BPI project
- Lack of commitment to resolve problems that arise or remove barriers to project completion

Through leadership support, those higher up in the organization than the project manager can more easily influence others to contribute to, and support, BPI projects. However, reliance on the sponsor and other key leaders alone is not sufficient. The project manager should utilize the power of the steering committee to assist in securing this leadership support.

The Importance of Building and Maintaining Relationships throughout the Organization

As soon as Jackson joined the company as a project manager he began to develop relationships with others. Not just within the Project Management Office, but throughout the organization. He has done this through introducing himself to colleagues, asking to "listen in" at department meetings, and inviting coworkers to coffee or lunch in the cafeteria. He not only talked about himself so that others could get to know him on a personal level, but was obviously interested in getting to know his coworkers, and engaged them in conversations about themselves. He talked to others about challenges they were having and their successes in their roles. One of Jackson's coworkers, a project manager who had been with the company for five years, asked Jackson what he was doing. Jackson replied that he has learned that by taking the time to get to know others and building relationships, his project success rate has more than doubled. He noted that even the most challenging BPI projects he has led had gotten the support and commitment they needed because he took the time to understand others' challenges and understood what was important to them.

What every smart project manager knows is that when time is invested to build relationships throughout the organization, the chances of project success increase overall. And this holds especially true of BPI projects, which require *significant* support and commitment from others in order to be successful over the long term. When the project manager has established relationships with stakeholders throughout the organization, the following tasks are more easily accomplished:

- Negotiating and getting commitment for resources to work on the project
- Getting support and commitment for the BPI project, such as in responding to surveys or documenting current processes
- Managing conflicts that arise between or among stakeholders and the project team
- Influence others to get funding and/or other resources needed for project success

Consider it from this perspective; it is much easier to get others to assist the project manager in accomplishing project goals when he has already established a personal connection with them, similar to what Jackson did in the story. Building relationships with others is all about establishing personal connections. Think about how you work with others. Aren't you more apt to assist others and provide them support in accomplishing their goals when they have taken the time to get to know you and do the same in return? Of course—it is human nature.

Table 2.2 provides a variety of ways to build relationships within the organization. Do whatever is comfortable for you. It doesn't take significant time, just 30 minutes a week often suffices.

DEVELOPING THE BPI PROJECT CHARTER AND BUSINESS CASE

The sponsor of the BPI project formally authorizes the project's start by issuing a project charter. In some organizations the steering committee may take on this responsibility.

Unfortunately, not all organizations utilize project charters. In fact, in many organizations, the *project manager* is the one who develops the project charter, rather than the sponsor. Project charters should be used to gain agreement on what needs to be delivered for the BPI project in order for it to be considered

Table 2.2   Ways to build relationships

Use a variety of methods to build relationships throughout the organization...	
• Invite coworkers to coffee or out for lunch	• Ask about successes and challenges in individual roles
• Share information about yourself— successes, challenges, goals, and objectives	• When possible, attend department meetings to understand work being done within each department along with goals and objectives to be reached
• Get out of your office and have lunch in the cafeteria; in the mornings stop by the coffee machine or water cooler to chat with coworkers	• Get up and out of your office or away from your cubicle just a few minutes each day to talk with those coworkers you encounter in the hallways
• Offer to provide assistance to others who are struggling to meet deadlines	• Offer to help out on committees that are not normally part of your regular responsibilities (e.g., annual summer outing planning committee)

successful. Consider the project charter as the essential first document in initial BPI project planning.

Table 2.3 shows the relevant information provided in the project charter.

The next three figures are examples of a few select components of a project charter. A full example of a completed project charter is available for download from the Web Added Value™ (WAV) Download Resource Center at the publisher's website: www.jrosspub.com/wav (hereafter referred to as the J. Ross website). The project charter, upon initial receipt, should be considered only a starting point for a conversation with the sponsor. Rarely are project charters perfect when delivered to the project manager. They often raise a number of questions about the project.

In Figure 2.2, for example, the question raised is, "Has Accounting been notified of this initiative?"

Given the fact, as seen in the example charter in Figure 2.2, that Accounting is immersed in two other projects, it would be of value to determine if they have been given a *heads up* or if the project manager will need to spend time socializing the project with Accounting to get their buy-in.

In Figure 2.3, the project manager is prompted to ask for more details. What does the sponsor mean by *need data*? The project manager will want more information about what *need data* means. One assumption might be that it means the project manager needs to reach out to stakeholders in these two business units to understand the processes in more detail, and specifically, any challenges they are

Table 2.3   Project charter components

Component of Charter	Description
Project manager authority level	What are the responsibilities of the project manager for this BPI project? Will she have authority to source and manage project team members? Is she responsible for securing and selecting external vendors? Can she manage the budget or must approval be obtained before money can be spent against the budgeted amount?
Business case	Why is the BPI project being launched? Is it to reduce expenses, increase time-to-market for new products, or merge redundant processes within two divisions? There are any number of valid business reasons as to why a BPI project is being planned.
Project description	This section provides a brief 2–3 sentence description of the project. For example, enhance internal communication processes cross-functionally to enable improved transmitting of information about current projects underway within the organization. Included here, if available at the time of project charter development, will be specific high-level tasks associated with the project.
Project objectives and success criteria	Denote here the objectives of the project at a higher level, along with what is considered successful. For example, project will be completed within one year of launch or budget will not exceed a specified amount. Considering the example project description provided above, also included in this section might be a success criterion, such as departments will share information more readily and early on when projects are initially launched using a variety of approved channels.
Expected risks	When projects are launched, there are usually risks that can be expected. Risks might include difficulty in engaging stakeholders, reduced resources to commit to work on the project, or limited time for completion. Some organizations have common and consistent risks associated with every BPI project. For example, engaging the workforce to change might be a consistent risk within an organization if the workforce tends to resist change.
Department involvement and participation level	Early on in many BPI projects you will know who needs to be involved in the project. For example, if the BPI project is to evaluate Accounts Receivable processes, surely the Accounting Department will be involved in the initiative. Their participation level may include providing information on the current process, participating in design of a new process, and testing the new process.

Table 2.3   *(continued)*

Component of Charter	Description
Project benefits and business impact expected	List each desired project benefit in this section, along with the business impact expected. Be specific, ensuring goals are measurable. For example, improve collection of A/R, reducing time from 45 days to collect to 30 days within 6 months of new process launch.
Project milestones	Milestones are major events within the project. For BPI projects, milestones may include documentation of a current process, straw model design of a new process, or completion of stakeholder interviews.
Project expenditures	When possible for the project, provide an estimate (or approved budget allocation) for key components of the project. For example, $5,000 may be set aside to interview stakeholders or $50,000 to hire an external contractor to document the "to-be" process.

Project Description
Document current process for approving invoices received by HR from training vendors. Refine/develop new processes to reduce time for reviewing and approving vendor invoices by HR from 5+ days to no more than 3 days.

Project Objectives and Success Criteria
• Document current process • Refine/develop new process for A/P procedures • Complete project within 6 month time-frame • Work within allocated budget range of $10,000 - $15,000

Expected Risks
• Engaging Accounting in the project may be difficult as two other projects requiring their support are in progress (may impact 6 month time-frame for completion) • Formal documentation of current process may show other issues that will need to be addressed in this project

Functional Organization or Business Unit	
Name	**Participation Level**
Accounting/Finance	• Need data • Assist in documenting current and "to-be" process • Understand current challenges in receipt of information to process payment; impact on department

Figure 2.2   Project charter component snapshot

Functional Organization or Business Unit	
Name	**Participation Level**
Accounting/Finance	• Need data on use of process • Assist in documenting current, "could-be", and "to-be" processes • Understand current challenges in receipt of information to process payment; impact on department
HR	• Need data on use of process • Assist in documenting current, "could-be", and "to-be" processes • Understand challenges in processing invoices

Figure 2.3 Project charter component snapshot—stakeholders

Project Manager Authority Level
• Select project team resources • Manage budget for project • Determine stakeholders to be interviewed

Figure 2.4 Project charter component snapshot—project manager authority

having with the current processes. However, rather than make any assumptions about what the sponsor means, it is best to ask the question.

In Figure 2.4, the project manager will want more clarification and details concerning the project manager authority level.

The more detail the project manager has, the easier it is to perform the project manager role *and* to hold stakeholders and team members accountable during the project. For example, what specifically does *manage budget for project* mean? Does it mean the budget provided can be utilized as the project manager sees fit, or does each expenditure need budget approval?

Given that project charters often take the form of a memo or e-mail from a sponsor to the project manager, rather than a formal document, it is of value for the project manager to develop the official charter for the project on behalf of the sponsor. The project manager should utilize the information received from the sponsor about the project and, based on conversations with the sponsor, fill in the blanks until a charter is established that is agreeable to both the project manager and the sponsor. Of key importance here is the business case for the project. The project manager must focus on this area until it is perfectly clear why the BPI project is being launched. It is imperative that the project manager understand how the project is aligned to an organizational strategic goal so that the importance of the project and why the project manager needs others to be involved in it can be clearly and effectively communicated to stakeholders.

Depending on the organization, sometimes a business case is the charter, or the business case replaces the charter. Both documents may be used—taking information from the charter once it is approved and including it in the business case. For BPI projects, the business case should be focused on the specific business process to be refined. Figure 2.5 provides a template for a business case worksheet, along with descriptions for each field. This template is also available via download from the J. Ross website.

As a best practice, one of the authors, Gina, prefers to use the business case after both the charter and scope statement have been finalized and approved. For her, the business case worksheet pulls information from both of these documents and provides, in effect, an overview of what she is trying to accomplish with the BPI project. It enables Gina and the rest of the BPI project team to ensure that the project is aligned to the organizational long-term strategy. It is a great document to share with key stakeholders early on in the project and a great document for sharing with team members and stakeholders.

This enables the project manager to get the support needed for the project from throughout the organization. In the business case, details should be included about the current impact on the business or the customer. The project manager should focus on the monetary impact that is causing the BPI project to be launched, such as reduced revenue, increased expenses, decreased profitability, or loss of customers based on the current situation. This shows the urgency of moving forward with the project.

A project manager in a large software development firm was tasked with leading a process improvement initiative. She reached out to various stakeholders to explain that she needed information from them for the project. When she was asked what the project was about, she was unable to answer the question with anything more than, "I have been tasked with completing this project to improve our processes." When a few stakeholders asked specifically why this project was being undertaken now within the organization, since from their perspective, all was working well—the project manager was unable to answer the question. The result of the project manager's inability to effectively communicate the business case for the project was that many stakeholders were disengaged in the initiative causing problems in getting the BPI project completed successfully. The lesson learned by the project manager was that she needed to be able to sell the reason for the BPI project in order to get others to buy-in and commit to helping her achieve success.

BPI Project Business Case	
Project:	**Project Manager**:

Process(es) in which project will be focused:
<For this section, write the process or processes that this project will be focused on creating, refining, or updating. For example, the process to be updated may be deployment of an applicant tracking system.>
Problem to be solved:
<For this section, delineate *why* this project is happening. What problem or issue is the organization trying to solve by changing the process. For example, the problem to be solved by deploying an applicant tracking system is to automate recruiting and hiring processes which are currently manual.>
Measures/objectives of "to-be" process performance:
<Measurements may include: reduced expenses, increased revenue, quicker time-to-market, improved workflow, reduced rework, etc. For the example, measures might include: quicker time to hire talent, improved tracking of candidates in the pipeline, increased efficiencies in interviewing potential candidates, etc.>
What is required to move from the current ("as-is") process to the future ("to-be") process:
<For this section, consider the amount of time and effort to complete components of the BPI project, such as: analysis of current process time and effort, redesign of process time and effort, implementation via pilot group time and effort, organizational-wide roll out time and effort.>

Figure 2.5   BPI project business case worksheet

Take these best practice steps for developing the project charter for the BPI project:

1. Take the initial information provided by the sponsor and enter it into the charter template. This information may come from an e-mail, a meeting with a sponsor, or even a hallway conversation.
2. The project manager should fill in as many gaps as possible based on his or her knowledge of the BPI initiative and the organization. This is effectively taking educated guesses that will be validated in a conversation with the sponsor.
3. The project manager will then arrange for a meeting with the sponsor to review details of the project that will fill in the gaps in the charter.
4. The project manager will revise the charter with additional details provided at the sponsor meeting.
5. If more questions arise, a second sponsor meeting may be scheduled to ensure full understanding and sufficient detail to move forward with project planning.

6. Once finalized, the project manager will share the final version of the charter with the sponsor—getting sign off that the charter is complete and ready to be used to move forward with planning the BPI project.

As a best practice, the project manager will want to focus on ensuring a valid and detailed project charter before moving on to creating other documentation for the BPI project. The project manager and the team will refer to this charter throughout the BPI project implementation.

Determining Metrics for Success

Metrics for successful BPI projects may be customer-based metrics and/or organizational-based metrics.

Table 2.4 shows just a small number of potential metrics for success of a BPI project. The project manager's initial discussions with the BPI project sponsor should include discussion on metrics for project success. These metrics must be aligned to long-term organizational strategic goals. For example, if an organization has been having difficulty engaging existing customers to buy additional products and services, it may undertake an initiative to review the sales and marketing processes in place to engage existing customers as part of a long-term strategic goal within the organization to drive increased profitability from current customers.

Don't make the error of assuming the statement, "We want to increase sales to existing customers," is sufficient as a metric, however. The project manager's idea of success may be different from the project sponsor and any other number of stakeholders. Rather, when confronted with the statement, "We want to increase sales to existing customers," the seasoned project manager will probe for detailed statements (project benefits) such as, "We want to increase sales to existing customers *by 5% in the first 3 months, 8% in the next six months, and then by 15% within a year, through increased effectiveness in sales and marketing processes.*" Specificity in metrics enables the project manager to better determine potential problems in meeting the goal. For example, when considering the goal

Table 2.4 Sample potential metrics for BPI projects

Customer-based Metrics	Organizational-based Metrics
• Customer satisfaction	• Utilization of resources
• Service level	• Manufacturing line utilization
• Time-to-market	• Cost per unit for development
• Accuracy of customer orders	• Headcount
• Customer sales	• Reduced expenses

of increasing sales to existing customers as outlined above, the following potential problems come to mind:

- Are there sufficient new products and services to entice existing customers to make a purchase?
- Are there different processes in place by sales and marketing for *securing* new customers as opposed to *engaging* current customers?
- What marketing is currently done for existing customers to keep them engaged in the business and what is the frequency of that marketing?
- Has anyone surveyed customers to determine the effectiveness of that marketing?
- What are the sales processes for engaging existing customers in purchasing additional products and services?
- How are sales people compensated for new business as opposed to additional purchases made by existing customers?

When the potential problems in meeting a specific goal can be determined, the project manager is better able to plan his project to address those problems, should they arise. Understanding these potential problems enables better design of a process to meet the metric of the business. This is part of risk planning, which will be discussed later on in this chapter and in Chapter 3.

DEVELOPING THE PRELIMINARY PROJECT DOCUMENTS

Once the project charter is satisfactorily finalized—based on the project manager's meetings with the sponsor to gather more information and clarify information already received—work will begin on three other key project documents:

- Project scope statement
- Budget
- Schedule

Scope Statement

The project scope statement is the second key planning document for the BPI project after the project charter. Consider it a narrative description of the BPI project that builds on the project charter. The project scope statement is a document that describes:

- The scope of the project (what is to be done)

- The major deliverables associated with that scope
- Any assumptions made (or known *truths*) about the project, along with constraints (restrictions that may impact the project's success)
- Any other risks, issues, or concerns about the BPI project that the project manager and/or sponsor and other key stakeholders may have

When done correctly, a team member who joins the team mid-project will be able to understand what needs to be done and why, simply by reading the scope statement. Project scope statements also enable the project manager to better manage the stakeholders, ensuring the project stays within the scope defined. And, when a stakeholder wants to make changes to the BPI project, the project scope statement is the document the project manager will refer to when negotiating changes to the project.

Paul was in the middle of managing a complex BPI project that crossed several business units. It was at a critical point, as there were significant discussions going on with key stakeholders around the first draft of the "could-be" processes that were being designed. Paul was notified early one morning, the day of a stakeholder meeting to discuss the "could-be" process options, that the sponsor had resigned from the organization and another leadership member would be sponsoring the project. The new sponsor would be at the afternoon stakeholder meeting. Paul did what any smart project manager would do—he immediately reached out to the new sponsor and asked for a meeting to review the project. In the meeting, Paul shared the charter and the scope statement and used those documents to ensure he would get the support he needed for the project. This was especially important because Paul was sure the upcoming meeting would not run smoothly, as there were many opinions about how the new processes should be designed.

Project scope statements cannot be developed without an understanding of the project stakeholders and specifically their needs, goals, and expectations around the BPI project.

Table 2.5 describes the critical components of project scope statements.

The next three figures are examples of a few select components of a project scope statement. A full example of a completed project scope statement is available for download from the J. Ross website.

In Figure 2.6 notice that more details have been provided around the project overall, in the Project Justification and Project Description and Deliverables sections.

Table 2.5 Critical components of project scope statements

Component of Scope Statement	Description
Project Justification	This section should include why the BPI project is being launched—what problem is being solved or what business need is being addressed? This section may restate the Project Business Case section in the Charter, or provide further details, building upon what is in the Charter.
Project Description and Deliverables	This section should build upon the information in the Project Description in the Charter. Be very detailed in this section. This particular section is of value when stakeholders are pushing back on the project manager to expand upon the scope of the project. Include: who are the customers, what is the final deliverable, when will the project begin and be completed, where will the project deliverable be used? Include in this section objectives (or criteria for success) building upon the information provided in the Charter.
Project Constraints	This section details restrictions that exist or may potentially impact the BPI project success. Constraints are often around stakeholder engagement, resources to complete the project, budget monies, and timing. Certainly the Expected Risks section of the Charter should be captured here if, after review of the Charter with the Sponsor, it is determined that those risks still exist. Include also any additional constraints determined during the early stages of planning the project.
Project Assumptions	This section details known facts or "truths" about the project. This may include information such as: resources will be allocated to the project as needed, budget monies required will be allocated when needed, access will be provided to stakeholders to provide input, external resources will be hired as needed, etc.

This information would have come about through a conversation with the project sponsor requesting more details, or further explanation of information already provided. The more information the project manager can get about the project, the increased likelihood of a successful outcome.

Figure 2.7 shows potential constraints of the project. Review the downloadable example project charter and it is obvious that additional potential constraints have been identified and included in the project scope statement.

The budget amount of $15,000 is listed as a project assumption in Figure 2.8.

Project Justification

This BPI project is being launched in order to solve the following business problems:

- Amount of time required to process invoices received by HR from external training vendors
- Reduced customer satisfaction with vendor interactions with the organization

Currently invoices are processed for payment anywhere from 35 to 38 days after receipt. Turnaround time committed to within vendor agreements are 30 days for payment of invoices. Within the last year more than 50% of the vendors have complained about payment on invoices. New, or refined, processes should enable a reduction of time for reviewing and approving vendor invoices by HR from the current 5+ days to no more than 3 days.

Project Description and Deliverables

This project begins effective Jan. xx, 20xx and will run for a six month time period. The following deliverables are expected by no later than June xx, 20xx:

- Refined, or new processes, for HR A/P procedures to ensure that all training vendor invoices are paid within 30 days of receipt and the time for review and approval of vendor invoices by HR is no more than 3 days from receipt of invoice by vendor.

Budget allocated for this project is capped at $15,000.

Key stakeholders, or customers, of this project include:

- HR
- Accounting/Finance
- Training vendors

This project requires the following high-level tasks to be completed:

- Documenting of current HR A/P process, looking for gaps within the process, or "trouble spots" that are creating a delay in processing payments to vendors
- Survey to training vendors to understand concerns from their perspective
- Review of current training vendor contracts to determine commitments made around payment of invoices
- Development of new, or refinement of current process, for HR A/P procedures
- Testing of new process
- Finalizing and roll out of new process

Figure 2.6   Project scope statement component snapshot

The budget amount could have just as easily been listed as a constraint. It is difficult to determine if the budget assigned is appropriate until sufficient project planning has been done for the BPI project.

Project Constraints
The following are potential constraints to the project:
<ul><li>Accounting support is required on two other major projects that are ending during March, 20xx. This may impact the timeline for this project.</li><li>Other issues may be determined once the current HR A/P process is outlined which may impact the timeline for this project.</li><li>Other issues may be determined when a vendor survey is completed that may impact satisfaction more than this issue is impacting satisfaction.</li><li>HR staff will be launching the annual review process beginning in mid-January, potentially impacting their ability to devote sufficient time to the project.</li></ul>

Figure 2.7   Project scope statement component snapshot—potential project constraints

Project Assumptions
<ul><li>$15,000 is sufficient to complete the initiative since much of the work is being done internally with only minimal external support.</li><li>The project timeline can be extended if needed to manage constraints noted above that may come to fruition.</li><li>The project sponsor will be available to contribute to solving problems that may arise with getting support for this project.</li></ul>

Figure 2.8   Project scope statement component snapshot—potential project assumptions

I have learned that determining if something should be listed as an assumption or a constraint is often based on the perceptions of the sponsor and other key stakeholders, and how they may react. For example, one of my clients always sets a budget up front for all BPI projects. He is not open to discussions that the budget may be a constraint on the project, since sufficient information about the project is not yet available. So, in order to "keep the peace," the budget amount is always listed as an "assumption," along with the statement "it is assumed that the budget is sufficient to manage the project as delineated in the charter."

As a best practice, the project manager should ask someone who has *not* been involved in the development of the scope statement to review it to determine the following:

- Does the reviewer understand why the BPI project is being completed? (Is the business case clear and concise?)

- Are the project deliverables clearly defined?
- Is anything in the scope statement unclear or confusing to the reviewer?
- Is there information missing that they believe would be of value to them in understanding the project?

Refine the project scope statement based on input from the reviewer and distribute it, one more time, in its final form.

Budget

The budget may be an overall estimated cost for the BPI project or may be broken down into cost per major project components. For example, there may be a budget for initial interviews of stakeholders—one for documenting current processes, one for preliminary design of new processes, and so on. BPI projects are ideally estimated at the onset, or a range provided such as $20,000 to $30,000 rather than simply $25,000. As the project manager digs further into the project and learns more about it, budgets may need to increase to accommodate meeting the project goals based on additional information learned in the early interviewing stages. It may be that a budget number is not even included in the project charter and further research about the project is requested for a budget number to be determined and then reviewed with either a go or no-go decision made about the project.

Janice was reviewing the budget that was approved for her BPI project by the sponsor. It was in the range of $45,000 to $65,000. She was concerned about the range provided as, without doing more research into the project, she just didn't know if it would be sufficient. Janice reached out to the sponsor who told her that the range was set by the executive steering committee and they felt confident it was sufficient based on past experiences with BPI projects within the company. However, he understood her concerns and suggested that she do her due diligence and, if she felt the budget was unsatisfactory, to make the business case for additional budget monies.

Budgets, once set, should be baselined for comparison as the project progresses and for analysis for future BPI projects. *Baselines* are approved first versions of a budget or schedule or another project management document that, once baselined, should be changed through a formal change control process. The original, baselined version of the document is then used as a comparison as the project progresses and is a great tool for lessons learned!

In most situations, at this point in the project, the project manager knows what budget amount has been allocated for the BPI project by senior leadership. Of course there are some situations where the project manager is asked to determine the amount required for the BPI project.

On a recent BPI client project, the client assigned a budget of $75,000 for the project. As the contract project manager brought in to manage the initiative, I immediately listed the $75,000 as a potential constraint or risk in the project scope statement. The project sponsor was shocked that I would consider that budget as a constraint to the project, as that was the amount that was set aside earlier in the year for a smaller BPI project initiative. He really was not sure if more money could be allocated. I explained that without truly understanding the project in detail yet, since we were in the early planning stages, it was difficult to determine if the budget was sufficient. Therefore, it was listed as a potential constraint on the project. This enabled me to look closely at what needed to be accomplished for the project to be successful. Of course, I intended to do all I could to develop the project to fit within the budget; however, by listing it as a potential constraint, it opened the door for raising a "red flag" to the sponsor that the budget may not be sufficient and may impact the desired scope of the project.

In the ideal situation, the preliminary budget number provided to the project manager would be developed based on sufficient research into what is required to complete the BPI project and based on project final budgets expended on similar past projects. Often a project manager is asked to contribute his expertise to such discussions. As a best practice, when a budget figure is provided to the project manager who has not been involved in discussions prior to a budget being set, the project manager should ask the project sponsor how the budget number was derived. Then, the project manager would want to do research to determine expenses that may arise based on the initial project description and past experiences on projects to determine if the budget number may be sufficient.

Figure 2.9 displays the estimated expenses shown in the example project charter. In this figure, estimated expenses include in-person stakeholder meetings ($3,000) and contractor support to assist in documenting/designing processes ($5,000). The project manager's assumption should be that these will *not* be the only expenses on the project. Inevitably, issues will arise that may require financial support to resolve. Certainly, as the project scope is finalized, additional expense needs may be determined.

Project Expenditures	
Expenditure Types Expected	**Estimated Cost**
In-person stakeholders meetings	$3,000
Contractor support to assist in documenting/designing processes	$5,000

Figure 2.9   Project scope statement component snapshot—estimated project expenditures

Even if a budget figure is provided for the BPI project and it is stated that the budget is a final number and not negotiable, as a best practice the project manager should take the time to determine expenses associated with the project. This is simply a best practice in project management! When this is done, it provides the project manager some ammunition to make the case for increased budget monies if needed, or for a reduction in scope to work within the budget already set aside.

In the preliminary BPI project planning stages, the project manager should consider if any of the following will be necessary for the project:

- The need for external contractors to work on project tasks
- The need for external resources because BPI expertise does not exist or is lacking in the organization
- Any professional services required to survey or interview users
- Training required on new technology or tools to be used to manage or deliver the project
- Training required based on the project deliverable (e.g., use of new processes, use of new technology to be implemented as part of the processes)
- Development of documentation for mapping current processes and/or designs of *to-be* processes
- Travel to remote sites to engage key stakeholders, gather necessary data or for team meetings

If any of the above holds true for the BPI project, the project manager should include the information in an updated project charter. Later on in this book we'll discuss a variety of ways to develop project budgets.

Schedule

The project schedule includes information on the tasks to be completed, including start and end dates, resources associated with completion of those tasks, and project milestones. Similar to budgets, project schedules should be baselined for comparison as the project progresses.

The project manager should keep in mind these documents will be considered works in progress and will be updated as the BPI project progresses. The project charter, however, will be finalized by this point and should not be a document revisited except under very special circumstances.

Unless the project manager has sufficient time to develop a high-level schedule for the BPI project prior to a due date being determined, the due date for the project is either a constraint or an assumption is made that the project timeline can be extended if needed to complete the project as defined. Alternatively, this information may have been documented as the following assumption: *the timeline is sufficient to complete the project*, or as a constraint, *the timeline is a potential risk and may be unable to be met due to other projects in progress within the organization.*

Unless there is a pressing need for a specific timeline, such as to meet contractual or regulatory requirements, the project manager may be able to negotiate the project timeline *provided* a business case for doing so is made. This will be discussed further in Chapter 3.

The project manager will develop the project schedule utilizing the high-level tasks delineated in the Project Description and Deliverables section of the project scope statement along with the project milestones information in the project charter. Certainly, as a best practice, the project manager will want to work closely with the team to develop the schedule. However, sometimes in the preliminary project planning stages the project team members may not yet be selected and the project manager may be working alone to develop the initial project schedule at a high level. As a best practice, the project manager should reach out to colleagues throughout the organization (and potential likely team members) to get their thoughts and any feedback on the preliminary schedule.

Figure 2.10 is an example high-level project schedule, in an outline format, based on the downloadable examples of the project charter and project scope statement.

Certainly as the project team meets for the first time to review the project (noted as the team kick-off meeting, main task VII on the high-level project schedule outline in Figure 2.10), this schedule will be further developed to show additional sublevel tasks under each major task. At this time, the schedule will also reflect dependencies, assigning of resources to tasks, due dates and major milestones.

HIGH-LEVEL RISK IDENTIFICATION

Identifying the risks associated with the BPI project is essential to managing the project effectively through being prepared to address risks that may derail the

Example: High-Level Preliminary Schedule in an Outline Format

I.	Project kick off (Jan. 20xx)
II.	Completion of Project Charter
III.	Develop Project Scope Statement
IV.	Develop preliminary budget and high-level schedule
V.	Develop high-level risk identification
VI.	Select project team members
VII.	Team kick-off meeting
VIII.	Develop budget and schedule (baseline)
IX.	Stakeholder meeting/data gathering
X.	Review of current training vendor contracts
XI.	Document current process
XII.	Feedback from stakeholders on current process (ensure accuracy)
XIII.	Survey training vendors
XIV.	Finalize current process documentation (based on feedback)
XV.	Design "could-be" processes
XVI.	Assess training needs
XVII.	Feedback from stakeholders on "could-be" processes
XVIII.	Select "to-be" process
XIX.	Test "to-be" process
XX.	Roll out training program
XXI.	Roll out finalized process
XXII.	Lessons learned
XXIII.	Evaluate new process

Figure 2.10   Example high-level project schedule

project and impact its overall success. Within an organization, when projects are launched, there may be common risks that are associated with each project.

Allen is a project manager at a mid-size pharmaceutical company. He has been selected to lead a new project that will review and refine the processes used to launch new products to the public. He immediately records the following as potential risks on the project based on experience with such projects in the past:

- *Federal Drug Administration (FDA)—approvals processes required by the FDA, regulations in place, etc.*

- *Budget—since each project launched at this company is often underfunded*

- *Schedule—since each project launched at this company is given very tight deadlines to meet in order to keep up with the competition*

> • *Resources—a recent lay off has reduced the number of resources available to work on projects*
>
> *While some of these risks are issues he and the team will have to manage—such as reduced budgets and tight deadlines—he has learned to effectively mitigate the FDA potential risks through providing training to team members on regulations and understanding of the FDA approval processes. He also assigns a more senior team member to manage interactions with the FDA and relies on senior leadership support if issues arise.*

Table 2.6 provides an example of questions to ask to determine the amount of risk to the project and provides some possible responses, along with the risk impact associated with each response.

Let's look at a couple of the questions and responses shown in Table 2.6 in more detail. If the complexity of past BPI projects has been low, but the current BPI project to be launched will be a high complexity initiative, risk increases

Table 2.6   Questions to ask to determine BPI project risk

QUESTION TO CONSIDER	IF THE ANSWER IS...	RISK IMPACT		
		Low	Med.	High
How many BPI projects have been successfully completed within the organization?	Of the 15 BPI projects over the last 10 years, only 5 have been successful			X
How effectively have stakeholders been engaged in the early stages and throughout previous BPI projects?	Stakeholders seem to be engaged early on in the project, but are rarely kept apprised of the project as it progresses.		X	
What complexity of BPI projects have been launched in the past within the organization?	Low complexity (but the current project will be a high complexity project)			X
What experience do team members have with BPI projects?	Significant—each team member has at least 3+ years working on BPI projects	X		
Is there access to business process management expertise within the organization at the leadership levels?	No or very limited			X

on the current project. We can assume that there is limited, if any, expertise within the organization around working on high complexity BPI projects. As a project manager, I would record this as a *high-risk* potential, but then I would dig deeper to understand if those involved have had experience in high complexity BPI projects at other organizations. If I find that many members of the team do have expertise with high complexity BPI projects, as do many of the key stakeholders/leaders who are impacted by this project, I would reduce that risk impact to medium. I would not consider it low risk because, undoubtedly, this organization is different than others—with a different culture, risk tolerance, etc.—and while individuals may have experience with high complexity projects, that experience is not in this particular organization.

Let's also consider the question: *Is there access to business process management expertise within the organization at the leadership level?* Recall that leadership support is essential to BPI project success. If there is limited business process management expertise within the organization at the leadership level, this will create a higher risk situation for the BPI project to be launched. As a project manager, I would be concerned about whether leadership truly understands what is involved in launching and leading BPI projects, and would be concerned about whether I would be able to get the support I need for a successful BPI project.

By exploring these questions further, the project manager is better prepared to manage the potential risk to the project. It is easier to develop a plan to manage risk when the project manager understands what is ahead. Too frequently, project managers jump into the *how* to get the BPI project completed and do not spend sufficient time in understanding what needs to be managed, or addressed, *prior* to the start to avoid increased risk to the current BPI project.

Let's look further at the example project discussed earlier in this chapter regarding *improvement in HR A/P processes*. Figure 2.11 shows the potential risks of this project based on initial discussions with the project sponsor, known information, potential constraints and past experiences within the organization.

The risks in Figure 2.11 were taken from the downloadable example charter scope statement. Undoubtedly, other risks will be identified once the project is officially *kicked off* and is underway. Risk planning will be discussed in more detail in Chapter 3.

KEY CONSIDERATIONS FOR PROJECT MANAGERS

A big challenge for project managers who are managing BPI projects is in the effective communication with, and engagement of, stakeholders. Additionally, challenges frequently arise in trying to move forward with what are effectively

Example: Potential Project Risks – Initial List

Category: Resource-related

- Accounting support on project: two other major projects in progress that involve Accounting, may impact Accounting's ability to support this initiative
- HR staff support on project: launching annual review process that may impact ability to participate in and devote sufficient time to this project

Category: Schedule-related

- There is a short timeline to complete the initiative

Category: Other

- Formal documentation of processes may show other issues (and therefore impact the budget and timing)
- Vendor dissatisfaction may not be solely based on payments made (and therefore impact the project overall)

Figure 2.11   Potential project risks

change projects while keeping the business moving forward. The work can't stop simply because processes are being evaluated and are going to be changing. We briefly discussed in Chapter 1 the importance of critical, or soft, skills as essential to BPI project management success. Leadership skills in general are essential to the successful BPI project manager.

Alison has been managing very complex BPI projects for the last five years. She noted that over the years she has learned that the ability to engage people from throughout the organization has helped to increase the "sticking power" of the BPI projects she has led. Through building strong relationships with others, she has been able to help stakeholders accept and embrace change and support BPI initiatives by sharing information, testing new processes and utilizing new processes. Now, when she leads BPI projects, she has no trouble getting stakeholders involved in the initiative. They trust her!

The ability to build strong relationships, in particular, facilitates the following results as they relate to managing BPI projects:

- Getting senior leadership and other executive support for the BPI project

- Getting support from stakeholders in providing data, responding to surveys and engaging in conversations about designing new processes
- Getting honest input in the design of *to-be* processes and in conversations concerning what works or does not work
- Converting stakeholders from resisters to the BPI project to champions who actively support the BPI project
- Getting others to participate in the project by taking on assignments and completing tasks to meet project goals

Even more essential than expertise in business process management is the ability to have others see a vision for the future that engages them and enables them to move forward embracing change.

David recalls his very first project working as a member of a BPI project team focused on changing processes to accommodate the release of a new financial system. This is the project where he learned the importance of a strong project manager to lead the team to success. The project manager, from David's perspective, was not as strong a leader as he believed was necessary for such a major BPI change initiative. Finance had been using the current system for over 10 years. The new system was dramatically different than the current one, requiring all processes for A/P and A/R to change completely; significant training had to be done to ensure employees could utilize the system. The project manager, when confronted by stakeholders who were concerned about the timing of the project and the type of training they would receive, responded by telling the stakeholders that they would need to "adjust to change." From that point on David realized the project was in serious trouble because the stakeholders were not happy!

As noted earlier, just because a BPI project has been approved from the leadership level, has an executive sponsor, and is moving forward does not mean that employees (the stakeholders) will accept the project. The project manager must *sell* the project to the stakeholders—this requires understanding the vision for the project and conveying that vision to the stakeholders in a way that engages them. Let's consider David's story. How might the project manager have sold and engaged key stakeholders—the employees of the financial department—in the project? Consider the following steps that the project manager may have taken to increase the comfort level of the key stakeholders toward the initiative:

- Facilitating a stakeholder meeting with the entire finance department to discuss the benefits of the new financial system and specifically how it will be of value to the employees in improving how the job gets done (e.g., reduce time to process A/P or A/R)

- Meeting with smaller groups of stakeholders, or one-on-one, to answer any specific questions that stakeholders may not feel comfortable asking during a larger group meeting
- Highlighting transition time to move to the new system and training which will be done to ensure comfort in utilizing the system

Obviously the ability to facilitate discussions is essential toward accomplishing these tasks along with understanding how change impacts people. Chapters 3, 8, and 12 will focus on change management and the people-side of change as BPI projects can only be successful when the project manager invests significant time in this key area.

Table 2.7 lists a variety of key critical, or soft, skills required for success when managing BPI projects. Project managers with the leadership skills listed in the table are more likely to lead BPI projects to a successful conclusion because they are focused on the *people-side* of BPI projects rather than just focusing on getting the project done—or the *how* of the project. Leadership skills will bring about a better understanding of people and how the team must interact with people in order to achieve success in implementing BPI projects.

In Chapter 2 the focus was on developing the initial plan to begin the BPI project. This early planning improves the chances of the BPI project being a success—meaning it meets its goals and meets the needs and expectations of the stakeholders. An assumption is often made that the sponsor and other key stakeholders are excited about the project and want to support it. This is not always the case. They may have had the project tossed at them by someone more senior or even by a Board of Directors; or they may simply believe that sponsoring a project means assigning it to someone else. Engaging the sponsor and other key stakeholders is essential as they will need to support the project in any number of ways—such as clearing barriers, securing resources, and providing funding.

The use of a project charter and project scope statement was covered in this chapter—documents that project managers are undoubtedly quite familiar with. However, a refresher course is always of value, and likely the reader has gathered a few tips and best practices that may be used on an upcoming BPI project.

And, of course, the ability of the BPI project manager to have strong soft, or critical, skills is a necessity. Yes, technical skills are needed to manage a project; but even more important (the authors would suggest) are those soft skills that enable the building of relationships, engaging stakeholders, and more effectively communicating with a variety of individuals in a variety of roles within the organization.

Table 2.7 Key critical, or soft, skills required for BPI project managers

Critical Skill	The Value of the Skill
Influencing others	Influencing others is an essential communication skill. When a project manager is able to influence others, he is better able to get support and commitment for BPI projects. The ability to influence others is essential because project managers often are working across the organization, and leading a project team, with whom they have no direct authority over.
Team building	Team building skills are essential to get a group of people to work together and function as a team in order to achieve the goals and objectives of the BPI project.
Team leadership	Effective team leaders are able to get a team through the four stages of team development to ensure effectiveness in working together as a team to achieve goals. They do this by spending time getting to know each member of their team to understand how they work with others. Chapter 3 will discuss the 4 stages of team development in more detail, focusing on the responsibilities of the project manager of a BPI project in leading the team through the four stages.
Negotiation/conflict management	Conflicts will arise on every project team and with stakeholders. The ability to manage conflicts by negotiating to come to consensus on how to move forward is essential to success on projects. While there is no statistic to share, BPI projects frequently generate more conflict among stakeholders especially when they do not feel as if they have been involved in the project or they are feeling threatened or worried about the change.
Facilitation	The ability to facilitate discussions around processes, process design meetings, and general meetings with stakeholders and team members is a necessary skill for project managers. Facilitation skills also enables helping to resolve conflicts.
Communication/ presentation	Communicating up, down, and across the organization is necessary to get support for and engage others in BPI projects. This includes the ability to communicate and present information in ways that work for others, utilizing a variety of modes. Communication will be discussed further in Chapters 4 and 8.
Decision making	A variety of decisions will need to be made on the BPI project, some of which will be made at the executive level, others at the project manager level and still others will need to be made among the team and/or stakeholders. The ability to drive decision making within a team environment enables buy-in and the commitment to resolve issues that arise and to move forward with the BPI project.
Navigating politics	The ability to navigate politics within the organization is certainly necessary when managing any project, but is going to be key in managing BPI projects. The project manager in charge of leading BPI projects may find that stakeholders will attempt to pull strings or go around the project manager and the sponsor in order to be exempt from being involved in the initiative. This might include refusing to provide necessary data, not responding to surveys or not participating in utilizing new processes. The ability to understand and negotiate the politics of the organization will enable increased effectiveness in getting the necessary participation on the project and in getting decisions made since politics includes understanding who has influence within the organization and who can make things happen.

3

TAKING A PROJECT MANAGEMENT APPROACH TO BPI PROJECTS

As with any project, taking a systemized approach to managing business process improvement (BPI) projects is a method of ensuring increased success. Chapter 3 will focus on a six-phased approach to managing BPI projects, along with diving more deeply into planning your project. Later chapters will focus on each step in particular, enabling the reader to be comfortable with this six-phased approach to managing their BPI projects.

At this point in the project, the project manager is still in the project-defining and planning stages. Remember, the more time spent here, the less time spent resolving problems later that will derail the BPI project or cause it to fail outright.

OVERVIEW OF A SIX-PHASED APPROACH TO MANAGING BPI PROJECTS

Figure 3.1, initially introduced in Chapter 1, is a six-phased approach to managing BPI projects.

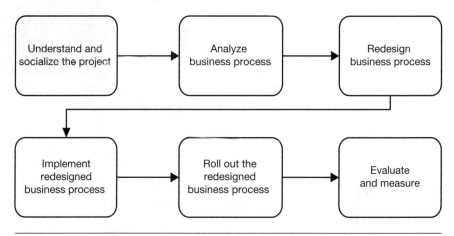

Figure 3.1   Six-step process for BPI projects

It is essential to project managers as they move through these six phases of executing and controlling their BPI projects to ensure that they have team members who are skilled in a variety of areas, including:

- Mapping, analytical, and process design techniques
- Research, interview, and group facilitation techniques
- Communication and change management
- Ensuring all business units affected by the BPI project are fairly represented
- Trainers who can train others during implementation of the BPI project

Note that communication and change management are a component of all six phases. Communication and change management plans are developed early in the BPI project life cycle and revised throughout the life cycle as the BPI project is implemented.

These six phases prompt the project manager to take a more hands-on approach to the management of the BPI project. Although a project manager never wants to be totally *hands off* from any project, most certainly it is not possible to be *hands off* of BPI projects. Failure to stay involved in the project through regular monitoring and constant attention to detail will only serve to derail the project.

Table 3.1 provides a brief description of each phase of managing a BPI project.

There is nothing earth-shattering about the phases shown in Figure 3.1 and described in Table 3.1. They are exactly how you need to manage a BPI project. The authors have used this six-step approach for every BPI project they have led, from the most simple to the more complex. This approach for managing projects allows for more effective initial preparation and planning of the project. Share these phases and what happens in each phase early on when engaging team members and stakeholders—it provides them an increased comfort level and confidence in the BPI project and provides structure for how the project will be accomplished.

Table 3.1   Brief description of the six steps of managing a BPI project

Phase	Brief Description
Phase 1: Understand and Socialize the Project	Phase 1 requires further developing, fine-tuning, and finalizing all project plan components. Getting the right people involved at the start is essential in Phase 1. Here is where socializing the project begins.
Phase 2: Analyze Business Process	Phase 2 looks closely at the process ("as is") that has to change as part of the BPI project. It may already be documented, and if so should be reviewed for accuracy. Otherwise, document the "as-is" process in this phase.
Phase 3: Redesign Business Process	Phase 3 focuses on the "could-be" options. Designing options for what the process might look like.
Phase 4: Implement Redesigned Process	Phase 4 entails designing the "to-be" process for testing. It takes the "could-be" process options and develops one "to-be" process that will meet all the objectives of the BPI project. The pilot group is engaged in testing the "to-be" process in this phase before it is rolled out organization-wide.
Phase 5: Roll Out Redesigned Process	Phase 5 rolls out the final process organization-wide. Training programs are put in place and documentation on the new "to-be" process is available. For larger BPI projects, a staged approach to roll out may be utilized.
Phase 6: Evaluate and Measure	Phase 6 entails evaluating and measuring the success of the final, new process. Did it meet its objectives? Are efficiencies being realized? Are the stakeholders continuing to use the process?

AN INITIAL LOOK AT KEY STAKEHOLDERS

Early on, project managers should be able to easily identify key stakeholders of the BPI project. Certainly, this includes the sponsors of the project, team members, and those departments who will be impacted by the BPI project. Recall that in the downloadable project charter in Chapter 2, the project involved changing how the Human Resource (HR) department processes invoices from training vendors. In the charter, the sponsor identified two key stakeholder groups, Accounts Payable and HR. Unfortunately, far too often project managers stop here and do not identify additional stakeholders that will be impacted by the BPI project being undertaken.

Investing time to identify *all* potential stakeholders is essential to ensure that the project manager gets the information necessary and gets the right buy-in and commitment for a successful BPI project.

> *Jackson was tasked with managing a BPI project that required changing how the company's Events Planning Team would select which events to attend to display the company's products. While he realized that, initially, the Events Planning Department would be key stakeholders, he also began to understand that key stakeholders included the Marketing and Sales Departments. He couldn't possibly work with just the Events Planning Department to determine criteria for selecting events without understanding how Sales relied on these events and how Marketing promoted the company's attendance at such events. They needed to be involved in the discussions early on. Jackson also knew that as the project got underway, even more stakeholders would likely be identified.*

Use the checklist in Figure 3.2 to determine who is a stakeholder of the BPI project.

These questions also aid in determining if a stakeholder is a *champion* or a *resister* to the BPI project. Champions support the BPI project—they are excited about the change that is about to occur and see the value and benefit in the BPI project. Resisters, on the other hand, do not support the effort—they may be vocal about their lack of support or be quiet saboteurs of the effort. The more vocal resisters are certainly easier to identify and to manage.

A Preliminary Stakeholder Assessment (see Figure 3.3) helps to identify potential resisters and determine how much a project manager will have to *manage* a resister to the BPI project.

Determine stakeholders for the BPI Project

Consider the following questions...	Stakeholders (by Group or Individual)
Who needs to provide data for the project?	
Who benefits from changes to processes?	
Who is negatively impacted by changes to processes?	
Who needs to change how they complete their tasks based on this project?	
Who needs to manage, utilize, or maintain the process once implemented?	

Figure 3.2   Questions to determine stakeholders for the project

Figure 3.3, for example, identifies two key stakeholders for the BPI project which were used as examples in earlier chapters—HR and Accounting/Finance. Both groups are critical to the BPI project and are identified as preliminary stakeholders for the effort. Certainly, the information contained in this example is preliminary and, as the project manager and his team meet with the stakeholders, more information can be added, and this information may change. Assumptions are often made based on:

- Knowledge of other BPI efforts within the organization
- Timing of the particular BPI effort compared to other activities happening
- Longevity of stakeholders (the longer a stakeholder has been within the organization, the more likely they are *settled* and more adverse to change)

It is perfectly acceptable and wise to make assumptions based on the project manager's knowledge; just be prepared to test the validity of those assumptions through meeting with stakeholders and discussing the BPI project in more detail.

In the example in Figure 3.3, an assumption might be made that the HR department might resist this change because they have been utilizing the current process for a long period of time. An assumption might be made that the Accounting/Finance group is a champion of the effort because it is known that

Example: Preliminary Stakeholder Assessment

Stakeholder group identified	How are they impacted by the BPI project?	How critical are they to the success of the BPI project (low, med, high)	How much effort is required to change how they will need to work? (low, med, high)
HR Department	Will need to assist in designing new processes and in documenting current processes. Will need to change how they process training vendor invoices.	High – they are the ones who utilize the current process and have developed the current process.	Medium effort – changes are not very impactful, however individuals have been utilizing the current process for a significant period of time. HR staff launching annual review process which may impact commitment.
Accounting/Finance	Will need to assist in designing new processes and in documenting current processes.	High – must get agreement on new process to be used.	Low effort – motivated for project because late payments to vendors are impacting department metrics. Accounting support required on two major projects which may impact commitment and timeline.

Figure 3.3   Example preliminary stakeholder assessment

late payments to vendors are impacting their department's metrics. However, both of these assumptions may be proven inaccurate upon conversations with stakeholders.

Remember that stakeholders are *key* to your project. Stakeholders will drive the success—or failure—of the BPI project. Successful project managers take the time to understand their stakeholders in detail, in order to engage them as champions of their initiative. Chapter 4 will further discuss how to manage champions and resisters to the BPI project, including the use of a further refined Stakeholder Assessment once the project manager and his team have gotten to know the stakeholders a little better.

Paul has been managing process improvement projects for over 15 years. He quickly learned the importance of getting to know his stakeholders early on in the project and continuing to keep in touch with them throughout the project implementation. Here's his story: "On the first major BPI project I led, I assumed that because I had sponsorship at the C-level, I was all set! When I heard rumblings from a few stakeholders that they weren't happy and this project was not a good idea, I ignored them. After all, the Chief Technology Officer sponsored the project and wanted it completed. Boy was I wrong! Those few stakeholders grew. Soon nearly all of the stakeholders were against the project. Bottom line, the project failed because I couldn't get the stakeholders to move forward and implement the changes. They worked against me from the start. The Chief Technology Officer blamed me for the failure since he got grief from the Board of Directors. I learned my lesson! Stakeholders are needed if the project is going to be successful because it doesn't matter if the sponsor is high up the ladder."

Choosing a Stakeholder Support Team

Stakeholder support teams provide a point of connection to stakeholders for the project manager and can also function as the primary communication channel (or the *go-to* person) for large stakeholder groups.

Your stakeholder support group should be comprised of a variety of individuals, and not *solely* of individuals who are in a leadership role. These individuals should be representatives from each department or business unit impacted (either positively or negatively) by the BPI project. Choose individuals who are champions of the project. The project manager needs individuals who can talk about the benefits of the project and its value, both to the organization and their coworkers.

Dana was concerned because the project she was leading involved seven departments and over 100 employees. She didn't know how she would manage all those stakeholders. Then another project manager told her to ask a few stakeholders to be part of a support team—helping to convey information to the others and share information on the project. These individuals could also assist Dana by sharing information from the stakeholders back to the project team. Dana relaxed. She didn't have to communicate with so many stakeholders after all. A stakeholder support team could help her with communications.

As a best practice, project managers need to be sure that the responsibilities of stakeholder support teams are clearly outlined. These responsibilities include:

- Responsibility for specific stakeholders (e.g., representative from the Marketing Department will be responsible for sharing information with all other members of the Marketing Department)
- Attendance at stakeholder status meetings to represent the larger stakeholder group
- Attendance at certain project team meetings where their input/expertise may be required
- Utilize standard communication channels to communicate news and status about the project, back to the greater stakeholder group
- Share information from the stakeholders, back to the project manager and project team
- Assist the project manager in communicating the value and benefit of the BPI project to the individuals impacted to help convert resisters to champions

The stakeholder support team members are key in helping to convert resisters to champions, or at least to *neutralize* them so they do not work actively *against* the project. They can best perform this role by being involved in project team meetings as well as stakeholder status meetings.

DEVELOPING INITIAL PROJECT RESOURCE NEEDS

In the early stages of the BPI project, the project manager will begin to work with the sponsor to determine resource needs for the project. Earlier in this chapter specific skills required of project team resources were delineated. This included modeling and process design skills, facilitation skills, communication skills, and change management skills. The project manager should reach out throughout the organization to find project team members who have the skills necessary to assist on the BPI project. In the beginning, some skills may be more necessary than others. Initially the project manager will be focused on finding resources that have skills around analyzing current processes, as these will be more important at the outset than having resources with skills around designing new processes.

When the project manager considers *when* they will need resources as well as the *types* of skills needed, they will be better able to make the case for project resources. For example, it is much easier to request resources by determining when resources are needed rather than requesting all resources at the immediate start of the project. For example, the project manager may request of the sponsor that there is a need for five team members with specific skills at the early stages of the project and then, once the project is being implemented, an additional five resources will be needed. It is easier to get approval for resources when the project manager is clearer about *when* resources will be needed rather than requesting *all* resources immediately up front and having resources sitting on the bench with no work to complete.

Let's think back to the project used as an example in Chapter 2 (see downloadable example of the project charter and project scope statement referred to in Chapter 2). Certainly, as a preliminary team, the project manager for this project would want to request:

- Team members from HR and Accounting/Finance (subject matter experts who utilize and understand the processes currently in place).
- Management from HR and Accounting/Finance (senior representatives who can help in resolving conflict, keeping the departments focused on the business object of the project and can help make decisions).
- A team member who has expertise in process documentation and analysis. While other individuals with this expertise may be needed for complex projects, at least one person should function as the lead role here to work closely with subject matter experts and senior representatives in HR and Finance/Accounting.
- Team members with expertise in business process management.
- A team member who can assist in developing and implementing a survey to vendors. In this particular example, the project manager is tasked with surveying vendors to gather additional information. The project manager would want someone on the team to manage this process.
- A team member who has expertise in change management and can assist in the early stages in socializing the initiative as well as throughout the BPI initiative.

Certainly other team members may be needed at some point in this BPI project, but initially these individuals are essential in the early stages. As a best practice, keep the core BPI project team to no more than 5 to 8 team members. If teams get larger than this, they will be more difficult to manage day-to-day; sub team-leads should be assigned to help in management of larger teams.

Two support teams that are essential to BPI project success include:

- **Process advisory team**: These are individuals who represent the perspective of a particular department, division, or business unit that is being affected by the BPI project. These individuals may serve on the pilot test group and are individuals that the project manager and other project team members can bounce ideas off of and get input from on how a particular component of the project may impact them. The process advisory team may not be involved in day-to-day team meetings, but certainly should be invited if particular topics of interest to them, or which require their input, were on the agenda.

- **Checkpoint review team**: These team members help to make recommendations to proceed with aspects of the BPI project—*go/no-go* decision points. The checkpoint review team members are separate from the day-to-day project team and assist with quality testing, communications, and risk identification. They also provide general guidance to the project manager.

These support team members should be identified as early as possible in the BPI project and will be involved throughout much of the project life cycle.

Project resources will include not just people resources, but also equipment needs, facilities, any materials and supplies, and external services (such as consultants) that are needed for the BPI project. For all necessary resources, capture:

- Resources needed
- Cost estimates
- Availability of resources
- Quantity of resources

All of the people resources are rarely needed for the duration of the entire project. During initial resource planning, the BPI project team should estimate when resources are needed. For example, a specific resource may only be necessary during the first two weeks of the BPI project through Phase 3.

Picking the Best Team for the Project

The best team members for any BPI project are individuals with diversity in skills, experience, and qualifications and with a variety of areas of expertise.

Although it is easiest to work with team members we know and with whom we are friends, I have learned through 20 plus years of project work that the best team members are often those who don't agree with everything the project manager wants to do. We need that diversity on a team—members with a variety of skills, expertise, experiences, and ideas on how to implement the BPI project—in order to increase the success of our BPI project.

Consider also requesting support from individuals who are not necessarily champions of the BPI project. Although resisters are much more difficult to manage, people often resist for very valid reasons. A resister enables the project manager to see a different perspective of the project and may provide insight as to how the project might be implemented to secure increased buy-in from other resisters.

Knowing What Skills Will Be Needed

The skills needed on the BPI project team will be determined based on information in the charter and the scope statement and also based on the major tasks outlined in the initial project schedule. If the project requires the facilitating of interviews in order to document current processes, a team member with strong facilitation skills is necessary on the team, or someone from outside the team should be brought in to facilitate. If the project requires interacting with external vendors to negotiate contracts, a team member with expertise in contract negotiations should be serving on the project team and working closely with the legal department.

The preliminary project schedule, detailing major tasks of the project, will also drive selection of team members. If application development work must be done as a component of the BPI project, then certainly an application developer must be part of the project team. This individual would be responsible for leading the tasks associated with application development.

While the project manager may not be able to select the *specific* team members desired, he should make the case for specific skills levels. For example, if an individual with the ability to communicate across a broad range of stakeholders is required because the BPI project requires input from a variety of individuals across the organizations, ask for a team member with exceptional communication skills who has interacted throughout the organization with a variety of business units and has served on complex projects. The project manager would not want someone assigned who is new to the organization and more junior in experience. If the project team will be working virtually, then ideally the project manager will want team members who have worked on virtual BPI project teams.

Remember, the more specific the project manager is about the skills, experiences, and required background of the project team members needed to work on the project, the increased success on the BPI project overall and the less time spent in oversight of team members' work efforts.

A best practice is to use a responsibility assignment matrix (RAM) to determine high-level assignments for project team members. RAMs may also be called RACI grids for the terminology used in the chart: Responsible (individual responsible for getting the task done), Assists (individual(s) who assist the individual responsible for getting the task done), Consult (individuals who need to provide input or data to complete the task—this might be core team members and/or stakeholders), and Inform (individuals who need to be kept up-to-date on the progress of the task—this might be core team members and/or stakeholders). There are a number of examples of RAMs and RACI grids available on the Internet. Figure 3.4 provides just one potential example.

Figure 3.4 is an example of a partially completed RAM for the project discussed in earlier chapters, *Improvement in HR A/P Processes*. In this example, the tasks are aligned to the High-Level Preliminary Schedule (see Figure 2.10.) As can be seen in the example, Jack is responsible for task X: Review current contracts. He is assisted by Lisa and will get information/data from Samantha, Sarah, and Alison. Jack needs to inform Joe when he is finished with the task. This may be because Joe will then take this information and utilize it on a following task.

RAMs might also be used by sub-team leads to delineate responsibility for subtasks (tasks that must be completed as part of a major task.) RAMs provide a great overview of how the team members are assigned to the project and can highlight situations where some team members have more tasks assigned than others and therefore may impact the project if they fall behind in completing tasks.

THE TEAM KICK-OFF MEETING

The team kick off is absolutely essential to getting the BPI project off on the right track. This is the first opportunity for the team to get together to build relationships with each other and learn about the project in detail. This is also the time to begin work on further refining and developing project plan components.

Example: Responsibility Assignment Matrix

TASKS	TEAM MEMBERS					
	Lisa	Jack	Joe	Samantha	Sarah	Alison
10.0 Review current contracts	A	R	I	C	C	C
11.0 Document current process	I	A	A	R	C	C
13.0 Survey training vendors	R	A	I	C	C	C

R = Responsible; **A** = Assist; **C** = Consult; **I** = Inform

Figure 3.4   Example responsibility assignment matrix (RAM)

Use this initial meeting to accomplish a number of goals:

- Enable the team members to get to know each other through sharing information and through use of team-building activities
- Share project information including the charter and alignment of the project to the organization's long-term goals
- Develop team roles and responsibilities including how team members will share workloads and be accountable to each other
- Establish common goals and a common approach to complete the activities associated with the BPI project
- Develop processes around how the team will work together, share information, solve problems, resolve conflict, and make decisions
- Develop processes around how the team will communicate with each other on a regular basis (outside of regular team meetings)
- Develop team norms for working together

Table 3.2 provides a list of areas in which team norms should be developed to ensure effective BPI project teams.

The team kick-off meeting needs to include the project sponsor(s) as well as all project team members. In situations where there are individuals assigned to participate on the project at a later time (for example, when training starts), still include them in the initial team kick-off meeting so they can become engaged in the project sooner, rather than later.

Key questions to ask the team during the initial team meeting to be sure there is common understanding of the BPI project and how to accomplish the project include:

- What is the team's understanding of what they are tasked with doing for the BPI project?
- How will the team accomplish the goals of the BPI project? What tasks will need to be accomplished?
- How will the team know if they have successfully accomplished the tasks assigned?
- What skills, tools, and resources will be needed to ensure success in meeting the BPI project objectives?
- What are the priorities of the project?

Making the Case for an Off-site Meeting

While certainly technology facilitates virtual team meetings, make the business case for the initial kick-off team meeting to be face-to-face. Certainly

Table 3.2   Areas in which to develop team norms

Develop team norms in these areas...	Consider the following in developing team norms in collaboration with the BPI project team...
Internal team communications (use of voicemail, e-mail, instant messaging, conference calls, videoconferencing, project portal	• Response time for replying to other team members' inquiries • When to use what method for communicating (e.g., quick question via instant messaging, problem solving session via videoconferencing) • Best practices for using various communication modes • Timing for communications
External team communications	• What information is shared with stakeholders and others • When is that information shared • How is it shared (what methods) • Who has responsibility for sharing information • How is consistency of sharing information ensured
Team meetings	• Expectation for participation in team meetings • Attendance expectations • Share ideas and suggestions, respecting others' opinions • Sharing responsibilities at meetings (taking notes, tracking time, agenda development, etc.)
Decision making, problem solving, and resolving team conflicts	• Processes and procedures for making decisions, solving problems that arise and resolving internal team conflicts • Building consensus on the team • Escalation procedures for problems that arise
Passing of tasks or documentation from one team member to another	• Quality expectations • Providing sufficient time to review information provided by others • Processes for reviewing and commenting on project documentation • Use of project portals for storing and sharing information
Status reporting	• Team status reporting expectations • Proper reporting procedures • Timing for turning in status reports

face-to-face meetings initiate stronger relationships to be built among the team members. Relationships, as we all know, are essential for individuals to come together as a team to accomplish common goals and objectives.

Face-to-face meetings also activate increased engagement among meeting participants. This initial kick-off meeting will require participation by all project team members in order to build the project plan and make decisions on processes, procedures, and best practices for working together to accomplish goals. Participation in such activities increases buy-in and commitment from the project team members.

After her first meeting with the project sponsor to discuss the BPI project and to discuss a budget for the project, Jessica asked the sponsor if he would be willing to add some additional funding for a two day on-site meeting to enable the project team members to get together to kick off the project. She shared that when team members have time to get to know each other, they become more effective as a team sooner, rather than later; meaning, they get to work on completing the tasks of the project much quicker. She also reminded the sponsor that the last project launched took a long time to get off the ground because the team members had difficulty figuring out how to work together effectively. Team members were easily distracted during a virtual team kick-off meeting and many decisions that needed to be made early on were not made effectively or not at all. Given the short timeline of the current project, and the sponsor's personal experience with the last BPI project time, he agreed to her request for a face-to-face team kick-off meeting.

Tie benefits to what will impact the project and, ultimately, the bottom line. These benefits include:

- Stronger relationships among team members—which equals the individuals coming together as a team much sooner.
- The ability to engage team members more easily in making decisions on how they will accomplish the project goals and work effectively as a team—which means that the team can begin the actual work of the project quicker than a team who is struggling to learn how to work together.
- Ensuring understanding of information shared about the BPI project, such as the mission, alignment to the organization's long-term goals, scope of the initiative, and overall objectives to be met. Team members are more apt to ask questions when they are together, and, it is much easier for the project manager to see those who may not grasp the goals of the BPI project when everyone is face-to-face.

Developing the Agenda

Get input from project team members in developing the initial kick-off team meeting agenda. The ideal initial meeting is at least a half day in length, and longer for more complex projects. When getting the team together face-to-face for the first time, allocate some time for socializing outside of conducting the business of the meeting. For example, for an initial face-to-face team kick-off meeting, ask team members to come in the night before the meeting for a team dinner and some *getting-to-know-each-other activities*. The following day will be the business of the meeting with a focus on the BPI project, along with additional team-building activities.

Consider the checklist shown in Figure 3.5 to use in ensuring key topics are covered during the initial team kick-off meeting.

As a best practice, develop the agenda for the meeting with some of the team members. This facilitates sharing of the project leadership role but also ensures a variety of perspectives are included in building out agenda topics to engage the team. Remember, team members are engaged when they have the opportunity to participate and contribute.

The agenda for the first team kick-off meeting might look like the example provided in the downloadable files. In this example, the team comes together the night before, to socialize and get to know each other. The entire next day is spent

Checklist: Key topics to be covered during the initial team kick-off meeting

Topic		Decision by Team Needed (yes/no)
☐	Information on the BPI project: charter, initial scope statement, goals and objectives, alignment to long-term strategic goals, key stakeholders	No
☐	Roles and responsibilities on the project team	Yes
☐	Develop team norms and ground rules; processes and procedures for how problems will be solved, how conflicts will be resolved, how decisions will be made, sharing of workloads and accountability to others on team, and how the team will collaborate and communicate with each other	Yes
☐	Team building activities	No
☐	Training in team repository/internal database/portal	No
☐	Scheduling of future team status meetings	Yes
☐	Question and answer session	No

Figure 3.5   Checklist: key topics for the team kick-off meeting

primarily on the business of the project along with some team-building activities; and the team leaves for their respective office locations the following morning. This is just one example of any number of agendas for an initial team meeting. Use this example to guide development of your own BPI team kick-off meetings.

Consider the following best practices to ensure all subsequent BPI project team meetings meet their objectives:

- Refer back to ground rules/team norms set at the initial team kick-off meeting on a bi-monthly basis or when needed, such as to get team members back on track when meetings begin to go astray.
- For longer or complex BPI projects, on a bi-monthly basis ensure objectives and goals of the BPI project are still clear to the project team members.
- Develop detailed agendas for all BPI project team meetings, including topics, timing for discussions, and whether decisions need to be made.
- Keep meeting minutes and track *to do's* (also called *action logs*) with decisions made, unresolved issues, follow up needed, etc.
- Keep a *parking lot list*. If meeting attendees bring up items not on the agenda, put it in the *parking lot* for discussion at the next meeting, for a sub-committee to manage, or for follow up after the meeting ends.
- Review status reports from the last meeting to show progress and find potential issues in the project progress.
- Assign a timekeeper to keep the project team on track and moving forward and to ensure agenda items are accomplished.
- Consider a round robin prior to the end of the meeting to ensure everyone has had a chance to share what needs to be shared. (A *round robin* entails the meeting facilitator going around the room and asking each meeting participant for any additional information they would like to share that may have not been on the agenda.)
- Before ending the meeting, draft the agenda for the next meeting based on the results of the current meeting.

Establishing the Team-building Activities

Having team activities early on in the project when the team is initially forming enables them to build relationships with each other, begin to get comfortable working together, and to develop confidence in each other's abilities. Remember, we feel more connected to those individuals about whom we know something personal. There are a variety of resources available for team-building activities and the reader will find this information in the WAV™ section of the J. Ross website (www.jrosspub.com/wav). Include a variety of team-building activities that initiate engagement of extroverted as well as introverted team members.

> *One activity that is of value at the start of a project is to pair up team members who have never worked together before and ask them to come up with four or five things they have in common. This should not be items such as they work together at the same company, or both have brown hair, etc. But rather it should be items such as, they have both vacationed at the same location, they have sons the same age, etc.; then switch pairs and start the activity again. Another great activity to get team members coming together for the first time is to have them complete a survey where they answer questions such as, "Where did you go on your last vacation?" "How many children do you have?" "In what state (or country) were you born?" "What is your favorite hobby?" etc. Take the responses and develop fact sheets that contain this information and then asks the team members to go around the room and determine who matches what fact.*

Don't utilize team-building activities *solely* at the initial team kick-off meeting. On a somewhat regular basis, especially for teams that are not co-located, consider including a team-building activity as an agenda item of a team meeting. As a best practice, the project manager might assign different team members with responsibility for leading team-building activities.

The Impact of the Four Stages of Team Development

Figure 3.6 shows the four stages of team development, which was developed by Bruce Wayne Tuckman in 1965.

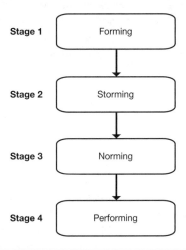

Figure 3.6 Four stages of team development

This theory is called *Tuckman's Stages* and was based on research he conducted on team dynamics. It holds true today and a number of subsequent team models have been developed based on his theory that every team goes through these stages in order to grow to a point where they can function effectively together as a team rather than a group of individuals and meet project objectives, delivering high quality results.

There is a fifth stage, *adjourning*, that was developed in 1977 by Bruce Wayne Tuckman in collaboration with Mary Ann Jensen. This last stage focuses on the team completing their project and moving on to other work. For the purposes of this book, we will focus on the first four stages, as that is where BPI project managers want to focus their efforts in achieving success on the project. Table 3.3 provides a brief description of each of the four stages along with the role of the BPI project manager at each stage.

Table 3.3   Brief description of four stages of team development

Stage	Brief Description	BPI Project Manager Role
1	This is the stage where the project team is just beginning to come together. The team members are unsure about each other and wonder how they compare to the others on the team.	The project manager must be very clear about the goals of the BPI project and provide clear direction to the project team. The project manager is very involved with the team in the early stages of the BPI project.
2	In stage 2, team members struggle for positioning on the team and for power. Differences of opinion are common as the team tries to figure out how best to work together.	The project manager can assist the team in moving past stage 2 by ensuring they listen to each other, understand each other's point of view, and respect differences. The project manager continues to remain very involved with the team.
3	In stage 3, the team is beginning to understand how to work together effectively. They have learned how to resolve differences of opinion and listen to each other. Each team member trusts the others on the team to perform their roles.	The project manager can be less involved in the day-to-day work of the team knowing that they are functioning as a team and not as a group of individuals. Of course, the project manager continues to monitor the team through regular team meetings to ensure the BPI project stays on track and the team stays focused.
4	In stage 4, the team performs at a consistently high level. They are focused on the goals of the team and in meeting the objectives of the project. They work together to solve problems and support each other.	The project manager during stage 4 serves primarily as the gateway between the project team and the project sponsor; helping to drive decisions from leadership and ensure the team has what they need to achieve success on the BPI project.

The quicker a project manager can move the team through the early going—Stage 1 to Stage 3, and then on to Stage 4—the more that gets accomplished on the BPI project. Team activities, as described earlier, assist in moving the team more easily through Stage 1. Ensuring time is spent during the team kick-off meeting in setting team norms and ground rules and developing processes and procedures for resolving conflicts, managing problems, and making decisions enables the team to move through Stage 2.

A CHANGE MANAGEMENT FRAMEWORK

BPI project changes are inevitable. Any deviation from the original scope of the project in terms of the project's deliverables, timeline, requirements, resources, budget, or quality requires a change to the project. For example, if a change is made to expand the scope of the project (such as adding functionality to a new software application to better enable tracking inventory), that change, if approved, may impact the following:

- The timeline (more time will be needed to complete the project for adding functionality and for testing the application)
- The number of resources (additional or new resources may be required)
- The budget (additional monies will need to be allocated to the project's budget)

Let's assume that the timeline cannot be extended, but the change must occur. In this situation, more resources will need to be thrown at the project for it to meet the timeline. This means that the budget must be increased. There will also be a risk of poor quality if sufficient time cannot be allocated for testing. As is obvious, any change to one area of the project *will* cause an impact in other areas.

Jeremy is a newly hired BPI project manager at a health insurance company. At his last organization, there were processes in place to manage changes that were requested in BPI projects. Leaders in that organization understood that a change in one area of the project would certainly impact other areas. Before a change was approved, an impact analysis was done to determine the positive and negative impact the requested change would have on the BPI project. In this new organization, Jeremy soon realized, changes were approved without analysis done and BPI project managers were expected to keep the project on schedule and within budget!

In the early stages of the BPI project, the project manager should work with the sponsor, key stakeholders, and project team members to determine a change management framework to manage changes to the BPI project. Many organizations have standards in place for how changes will be managed as they impact the project budget, timeline, and quality of the project. This might be through the use of templates or approval processes based on expected impact of the change.

What Kind of Change Is This?

The BPI project manager will need to evaluate the type of change requested in order to fully understand its potential benefits and impact to the project. Project complexity certainly impacts the type of change to the BPI project. The more complex the project, as shown in Table 3.4, the more likely any change requested will be quite impactful on the project overall.

However, do not minimize the impact of changes even on the smallest scale projects. Have a formal process in place for *all* changes requested; even if the change is minor and appears to have nominal, or no, impact to the project.

Chapter 11 will discuss change and people. A key area of concern of BPI project managers is in managing stakeholders' perceptions of change. This section, however, will focus on developing the plan to manage requested changes to the BPI project. It is essential that the BPI project manager makes sure that the project team and key stakeholders are aware of, and versed in, the change management plan for the project. This helps to promote the process for changes requested to the project and ensures consistency in making decisions on changes to be implemented.

Table 3.4   Project complexity

Type of Project Complexity	Large scale and complex: impacts most all business functions; requires employees to dramatically change how they work.
	Moderate in scale: impacts several functions; requires new skills and behaviors of employees.
	Small scale: impacts only 1-2 functions; requires minor changes to how employees will do their work.

Gina was working with a new client co-leading a moderately complex BPI initiative. During a stakeholder meeting one of the leaders in the organization thanked her for moving forward with a change he requested to the project. She was surprised and caught off guard. The team had just had a team meeting a day earlier and nothing was raised regarding changes requested by stakeholders. Certainly Gina had not seen any paperwork come through on the requested change. She pulled the team together for a quick meeting later that day to inquire about the change. Jeffrey, one of the team members, mentioned that he had made the change and that it was no big deal, "It only took 5 minutes." He explained the change he made. Suddenly, Roger perked up and noted, "That's why my part of the project is no longer working!" The change that Jeffrey made—that small change that only took 5 minutes—effectively "broke" Roger's component of the project. That simple 5 minute change meant that Roger had spent 2 full days trying to fix what went wrong with his component of the project, thereby putting the rest of Roger's task completion dates in jeopardy.

Develop the Change Management Plan

The change management process can be developed to support any complexity of BPI project. Differences may occur in approval processes, with more approvals in place for more complex BPI projects and less approvals required for simpler initiatives. But as a best practice, try to utilize the same change management plan in order to keep it simple.

For each change requested by a stakeholder, gather the information that is shown in Table 3.5. When the BPI project manager obtains this information from the stakeholder, it should be evaluated against the information shown in Table 3.6.

The resulting information would be used in order to get approval to move forward with the requested change for the BPI project. A change request template is downloadable from the Web Added Value™ (WAV) Download Resource Center at the publisher's website: www.jrosspub.com/wav (hereafter referred to as the J. Ross website).

Part of the change management plan includes how *yes* or *no* decisions will be made regarding requested changes. Consider any of the following options for decision making around requested project changes:

- The project manager is allocated authority to approve any change that impacts the project by no more than 3 additional weeks and by an

Table 3.5 Information to gather on change requests

Information Required for Each Change Requested	Example
Description of desired change	Additional component needed in the software application being developed—an inventory tracking component.
Reason for change (benefit)	This additional functionality will allow for sorting inventory by vendor, auto-removing from inventory materials used in development of product, and tying inventory into vendors' systems for auto-reordering capabilities. This will eliminate the need to count inventory on a monthly basis and will enable more effective tracking and reordering of inventory.
Impact if change is not approved and does not occur	The process will continue to be done manually. Analysis has shown that the last three major client projects were delayed due to lack of sufficient inventory on hand because of delays in counting and ordering inventory.

Table 3.6 Example of a change impact on a BPI project

Impact on Project	Example: Option 1: Contractor Hired
Scope	The project scope will increase by the addition of another component being added to the software application.
Schedule	The schedule will have to have at least 3½ weeks added in order to support requirements gathering, development and testing of the new component.
Budget	The budget will need to increase between $25,000 and $45,000 to incorporate this change. Additional cost may be added due to delay of release of application.
Resources	Application development contractor needed to support in-house developers and keep time frame to no more than 3½ weeks. (Included in $25,000-$45,000 budget.)
Quality	Refinement of testing plan required to include testing of this additional component. This will take ½ day to complete and will have no material impact on the project scope, schedule, budget, and resources.

increase in budget of no more than $5,000; any changes that fall outside of the 3 weeks or will cost more than $5,000 must be escalated for approval to the project sponsor.

- The project sponsor makes all decisions regarding project changes.

- A key group of stakeholders representing each business unit impacted by the BPI project are authorized to make decisions regarding project changes.

In each situation, the project manager is responsible for working with the project team in order to determine the impact of the requested change, developing a number of options or alternatives, and presenting the best option or a recommendation to not move forward based on impact areas (budget, timeline, resources, quality).

Refer back to Table 3.6. This may be *one* option to address the change. This option may assume an outside contractor is hired to make the change. Another option may impact the project in the following way (Table 3.7).

Certainly other options are possible—such as:

- Hold off on implementing change until Phase 2 of the project
- Do not make the change at all and continue as current (manual inventory process)

When a change is approved, be sure that all relevant project documentation is updated to incorporate information about the approved change. If a change is rejected, be sure to track why the change was rejected and any further action required.

Table 3.7 Example of a change impact on a BPI project

Impact on Project	Example: Option 2: Work Done In-House
Scope	The project scope will increase by the addition of another component being added to the software application.
Schedule	The schedule will have to have at least 9 weeks added in order to support requirements gathering, development, and testing of the new component.
Budget	Internal application development resources salary & fringe for extended period of time working on BPI project. Additional cost may be added due to delay of release of application.
Resources	Application development internal resources will be required for the additional 9 weeks.
Quality	Refinement of testing plan required to include testing of this additional component. This will take ½ day to complete and will have no material impact on the project scope, schedule, budget, and resources.

Communicating Your Change Management Process

Every project team member and every stakeholder *must* know about the change management process in place *prior* to the start of the BPI project. Consider a variety of ways to communicate:

- To the project team via the team kick-off meeting
- To the sponsor via an in-person meeting or via e-mail
- To the stakeholders via a project portal, e-mail, or at the initial project kick-off meeting

The communication should include information about how changes must be submitted, evaluated, decided upon, and managed; who is involved in the decision-making process; and any appeal process that may be in place.

For larger, more complex BPI projects, the project manager may assign a sub-team lead and 2 or 3 team members to manage all project change requests that are submitted by stakeholders. This practice is of particular value for projects that have significant changes due to any number of reasons, even if they are not complex BPI projects.

SOLVING PROBLEMS AND RESOLVING CONFLICTS

Earlier in this chapter we discussed the need to develop a plan for how problems will be resolved and conflicts addressed during the initial team kick-off meeting. Let's explore this topic further. Problems and conflicts will inevitably arise on every project team. Recall the discussions around the four stages of team development. Certainly the project manager will experience a variety of problems and conflicts in the early stages of the team coming together to work on the BPI project. The sooner a plan is put in place to resolve problems and conflicts that occur on the team, the more likely the team members will resolve problems and move past conflicts without disrupting the flow of the project.

Alexandria and Jonathan were co-leading a complex BPI project that involved developing new processes to support two newly merged organizations. At the onset of the project a variety of problems surfaced. This included stakeholders who refused to participate in data gathering sessions and turf battles between team members from each of the organizations. Both Alexandria and Jonathan knew that they had to resolve the situation quickly before the project failed. Unfortunately, they had never discussed how to resolve problems and conflicts and needed to spend time coming to agreement between them on how to do so.

For more complex BPI projects, or for BPI projects that involve team members who work virtually, consider utilizing special, smaller teams with expertise in specific areas of the BPI project who come together to resolve problems that arise. For example, 2 or 3 individuals with technical expertise may come together to resolve any technology-related problems that arise on the BPI project. This expedites management of problems by team members who have the skills and expertise necessary to solve the problem and enables the rest of the team to continue to focus on moving forward with completing the tasks of the project.

Plan before Problems and Conflicts Arise

Through risk planning, the project manager is better able to plan for problems that may arise during the course of the BPI project. Let's think back to the project discussed earlier, *Improvement in HR A/P processes*. Recall from the downloadable project charter that Accounting is involved in two other initiatives. This has already been identified as a risk to the project. A potential problem arising from this risk is that the project manager will not have sufficient support from Accounting for this HR BPI project, thereby delaying the launch of the final process. Through risk planning, this potential problem is highlighted and can be planned for *before* it becomes an actual problem. Consider the other risk identified in this downloadable project charter—*formal documentation of current processes may show other issues that will need to be addressed in this project.* As the project progresses through documenting the current HR A/P process, other issues may arise that will create problems for this particular initiative. Bottom line, project managers must look carefully at the identified risks to the BPI project since these risks are, effectively, potential problems that may derail the project.

In addition to the identified project risks, consider other potential problems that may arise on the BPI project. For example, team members that may be pulled off the project to work on initiatives, the sponsor or key stakeholders may leave the organization, priorities may change, funding for the BPI project may be pulled, etc. These are all potential problems that may derail the BPI project. While it is not practical that the project team prepares for *every* conceivable problem that may arise, having a plan in place to deal with problems *before* needed is always a best practice. The same goes for managing conflicts. Problems and conflicts are more easily managed when the BPI project team has agreed on processes for managing them beforehand.

Melissa was managing a BPI project that was expected to have a number of issues that would arise as the project got underway. She got the project team

> *together to discuss the potential issues and develop a plan to address each one of them. About three months into the project, Melissa gets a call from Sammy who tells her that a number of risks were coming up in designing "could-be" process options. Sammy seemed a little panicked. He told her that a few key stakeholders were not very happy. Melissa reminded Sammy that these issues were expected and suggested he review the risk management plan the team developed at the project kick off. All of the answers would be found in that document.*

Table 3.8 provides a process for managing problems that arise on the project, in collaboration with the project team and stakeholders. This table focuses on bringing options to solve a problem to the decision makers for a final decision to be made—basically, which option of those recommended by the BPI project team should be moved forward to solve the problem. However, let's assume that the decision can be made at team level and doesn't require a sponsor or other leader in the organization to be involved. This may be the case, for example,

Table 3.8 Process for managing problems

Step	Description	Who is Involved
1	Present the problem to the team and ensure common understanding of the situation.	Project manager
2	Brainstorm creative ways to solve the problem. Note all possible options brainstormed. Spend no more than 30-40 minutes on Step 2.	Project manager, project team, stakeholders
3	Reduce the list of ways brainstormed by eliminating those options that are not practical or possible given the environment. Leave Step 3 with no more than 6-8 options for solving the problem to explore further.	Project manager, project team, stakeholders
4	Evaluate the 6-8 options against a variety of factors: cost impact, scope impact, timeline impact, introduction of further risk to the project, resources necessary to implement the option, quality impact on the project.	Project manager, project team, stakeholders
5	Choose the top 3-4 options to move forward for approval. Develop the options focusing on "pros" and "cons" of each option.	Project manager, project team, stakeholders
6	Provide the decision makers (sponsor of the project, key stakeholders, etc.) with a grid comparing each possible option to resolve the issue.	Project manager

with minor problems that, when a solution is implemented, will not substantially impact the timeline, scope, or budget of the project.

Table 3.9 provides a variety of options available for making a decision within the BPI project team.

Let's look at managing conflicts that arise on the project team. Regardless of how well the team gets along, conflicts will arise.

Table 3.9 Options for making decisions

Decision-making Option	Brief Description
Unanimous	In this situation, the entire team agrees with the decision to be made. Unanimous decision making works well when the problem to be solved is minor. In many cases, there is only one clear solution to the problem and everyone can agree on it easily.
Compromise	This is a negotiated approach to decision making and might be used when two or more options exist to solve the problem. Compromising is a process of give and take until a solution arises that everyone can agree on (win-win). However, at times in using the compromising approach, individuals may feel as if too much has been given up, or lost, in order to come to a compromise and then it appears as a lose-lose situation. Compromise, however, does work well when there is no clear agreement on one option over another.
Criteria Ranking	In this approach, options for solving the problem are ranked by agreed upon criteria to determine the best choice of all the options available. This is an objective and democratic approach to making decisions on which option is the best choice to move forward with to solve the problem. This option does require agreement on criteria to be used for ranking the options. Criteria is often best developed before it is needed to solve a problem.
Consensus/Collaboration	In this approach, those involved in the process develop a solution to the problem, based on everyone's input, that all can agree with. This collaborative approach to problem solving enables for commitment and buy-in to the solution. It is time consuming and requires strong facilitation to be effective. This is, however, the best method to use to keep a team strong and ensure everyone feels like they have contributed to the solution.

Samuel was a seasoned project manager, leading his 10th BPI project in the organization. He was well-versed with conflicts arising on project teams. It barely fazed him any longer. On this recent project, his team had been working well together for a while now; but recently there have been a number of conflicts. First, Jack and Sara began arguing about whose approach to resolve a problem was the best. They were working through it, so Samuel knew it was best to let it be and let them collaborate on a solution. Then Sally and Barbara began arguing about the best way to communicate the newly documented process. However, they resolved this rather quickly, as they usually do when they work together. But then Rob and Elana began arguing, and it was unclear what the issue was with these two team members. Within a day, however, it escalated and a number of other team members were taking sides. Samuel realized it was time to step in and get involved in resolving this conflict.

The BPI project manager does not, and should not, get involved in every conflict that arises on the team. It is impossible to do so and effectively manage the project. Rather, consider the situations in which the project manager should *definitely* get involved to resolve the conflict and keep the team and project moving forward—for example, is the conflict:

- Affecting the performance of the team overall?
- Affecting the project overall by impacting timelines?
- Interfering with regular communications on the team by inhibiting others?

Additionally, has the conflict been going on for a period of time with no progress being made between the parties or have the parties stopped communicating altogether? If any of these conditions exist, the project manager must get involved in managing the conflict toward resolution.

Table 3.10 provides a process for managing conflicts that arise on the team.

Sally learned early on in her career as a project manager that enabling time for the project team to get to know each other at the very start of the BPI project resulted in fewer conflicts between team members. Certainly conflicts still occurred; however, Sally found that when they did occur the team members either were able to easily resolve them on their own or, when she did intervene, they came to agreement quickly.

Table 3.10   Process for managing conflicts

Step	Description	Who is Involved
1	Get the team members involved in the conflict together in a room.	Project manager, those involved in conflict
2	Set ground rules for the conflict resolution discussion	Project manager, those involved in conflict
3	State the conflict clearly and ensure understanding about the conflict (keep the conversation neutral); ensure understanding as to how the conflict is impacting the BPI project goals and/or the rest of the project team.	Project manager, those involved in conflict
4	Discuss areas where the team members agree (no conflict) and areas where they disagree (where the conflict still exists).	Project manager, those involved in conflict
5	Enable each team member to discuss the conflict from their point of view, ensuring they listen to each other and don't interrupt or negate the other's feelings about the conflict.	Those involved in conflict, project manager (monitoring)
6	Develop alternatives to resolve the conflict (the project manager should collaborate with those team members involved in the conflict to develop alternatives).	Project manager, those involved in conflict
7	Evaluate the alternatives and look for a win-win solution and have those involved in the conflict agree on the solution	Project manager, those involved in conflict
8	Establish an action plan to move forward with implementing the solution to the conflict	Those involved in conflict with project manager support

Keeping the Team and Project Moving Forward

During any conflict that arises or problem that must be solved, it is essential that the project manager does not permit the entire team, and himself, to get so wrapped up in the situation that the project comes to a grinding halt.

Consider these best practices for keeping the team and the project moving forward during times of conflict and/or problems arising that must be solved:

- When a problem arises, check to see if the problem was on the risk list and whether it was planned for. If so, simply work the plan.
- When a problem arises that has not been identified previously on the risk plan, get together with those individuals who have the expertise to

resolve the problem, along with those who are involved in the problem or being impacted by the problem, to develop a solution. The entire team likely does not need to be involved in the solution discussions.

- When conflicts arise, let those involved in the conflict know that they need to resolve the conflict between them as quickly as possible before they impact the rest of the team and/or the project. Continuously monitor the situation to be sure those involved in the conflict are talking and moving toward resolution.

Consider, early on in the project as roles and responsibilities are being assigned, allowing those individuals with expertise in specific areas to be tasked with joining together to resolve a problem that might arise. For example, if the BPI project involves the rollout of new technology, ask those individuals with expertise in that technology to be part of a *special forces* team that will be called upon to resolve problems that arise with the technology. This enables the rest of the project team to move forward with the project and the *special forces* team— the individuals with the appropriate expertise—to come together to resolve the technology-related problem.

BEGINNING TO SOURCE YOUR PILOT GROUP

Let's define the *pilot group*. The pilot group is the group of individuals selected to try out the new process, in its entirety, from start to finish. Their goal is to find any issues with the process before it is rolled out organization-wide. The pilot group is effectively testing out the new process, looking for situations where it may fail or not be robust enough to support continued use. Prior to roll out of the new process throughout the organization, the project team will make any changes to the process based on the feedback from the pilot group. The project manager should begin to source the pilot group who will test the new process to be implemented early on in the project. This enables them to be involved in the initiative from the beginning and to provide feedback as the project progresses.

Sufficient time must be left for testing of the process by the pilot group. Shortchanging the time needed to fully test the new process will only increase the chances of non-acceptance during full organizational-rollout.

Selecting the Right Pilot Group Members

The pilot group should be comprised of a number of individuals from across the organization who are impacted by the process improvement project. This will include individuals who will use the process regularly, as well as those who may only use the process on occasion. They should come from all levels within the organization—individual contributors up to anyone in a management role. Additionally, the project manager should ensure that the pilot group includes individuals who are champions of the BPI project (meaning they are excited about the upcoming change and see the need for it) as well as those who are resisters to the BPI project (don't see the need for change and would prefer to see the process remain as-is).

The diversity of the pilot group generates increased effectiveness in evaluating the *to-be* process before full roll out and also increases the acceptance of the process once it is rolled out.

Keeping the Pilot Group Engaged from the Start

Earlier in this section it was noted that getting the pilot group selected early in the project is preferred. Doing so not only enables the pilot group members to be more participative in the BPI project, but also facilitates increasing their engagement in the initiative.

Consider these best practices to keep the pilot group engaged in the BPI project:

- Involve the group in the initial kick-off meeting when the project is discussed in detail, including the vision and business case for the project.
- Keep the group updated on the project through inviting them to attend stakeholder meetings and team meetings, and through providing them access to any internal sites used by the project team to collaborate and share information on the project.
- As it comes closer to time for testing the new process, have regular update meetings with the group on what will need to be done for testing, timing involved, and how feedback will be gathered.

As with anyone involved in the project, keeping the pilot group engaged from the beginning promotes increased commitment to the project overall and generates a better solution to the BPI project.

FINALIZING AND BUILDING COMPONENTS OF YOUR PROJECT PLAN

In the early stages of the project, the project manager, working collaboratively with the project team and the sponsor(s), will continue to build upon and finalize components of the project plan. Certainly at this stage the project charter is finalized and it has been shared with the project team. There is an understanding of why the BPI project is being launched—its business case and link to long-term strategic goals within the organization.

Project Scope

In Chapter 2 the scope statement was introduced. While it is, at this point, fairly well developed, a review of the scope statement with the project team may highlight some areas where additional information is required. Recall that the scope statement is *the* document used to implement the project—it is the working document for each member of the team and enables the project manager to better manage the expectations of stakeholders. During the kick-off meeting for the BPI project, the project team should take one final review of the scope statement to ensure clarity and understanding.

Schedule

While the schedule was initially developed at a high-level overview, as previously shown in Figure 2.10, the project manager will work with the team to look at it in much more detail. As any good project manager knows, timelines are not given to tasks *without* the involvement of those team members who will be performing that task.

Jessica is a member of a BPI project team that is responsible for documenting processes of a current process. This information will be used to find issues in the process that are causing delays in processing orders for customers. She has done this work before; in fact, she is often called in to perform these tasks—as she has expertise in documenting processes—and this particular process is a thorny one, with much to consider. When she reviewed her task on the schedule, she saw that the project manager had only allocated two days for the task. First, she couldn't work on it 100% of the time; she was also assigned to another project. And second, there is no way this could be done in only two days, it would require at least six days' effort and that assumes she can get everyone involved who needs to be involved.

Best Practices for Schedule Development

To develop an accurate schedule for the BPI project, work with your team, utilizing the high-level outline of the schedule as the starting point. This high-level outline provides the major tasks of the project.

Utilize the checklist shown in Figure 3.7 to develop a more comprehensive project schedule for the BPI project.

As a best practice, don't prioritize the tasks as the team brainstorms what tasks are involved in the project. It is easier to miss or forget key tasks if the team is focused on prioritizing at the same time as determining overall tasks. This is especially true for larger, complex BPI initiatives. Rather, wait until the list of tasks is developed, then prioritize them.

Consider also in developing the BPI project schedule:

- How many full-time employees are required to complete the activities? For example, the task may require one full-time employee on the project in order to complete the project in two days; but if the resource assigned is only available 50% of the time (part-time employee), then the task will take four days to complete unless another part-time employee can be assigned to work on the task also.
- What is the unit of time available for the team member to perform the task? Is 100% of the time equal to a 7-hour day or an 8-hour day?

A work breakdown structure (WBS) is an outline that is a hierarchical depiction of the tasks associated with a project. A WBS is developed by the BPI project team starting with first identifying the major tasks of the project and then breaking those tasks down to individual assignments. A WBS often resembles a flow chart of the work to be completed to accomplish the project objectives. Figure 3.8 is an example of a graphic WBS.

Checklist: Developing a Comprehensive Project Schedule

First...	
☐	Review the major tasks previously identified for the BPI project and add to the outline as needed.
☐	Prioritize the major tasks.
☐	Review each major task and determine sub-tasks (specific activities or work package) for each of those tasks. Cost to complete the task and duration of the task is calculated at this level.
☐	Prioritize sub-tasks under each major task.
☐	Review the prioritization and sequencing of all tasks and look for dependencies (a task that cannot be completed until another task is done).
☐	Look for the critical path (the tasks along a path that take the longest time to complete is the earliest possible time the project can finish).
☐	Determine key milestones (significant deliverables for the project) and assign dates for each milestone.
☐	Develop the Work Breakdown Structure (WBS).
☐	Develop the project schedule from the WBS.

Figure 3.7   Checklist to develop a comprehensive project schedule

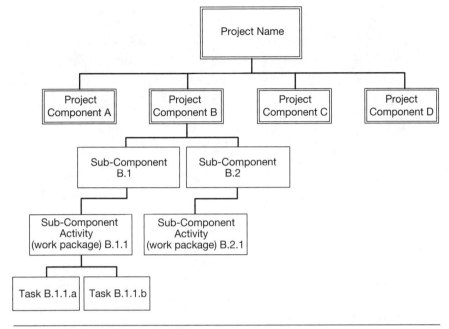

Figure 3.8   Example graphic WBS

1. Project Component B
    a. Sub-Component B-1
        i. Sub-Component Activity B.1.1
            1. Task B.1.1.a
            2. Task B.1.1.b
    b. Sub-Component B-2
        i. Sub-Component Activity B.2.1

Figure 3.9   Example outline WBS

A WBS can also be depicted as an outline format, as can be seen in Figure 3.9. Utilize the WBS to build out the BPI project schedule. The value of building the schedule in collaboration with the project team is that those team members with expertise in completing a task can provide a much more accurate timeline for completion. This generates a more accurate project schedule.

> *The first time I created a project schedule for a BPI project I thought I had considered everything. I worked with the project team to develop accurate timelines for completion of tasks and then proceeded to build the schedule.*

But I forgot to include planned vacation time and upcoming holidays when the office would be closed. Needless to say the team promptly fell behind in the schedule when a four-day weekend came up just three weeks into the project. That was two days that no work got done. Remember also that an 8 hour day may actually be only 7 hours if most individuals in the organization take their 1 hour for lunch. So setting up the schedule for a 9:00 AM to 5:00 PM workday means, really, that the schedule is 9:00 AM to 12:00 noon and 1:00 PM to 5:00 PM, or 7 hours in total. I have also worked with organizations where employees are given a 15 minute break mid-morning and another 15 minute break mid-afternoon; that is yet another 30 minutes that should be removed from the schedule. Our 7 hour day is now down to 6½ hours.

When developing the schedule for the project, be sure to do the following:

- Review upcoming planned company holidays or days off and block these off from the project calendar so they are not calculated in the schedule.
- Inquire as to planned vacation time for team members and block off this time for each resource.
- Be sure the calendar being utilized blocks off weekends and includes the appropriate hours for calculating tasks—for example, time to work from 9:00 AM to noon and again from 1:00 PM to 5:00 PM, Monday through Friday with 1 hour each day (noon to 1:00 PM) allocated for lunch and therefore no work on the project being completed.

As a best practice, I have learned that no resource is ever available 100% of the time. Something always comes up that distracts team members from completing project work. If a resource is assigned 100% to the project (meaning he is working on no other projects or other work during the duration of the BPI project), I calculate availability at 90% of the time. This enables me to build a better, more accurate project schedule.

BPI projects require significant involvement from stakeholders who are not part of the core project team. Their involvement is needed in documenting current processes, determining *could-be* processes and developing *to-be* processes. The BPI project team relies on these stakeholders to share documentation, information and to answer questions that arise. Understanding their successes and challenges as it relates to the process being evaluated is absolutely essential to the success of the BPI initiative. It is not possible to accurately develop a BPI project schedule without understanding this involvement necessary by stakeholders and considering how much time they have to commit to the project.

Let's consider Figure 2.10. One of the major tasks of this BPI project is to survey the training vendors. It is unlikely the project manager and his team will reach out to the training vendors to determine their time availability to participate in the project by responding to a survey. However, as a best practice, the project manager and the project team member(s) responsible for this particular component of the project will either consider past experiences with vendors in being responsive to requests and/or be sure to add additional days to the schedule in order to accommodate this unknown, or risk that the training vendors will not be responsive to requests for information.

Testing the Preliminary Schedule

Once the schedule has been developed, share it with the sponsor and stakeholders who need to be involved in the project (as mentioned earlier.) If the core project team worked on the schedule, but there are others who will be involved in the project—possibly coming on and off the project to work on specific tasks at specific times—share the schedule with these individuals also. The goal here is to have other sets of eyes on the schedule. These individuals may notice schedule issues that the project manager and core project team may have missed. Additionally, use these conversations around schedule review to obtain buy-in for participation on the project.

Baseline the schedule, but regularly evaluate progress toward the schedule as the project work begins. Adjustments may need to be made early on in the project. If this is the case, make updates to reflect a more accurate schedule and using version to keep the baseline schedule intact. These types of changes to the schedule may be common with BPI projects since there is a heavy reliance on others outside of the core project team to complete tasks.

When developing the schedule, review the questions in Figure 3.10 to determine if the project team has considered all possibilities of tasks required to meet project objectives and accomplish the BPI project.

In nearly every project, the project manager is assigned a due date without having the benefit of developing the project schedule. Only in a handful of cases are project managers asked to determine when they can deliver the project. Much of the time a due date is provided and the BPI project manager and his team back into the expected delivery date when developing the project schedule.

Much of the time, the project due dates can be adjusted. Naturally, in cases of federal or state regulations or other requirements, due dates may not be adjustable; but often, especially with BPI projects, some flexibility exists.

☐	Is the entire project scope included?
☐	Has a team member been assigned to each major task?
☐	Are all tasks (work packages) small enough to accurately determine duration for completion?
☐	Have tasks been included that are needed to mitigate any identified project risks?
☐	Are predecessors clearly defined?
☐	Are milestones clearly defined?

Figure 3.10   Questions to determine if all BPI project tasks are considered

As a best practice, the project manager should work with the project team to develop the BPI project schedule *without* considering the due date assigned for the project, at least initially. Once the schedule has been developed, determine areas that can be tightened up to reduce the overall timeline of the project. This might be done through negotiating with team members about durations for tasks or inquiring as to the possibility of an additional part-time resource to help another project team member to reduce the amount of time needed to complete a task or to enable completion of tasks that are not dependent on each other. It is much easier to make the business case to extend the timeline for a BPI project *if* the project manager has done everything possible to tighten up the schedule.

In developing the WBS, break down major tasks as much as possible to better understand what needs to be done. Figure 3.11 shows one of the tasks from Figure 2.10 broken down even further.

As can be seen in Figures 3.11a and 3.11b, the task, *Team Kick-off Meeting*, has been further broken down to itemize the sub-tasks and activities associated with that main task. The further a task is broken down, the more easily you can determine the time needed to complete each activity associated with the main task and, therefore, better develop the project schedule. There is, of course, no right way to break down a task. Break down a task as much as necessary to ensure understanding of the activities associated with the task and to better predict the amount of time necessary to complete the task. Assign a primary resource at the main task level.

Budget

While it is likely that an overall budget was provided for the project, it is still the responsibility of the project manager to utilize project documentation to more accurately determine the budget necessary to complete the project per the scope statement. This includes using the WBS, project schedule, scope statement,

VII. Team Kick-off Meeting (Resource: Ann Smith)

    Planning Committee Meeting

        Select team kick-off planning committee members

        Select date and venue

        Develop agenda

        Hold Planning Committee Meeting

    Team Kick-off Meeting

        Determine meeting participants

            Core team

            Extended team

            Key stakeholders/sponsor

      Logistics

            Date and time

            Venue

                Source venue

                    Evaluate options

                    Select venue

                        Contract with venue

            Catering

                Source caterer

                    Evaluate options

                    Select caterer

                        Contract with catering

Figure 3.11a   Example: team kick-off meeting task

resource list, and risk plan. The project manager may also be responsible for considering indirect costs, as well as direct costs. Figure 3.12 shows what comprises direct costs on a project and what comprises indirect costs.

There are a number of cost estimate methods that may be used to more accurately refine the BPI project budget. Table 3.11 provides a variety of methods and a brief description of each.

Some methods are more accurate than others. The method used is based on a number of factors, such as:

- Expectations of the sponsor and other key leaders
- Common methods used within the organization
- Information available about the project

Plan Team Kick-off Meeting
  Determine purpose and objectives
  Develop agenda
    Determine topics for discussion
    Determine timing
  Develop team-building activities
  Develop pre-work components
    Develop survey/skills questionnaire
  Prepare materials for meeting
    Compile documents to share pre-meeting
  Secure facilitator
    Evaluate facilitators
    Select facilitator
      Contract with facilitator
  Send meeting invitation
Travel
  Secure hotel for participants
    Contract with hotel for direct billing
  Make travel arrangements for all participants
  Send travel confirmation e-mails to all participants
Team Kick-off Meeting
  Conduct team kick-off meeting

Figure 3.11b   Example continued: Team kick-off meeting task

DIRECT COSTS	INDIRECT COSTS
• Internal labor costs • External labor (contractors, consultants) • Materials and equipment costs • Travel for team meetings • Training on the new process • Stakeholder meeting costs such as food and beverage, meeting room rentals • Contracting fees related to the project • Costs associated in documenting processes	• General administrative or overhead costs (electricity, air conditioning/heating costs) • Fringe benefits • Depreciation on equipment • Marketing and sales costs • Research and development costs

Figure 3.12   Direct and indirect project costs

Table 3.11 Example cost estimating methods

Estimating Methodology	Brief Description
Expert judgment	Expert judgment is based on the expertise of project team members who understand the costs associated with a particular component of the project. For example, if the BPI project requires development of software, a team member with expertise in the software may have knowledge as to the costs involved in the development effort.
Analogous estimating (also called top-down estimating)	Analogous estimating looks at past similar projects and what they cost to complete to determine the cost of the current BPI projects. For example, if a project is launched with a proposed budget, it is likely that similar projects have been used to determine the cost of the newly launched project. Analogous estimating is most commonly used early on in the project.
Parametric estimating	Parametric estimating uses quantitatively based information to determine project costs. For example, cost per hour for software developers or costs for using an application, such as cost per online survey developed. Parametric estimating is not commonly used for BPI projects but is common for technology projects.
Bottom-up estimating	Bottom-up estimating relies on the WBS being broken down into the smallest tasks, or work packages and cost being associated with each individual task. This information is then rolled up to the major task that the smaller tasks comprise.
Three-point estimates	Three-point estimates use three estimates to define a range for the cost of the task: • **Most Likely:** cost based on a realistic assessment of the required work and expenses associated with that work. • **Optimistic:** cost based on a best-case scenario for the task. • **Pessimistic:** cost based on worst-case scenario for the task.

There are a number of resources available on the Internet and via project management books on estimating costs for projects that provide further details and instructions on how to use each of the methods listed in Table 3.11.

When determining the project budget, the project manager should be sure to note what method(s) of estimating were used to determine or fine-tune the budget. Certainly if the project manager is trying to make the case for a higher budget for the project, this information will be required as well as the justification for a higher budget. For example, if the project cost does not include money for training, the business case might be that training cannot be provided on the new process unless additional budget monies are allocated to develop a training program. A lack of training would affect the roll out of the new process and its success overall.

Contingencies in budgets are common and allow for managing surprises that will inevitably arise on the BPI project. It is common for 10-20% to be set aside for management contingency. Contingencies are difficult, if not impossible, to include when bidding on government contracts for BPI projects, as they are often removed from the budget by the agency approving the bid.

Even at this stage of the BPI project, the budget should be considered an estimate. As more work is done in project planning, the budget will become further refined and then considered a final budget. It is important for the project manager to set expectations with the sponsor that, as the project progresses, more details may come to light which require adjustments to the budget.

High-level Communications Planning

An effective communication plan is a *critical* component for a successful outcome of the BPI project. Communication planning, however, is not easy with BPI projects. Given the wide variety of individuals usually involved in the project, there are just as many communication expectations. Each stakeholder will respond to communications differently, with some responding better to certain communication modes than others.

Jeremy learned early on while managing BPI projects that the need to use a variety of communication modes was essential in order to capture the largest group of stakeholders. This included using a combination of small group meetings, presenting at department meetings, and using e-mail as well as the internal company newsletter for communications.

As an initial first step, the project manager, working in collaboration with the project team, should develop a high-level communication plan for the BPI project. Early planning for communications will result in more effectively engaging the stakeholders to get their buy-in and commitment—ensuring their participation in the BPI project. It also facilitates:

- Improving requirements gathering
- Increasing understanding around BPI project goals and objectives

- Improving working relationships between stakeholders and the project team
- Creating better management of stakeholders' expectations of the project through regular sharing of information

Early communication efforts should focus on the following:

- Promoting the benefit of the BPI project being launched to stakeholders and its value to both the organization and individuals; providing a high-level overview of the BPI project.
- Communicating with each specific group of stakeholders—e.g., individuals from whom the project team needs information, individuals who will be impacted after the BPI project is complete, individuals who need to participate in documenting processes—as to specific needs on the project to engage them early on in the effort.

As communication plans are being developed, consider the following:

- How much will stakeholders be impacted by the BPI initiative?
- How long have those who will be impacted been in the organization and in their current role?
- How many BPI initiatives have individuals been involved in within the organization and how accepting have they been of such initiatives?
- How successful have past BPI initiatives been within the organization?

Answering these questions provides a level of detail about your stakeholders that enables a more effective structure for early and ongoing communications.

Figure 3.13 shows a potential overview communication plan for the BPI project discussed in earlier chapters, *Improvement in HR A/P Processes*. This format allows for a high-level overview of necessary early communications for the BPI project. Capturing this information in this format enables the project manager and the project team to ensure communications are done at the right time with the right individuals. A common mistake made in many BPI projects is a lack of communication with stakeholders. This particular communication plan would continue to detail other communications with these groups. For example, the project manager may add to the communication plan in Figure 3.13 that an e-mail is to be sent to select HR department employees with dates for shadowing employees to capture and document the current process.

Early Stage: Overview Communication Plan			
WHO	**WHAT**	**WHEN**	**HOW**
Human Resources	Overview of the project charter, scope statement, schedule and overall plan; involvement necessary in project	At project start	Presentation and discussion at HR department meeting (1 hour allocated for presentation and discussion)
Accounting/Finance	Overview of the project charter, scope statement, schedule and overall plan; involvement necessary in project	At project start	Presentation and discussion at Accounting/Finance department meeting (1 hour allocated for presentation and discussion)
Training vendors	Overview of project, value to training vendors in making process changes	After HR and Accounting/ Finance department meetings	E-mail from HR management to all training vendors, content to be provided by project team
Sponsor	Status report based on presentations and discussions with HR and Accounting/ Finance and communication sent to training vendors	After initial communications with involved departments and training vendors	Verbal update in one-on-one meeting with Sponsor

Figure 3.13   Example partial overview communication plan

Some project managers like to keep potential risks to the BPI project to themselves, thinking it will worry or scare off stakeholders. While they may be worried, I guarantee you they are also thinking about risks of the project. I have learned over the years in managing BPI projects that sharing information about risks that have been identified, and how the project team will manage those risks, increases the comfort level of stakeholders. When I communicate this information, they understand that the team has prepared for this project and are ready to move forward and tackle any issues that arise.

Communications planning and socializing BPI initiatives—which go hand-in-hand—will be discussed in more detail in Chapter 4.

Risk Management Plan

Risks are inherent in every project and are certainly prevalent in BPI projects. Given the reach that BPI projects may have throughout the organization, risk planning is essential to increase the success of the BPI initiative.

Risk management planning should be developed in collaboration with the team and key stakeholders. The diversity of the project team and key stakeholders in assisting in risk management planning provides:

- Increased identification of potential risks to the BPI project
- Increased engagement in managing risks when they arise
- Innovation in development of potential solutions to identified risks
- Increased commitment to supporting risk management activities throughout the project life cycle

Risk planning entails performing the following steps:

1. Developing the *risk management plan*
2. Identifying risks
3. Analyzing risks
4. Prioritizing and categorizing risks
5. Developing the risk register
6. Monitoring risks throughout the BPI project life cycle

The risk management plan is the document that delineates how risks will be identified and managed throughout the BPI project life cycle. The J. Ross website provides a downloadable risk management plan template. Table 3.12 provides a description of each component of the risk management plan.

Notice in this table that one component of the risk management plan is *funding*. Let's assume that the BPI project requires use of new technology within the organization. There are internal resources that are being planned for, in order to implement the new technology. However, none of the internal resources have ever worked with this technology before. A risk to the project is that internal resources will be unable to work with the new technology, given their limited expertise. The risk will be managed by hiring external contractors to develop with the new technology and train internal resources to maintain it moving forward. The cost of external contractors for this effort is estimated at $50,000 to $75,000. Monies will be set aside for this amount (risk reserve or contingency) in order to provide funding should external contractors be needed to utilize the new technology. If external contractors are not utilized, the money is *not* used for anything else on the project. It is set aside for this need only.

Table 3.12   Risk management plan components

Component of Risk Management Plan	Description
Risk tools/techniques	This section is where the project manager delineates how risks will be identified. This may be through brainstorming (most common), utilizing risk software, evaluation of past projects, experts, research, etc.
Risk owners/ responsibilities	Team members or stakeholders responsible for monitoring risks and updating the risk register. For example, John Smith may be responsible for all technology risks which includes monitoring for those risks to occur and managing the risk if it does occur.
Risk categories	Categories used to classify risks. For example, technology, financial, vendor, team resources, external.
Risk tolerance	Risk tolerance is related to how accepting the organization is of risk occurring. It may be tolerance in general (e.g., pharmaceutical companies are less tolerant of risk overall, regardless of the type of project) or risk tolerance for a particular project (e.g., a company may set aside monies for innovation and any projects related to innovation have a higher tolerance for risk). Risk tolerance could be classified as low, medium, high or using 1 (no tolerance) to 5 (high tolerance), or even 1 through 3.
Risk probability definition	This is the definition of probability (how likely is it the risk will occur?) to be used on the project. It may be classified as low, medium, high or 1-5 or 1-3.
Risk impact definition	This is the definition of impact (how seriously is the risk going to impact the project if it does occur?) to be used on the project. It may be classified as low, medium, high or 1-5 or 1-3.
Funding for risks	Any budget monies set aside to manage risks on the project should be included here. This money is used *only* to manage risks that arise. If it is not needed, it is not used for any other part of the project. This is the risk reserve.
Frequency and timing for risk management activities	How frequently will the team review project risks. It may be weekly (for very complex, riskier BPI projects) or monthly or as designated by the project manager and the project sponsor.

The other tool that will be used frequently on BPI projects is the *risk register*. The J. Ross website provides a downloadable risk register template. Figure 3.14 provides an example of a completed risk register.

Risk Register Example

Project Name: Improvement in HR A/P Processes	Date: January 20xx	
Risk ID/WBS Number WBS Number: IX	**Risk Description:** Engaging A/P in the stakeholders meetings to gather data. A/P is involved in two other projects that may impact their ability and willingness to participate in this project.	
Risk Category: Stakeholders		
Probability: 3	**Impact** 5	**Overall Rating:** 15
Priority Ranking: Medium		
How will risk be addressed? Will accommodate A/P schedules as needed to engage in stakeholder meetings, through one-on-one meetings, via survey or in other ways that enables A/P participation.		
Team member responsibility (name and role) John Smith, Project Team Member		

Figure 3.14   Example risk register

Recall that in the downloadable project charter for the sample project, *Improvement in HR A/P Processes*, one of the first risks identified is engaging Accounting in the project. This is a potential issue because Accounting has two other projects in which they are involved, reducing their ability, and potentially willingness, to be involved in yet another project. Figure 3.14 is the BPI project team's plan for managing this particular risk to the project. Notice the following in Figure 3.14:

- The WBS number is linked to the high-level project schedule shown in Figure 2.10. This particular risk is tied to WBS Number IX: Stakeholder meeting/data gathering.
- The probability of this risk occurring is a 3. This number will be determined by any number of factors, such as past history (in this case experience working with A/P on projects), conversations with A/P on how committed they are to the initiative, and/or how vested A/P might be in the project.
- The impact of the risk occurring is a 5. This is a high impact because A/P is *needed* for this project to be successful. The BPI project cannot be successfully implemented without A/P involvement.

- The overall rating is determined by multiplying the probability of the risk occurring (3) by the impact if it does occur (5), which equals 15 (3 × 5 = 15).
- This is considered a *medium* priority. This may be set by the organization (such as via a Project Management Office or Center of Excellence) based on tolerance of risk by the organization, by the sponsor of the project, based on past project history, or determined by the project manager in collaboration with the project team. Priority ranking may also be determined based on information about the stakeholders involved in the risk. For example, in this particular situation, the project manager and the team may know that A/P will find the time to be involved in the project because they are committed to improvements in processing of vendor invoices but are still setting the priority as *medium* because it is essential that A/P participate in data gathering/documenting processes.
- The team has decided to address this potential risk by working with A/P to accommodate their schedule. Table 3.13 describes four ways to address identified risks.
- A team member has been selected to be responsible for managing this risk. This individual's responsibilities may include, in this example,

Table 3.13   Ways to address identified risks

Addressing Identified and Prioritized Risks		
Address by...	**Description of method**	**Example of use of method (risk: A/P may not be engaged in stakeholder data gathering meetings)**
Avoid	Prevent or eliminate the risk from occurring by eliminating its cause.	Do not include A/P in data gathering meetings and rather get information needed from HR only.
Mitigate	Reduce the probability or the impact of the risk if it occurs.	Work closely with A/P to schedule times for data gathering that work for them.
Transfer	Shift the risk to a third party.	Have the sponsor be responsible for ensuring A/P attends data gathering meetings or hire a third party (consultant) to manage the data gathering process.
Accept	Accept that the risk will occur and it cannot be mitigated, transferred, or avoided.	Do nothing and hope for the best (the team has other options and therefore this option would not even be considered in risk planning).

working closely with A/P to accommodate their schedules for participating in data gathering.

In Figure 3.14, the risk method chosen for this identified risk is *mitigate*. In order to mitigate the risk of A/P not being available for stakeholder data gathering meetings, the team—and in particular John Smith—will reach out proactively to work closely with A/P to schedule dates for data gathering that are most convenient for them.

Refer back to the information on problem solving and decision making earlier in this chapter. Managing risks that arise *requires* problem solving and decision-making skills. The best practices provided earlier enable the project manager and his team to effectively think through risks that may arise on the project and how they will be handled should they actually come to fruition.

Keep in mind that when the team is planning responses to potential BPI projects, secondary risks may come to light. Secondary risks are risks that come about due to a planned response to an identified risk. These risks should also be planned for and part of the risk register. Additionally, residual risks may come to light. Residual risks are risks that remain after risk responses have been implemented. These risks will only be addressed and managed if they occur. The project manager might classify these as risks that are *accepted*. Figure 3.15 provides an example of a residual risk and a secondary risk.

Example: Secondary and Residual Risks

Secondary Risk	The project team may choose to hire a consultant to document current processes because there is no internal resource with skills in process documentation. The secondary risk associated with this action is developing the agreement with the consultant. The team would want to analyze this secondary risk and plan for it.
Residual Risk	The project manager may move forward and sign an agreement with a consultant that puts penalties on the consultant if deadlines are missed. However, just because there are penalties in place doesn't mean that deadlines will not be missed. If the consultant misses a deadline, the team will then deal with that situation. Nothing will be done about missing deadlines now other than putting penalties in place.

Figure 3.15   Example residual and secondary risks

Expanding on Your Initial Risk List

In Chapter 2 we looked at the beginning of identifying risks based on information in the charter, in the scope statement, and based on knowledge of the organization. The project manager will want to expand on this initial list of risks by collaborating with the project team and key stakeholders to identify any additional risks. There are a number of other ways to identify risks and expand upon the initial risk list, including:

- Lessons learned from previous BPI projects or research of similar BPI projects
- Research external to the organization (e.g., regulations)
- Brainstorming with the team/key stakeholders
- One-on-one or small group interviews with stakeholders
- Strengths, weaknesses, opportunities, and threats (SWOT) analysis (brainstorming strengths and weaknesses and then examining those strengths to find opportunities [positive risk] and the weaknesses [negative risks])
- Root cause identification (analyzing each risk and diving deeper to understand exactly what is behind that risk—its root cause)
- Surveying experts external to the organization (Delphi technique)
- Review of the critical path for the project

In most BPI projects there is uncertainty around the schedule, the budget set aside for the project, and the expectations and/or tolerance of change by stakeholders. These are all areas that the project manager and his team should examine for risks to the project. In identifying risks to the BPI project, review in detail each project resource and activity associated with the project to find risks associated with those areas.

Allan was leading a BPI project that included team members who were all assigned to other projects in progress within the organization. The most time any team member could commit to this initiative was 75%. The rest were available only 30 to 60% of the time. Allan knew project team resources were a risk to the project. The other projects in progress would impact his project because resources would be tied up to manage those and, should something occur on those projects, his resources may be pulled to commit more time to the earlier projects to which they were assigned. Additionally, as with any organization, something also happens that pulls a resource away temporarily. If too many resources are pulled from his project, or if their time allocated to his project is reduced, it will impact the probability of achieving the implementation goals set up by the sponsor.

All project managers have their own way of identifying risks. There is no perfect way to do so. Let's look in further detail at three options commonly used by project managers and the team to determine risks on BPI projects. These options allow for more diversity in the identification of risks, which leads to the likelihood that the most troublesome potential risks will be identified and planned for.

Brainstorming

Brainstorming is an excellent way to identify risks to BPI projects, but it does require strong facilitation skills to keep the group on track. Certainly some risks that are shared during brainstorming will not be practical or even likely to ever happen, but that is where the diversity exists in brainstorming resulting in the ability to identify more risks than the team might otherwise be able to do.

While brainstorming is often considered an activity where ideas are just shouted out; the process of using brainstorming for identifying risks to BPI projects must be well-structured. The project manager, or designated facilitator of the session, might focus the efforts of those involved in the process by identifying risks that occur in particular categories, or project areas—for example, risks that might occur concerning the specific technology used, external risks due to regulations or the marketplace, or customer-associated risks. For larger groups, or in cases where stakeholders are overly eager to share their thoughts, a *round robin* approach may work—where the facilitator of the session asks each stakeholder, in turn, to identify a risk to the project. This prevents shouting out ideas and better controls the process of brainstorming potential risks overall.

Interviewing

When conducting interviews, keep the group of those being interviewed small—no more than 5 to 8 per group—enabling for a better conversation overall. Similar to brainstorming sessions, these sessions should be well-facilitated and should enable and encourage participation from everyone involved. This is where the project manager, or other facilitator, may start by asking these three simple questions:

1. What could go wrong with this BPI project?
2. What are the uncertainties with this particular BPI project?
3. What don't we know that may impact the project or impact our ability to manage the BPI project through to implementation?

Expert Judgment

Reaching out for expertise on potential risks to the BPI project is another way to determine risks that may arise. These could come from industry reports, market research, competitor knowledge, or through any variety of internal or external sources. External experts could provide independent opinions about the risk associated with a particular BPI project. Utilizing a variety of expertise increases your chances of capturing as many potential risks as possible. The BPI project team will look for consensus among the experts to determine which risks are most likely and should be planned for.

All of these methods, when performed well, will help to capture the breadth of experience and knowledge that exists in the project team among key stakeholders and within external sources.

Quality Plan

The goal of this section is *not* to make the BPI project manager an expert in quality (think *Six Sigma*), but rather to provide a general understanding of the importance of quality and how to assure quality on BPI projects. The project manager does *not* need to be an expert in Six Sigma nor Total Quality Management (TQM) to lead successful BPI projects.

Although quality is certain of importance on *every* project, it is essential for BPI projects. BPI projects *are* about quality in all of these categories:

- Understanding stakeholder requirements for the process
- Documenting the current process to look for gaps or weak links
- Analyzing the current process against the stakeholder requirements
- Developing a new or refined process to meet stakeholder requirements
- Testing the new process to ensure it meets stakeholder needs
- Rolling out the new process organization wide

This is not dissimilar to a Six Sigma project that uses the define, measure, analyze, improve, and control (DMAIC) process as shown in Figure 3.16.

DMAIC is a data-driven method for improving, fine-tuning, and rolling out business processes. While DMAIC is used mainly for Six Sigma projects, it can be applied to any process improvement initiative. Figure 3.16 shows what each step of the DMAIC process entails at a high level.

Organizations undertake BPI projects to improve in some area of the organization. BPI projects that are not quality driven do not take into account the requirements of the stakeholders—those individuals who are actually working with the process.

Quality is assured on the BPI project through the following ways:

- Understanding quality expectations of the stakeholders
- Knowing the metrics for success—for example, reduce time-to-market, reduce manufacturing costs, improve customer satisfaction, etc.

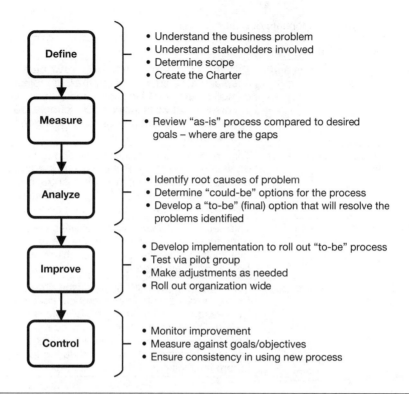

Figure 3.16 DMAIC Process

- Engaging stakeholders in the BPI project—from the start through the implementation

Table 3.14 describes key components of a quality plan. The J. Ross website includes a downloadable quality plan template.

Testing Plan

Developing the testing plan for the BPI project enables testing of the quality of the BPI project—basically to find out if the new process is sufficient to meet the goals of the project. For example, if the BPI project's objective is to reduce time-to-market of new products, does the new process, when tested, result in reaching this objective. This is where the pilot group comes into play. Testing plans must be developed early on in the project and the pilot group should be engaged from the beginning—*not* just when their work of testing the new process will begin.

Table 3.14   Key components of a quality plan

Component of Quality Plan	Description
Quality assurance approach and activities	This section describes how quality will be managed and assured throughout the BPI project as well as the activities associated with assuring quality. Activities include, for example, documenting the current process and testing the new process.
Testing plan and acceptance processes	This section further delineates testing to be done in relation to the BPI project. For example, utilization of a pilot group to test the new process and their responsibilities associated with testing the process is included here.
Quality audit activities	This section delineates what activities will be done to assure high quality on the project. This may include, for example, use of checklists for testing of a new process.
Quality management responsibilities	For larger, complex BPI projects, the project manager may assign team members specifically responsible for managing BPI project quality. These team members may be responsible for managing the testing process and ensuring issues are documented during testing before final roll out of the new process.

The testing plan should include details on what needs to be tested in the new process and what feedback is needed from the testers. In order to achieve effective testing, the testers need to understand the differences between the current (old) process and the proposed *to-be* (new) process. Additionally, they will need to be trained on using the process *before* testing begins. The project manager needs to be sure to allocate sufficient time for training of the pilot group and for testing the new process. Remember that it is very unlikely that the pilot group will be devoted 100% of the time to testing; rather they will be testing while doing their *day jobs*.

Training Plan

Even the smallest *tweak* to a process requires training for those who will use the process. Too many BPI projects fail because training is not conducted. It is expected by the BPI team and, more often, the sponsor that when the new process is rolled out, employees will just begin to use it—that never happens. Those who will be impacted by the new process—the stakeholders—*must* be trained in how to use the new process. As a best practice, ensure that stakeholders understand and know early on that training will be provided. The earlier that those impacted know about the plans to train them in the new process, the more relaxed they are about the upcoming change.

The ideal training plan includes a variety of options, especially for larger organizations where employees may be global or remote and BPI initiatives may be more complex, to ensure understanding of how to use the process. This might include:

- Small group training
- One-on-one training for those who will use the process daily
- Virtual training
- Self-paced e-learning
- Training manuals to reference

Roll Out, Measurement, and Evaluation Plan

Another plan included in the BPI project overall documentation includes the roll out, measurement, and evaluation plan. This plan comes into play *after* testing of the new process is done and any changes are made based on pilot group feedback. This plan includes information on:

- How the process will be rolled out throughout the organization. For example, will it be rolled out in stages and how much time, if at all, will the old process be available for use while the new process is being rolled out. This includes information about training on the process organization-wide.
- How the success of the new process will be measured and evaluated and the time associated with that. This refers back to the goals of the BPI project. For example, if the objective (or business impact expected) is to reduce from 5+ days to no more than 3 days the amount of time to submit an invoice for processing from HR to Finance, when is that expected to happen? Does the sponsor expect that the reduction in processing time will occur within two weeks or three months after the new process is implemented?

Even if the evaluation and measurement plan is being managed by a different group, it should be developed early on in the BPI project planning. Additionally, the individual or group that will be managing this component of the project should be involved in the project kick off.

Roll out of the *to-be* process as well as measuring its success will be discussed in more detail in Chapter 8.

PLAN EARLY FOR LESSONS LEARNED

The last meeting scheduled on my BPI projects is a lessons-learned meeting. I have learned over the years that unless the meeting is planned for and on the schedule early, it just doesn't happen. The project ends and everyone is off to work on the next one!

When project managers plan early for lessons learned, they and their teams are better able to evaluate the success of the project at its conclusion. By planning for lessons learned early on in the BPI project, lessons are captured throughout the project life cycle, and not simply at the end when the project team is ready to move on to the next BPI project and much is forgotten or details are sparse. As a best practice, at least on a monthly basis, the project manager should include an agenda item to evaluate the project to date: What is working? What is not? Include key stakeholders at these meetings. Additionally, for BPI projects that may last 6+ months, send a survey mid-project to stakeholders to check in on their perception of what is going well and where improvements are needed.

The Value of Lessons Learned

Lessons learned, when captured and applied on one BPI project, provide value to future BPI projects. Lessons learned provide future BPI project managers and their teams with a head start in a variety of areas including risk identification, planning communications, and developing the project schedule. For example, issues encountered on a past BPI project that was resolved satisfactorily provides information for avoiding, or planning for that issue, on a future BPI project.

One client the authors have worked with, who regularly launched BPI projects due to tremendous growth within the organization, started to capture lessons learned and developed a database to store the information captured to share with others. Each time a BPI project was launched, the project manager in charge immediately accessed the lessons-learned database to review past BPI projects. Within one year of evaluating the success of the lessons-learned initiative, the leadership team found that BPI projects were more successful overall—they were completed in less time, stakeholders were more engaged, and there were far fewer risks that occurred on the projects.

BPI projects, over time, are run more efficiently when lessons are applied from past projects. This assumes, of course, that lessons learned have been captured and shared.

Developing Your Lessons-learned Methodology

The lessons-learned methodology is how the project manager will work with the team to capture lessons learned and how that information will be shared throughout the organization on future BPI projects. In most organizations that embrace lessons learned, there is a common methodology used on all projects launched within the organization. If such a process does not exist, the smart BPI project manager develops his own methodology and shares with the team. If needed, that same BPI project manager will share his team's lessons learned from the BPI project via e-mail with future BPI project managers.

Lessons learned captured should share what went well on the BPI project and how those successes can be applied on future similar projects as well as what was less successful (e.g., issues encountered, poor decisions made, etc.) and how to avoid similar situations in the future.

A simple lessons-learned methodology will include a document that captures the following information:

- Area reviewed (e.g., team kick-off meeting, vendors/contractors, stakeholder management, communications, process documentation)
- Situation or issue encountered in the area reviewed
- Actions taken or alternatives considered to resolve the situation or issue
- What worked well (exceptional performance on the project)
- What can be improved upon in the future

When technology is used to hold and share lessons learned captured on BPI projects, the information should be categorized to enable ease of search. Examples of categories are *procurement, risks,* or *communications.* Additionally, the information should be searchable via keywords, such as *stakeholders* or *vendor/ contractor.*

USING TECHNOLOGY EFFECTIVELY

Technology initiates improved engagement of stakeholders, especially on BPI projects that have a global reach or where stakeholders are located remotely. This includes communicating with stakeholders, sharing information about the project, and otherwise keeping everyone updated. Additionally, technology enables project team members to better communicate and share information about the project. Technology ranges from things as simple as e-mails and conference calls to virtual meetings to using more complex tools such as project portals.

For global BPI projects, make sure that the technology selected is accessible to all team members and stakeholders. If the team has access to a number of technology tools, choose the best tool for the appropriate situation. For example, if the initial team kick-off meeting includes stakeholders and team members from a variety of locations and a face-to-face meeting is just not possible, the project manager might choose to use a virtual platform to *connect* the team.

Table 3.15 provides a sample of options for using a variety of technologies to meet objectives, or tasks, on BPI projects.

Project Portals

A project portal is an effective tool for sharing information on the BPI project, engaging stakeholders, and communicating about the project. The portal can also be a location for project documentation and lessons learned. The project manager can use the portal to enable BPI project teams to:

- Have access to roles and responsibilities on the project
- Provide contact information for each team member, including time zones if team members come from across the globe
- Display expertise/special skills that team members have that may benefit the project (such as technology skills, good problem solving, etc.)

Table 3.15   Options for using technology

Technology to Use	Objective		
	Sharing information with project team members and stakeholders	Stakeholder meetings to gather information on current processes, ask questions about processes being designed, etc.	Collaborative problem solving with project team members
Teleconference	X	X	X (small groups)
E-mail	X		
Virtual meeting	X	X	X
Project portal	X		

A portal can provide a dashboard for the sponsor(s) and key stakeholders so they can get updated information on the BPI project.

> *One BPI project featured 8 sponsors and 6 other key stakeholders that wanted a variety of information about the project. A project portal was used to set up dashboards for each of the leaders so that they were able to get access to the information they wanted, when they wanted it.*

In Chapter 3, we looked at the value of taking a systematic approach to BPI projects. In this chapter, best practices for engaging early on and kicking off the BPI project team were shared. This initial kick off allows project teams to get to know each other on a personal and professional basis. This only increases their comfort level working on the team and relying on each other to accomplish the goals of the project. This is not always easy to accomplish. With so much on the *to do* list of companies, there is often a push to get started immediately on the project and skip some important preliminary *getting to know each other* meetings. But these meetings are not all about fun and games, they are setting the stage for how the team will work with each other, with the stakeholders, and enable development of some key project documentation. When this documentation is developed collaboratively with input from all team members, the project manager sees increased buy-in toward sticking to processes and procedures agreed upon to work on the project.

Since requests for changes can really impact the project, if those requests are not managed, a process for a change management framework based on the complexity of the BPI project was shared. While, certainly, some of this information was a refresher for project managers, the authors cannot tell you how many times they have been called in to save a BPI project that has gotten way out of control because changes were not managed from the start. If a change management process already exists within the organization, share it with BPI project team members to ensure understanding of the process. If one doesn't exist, create one!

This book has free material available for download from the
Web Added Value™ resource center at *www.jrosspub.com*

4

UNDERSTANDING AND SOCIALIZING THE BPI PROJECT

No business process improvement (BPI) project can be successful if the project manager, the team, and the sponsors have not socialized the project to achieve buy-in and commitment throughout the stakeholder group. However, *prior* to socializing the project, the project manager and his team must understand the project themselves.

Jeremy had spent significant time with the sponsors understanding the purpose of the project and how it was aligned to the company's strategic long-term objectives. He was confident that he would be able to answer any questions that came up during his upcoming stakeholder meeting to introduce the project. During the meeting, the very first question that was asked was why the BPI project was moving forward now? Jeremy had it covered! Based on his conversations with the sponsor he was able to respond to the question by letting the stakeholder know the alignment to the strategic goal and the value in initiating the project now rather than later in order to meet customer needs. Additionally, he was able to explain why the project would be of value to individual stakeholders.

PHASE 1 OVERVIEW

Figure 4.1 depicts the first phase of the six-phased approach to managing your BPI projects, introduced in Chapter 3. In this chapter, the focus will be on *Understanding and Socializing the Project.*

In this initial phase of the BPI project, the project manager—along with his team—is:

- Developing an initial description of the problem to be solved by initiating the BPI project
- Developing the preliminary project plan to implement the BPI project
- Identifying stakeholders who will be impacted by changes to processes
- Determining the preliminary project scope
- Determining desired performance improvements in the business (goals to measure against)
- Preparing the preliminary communication plans
- Setting initial timelines and project budget
- Determining preliminary training needs and implementation/roll out plans

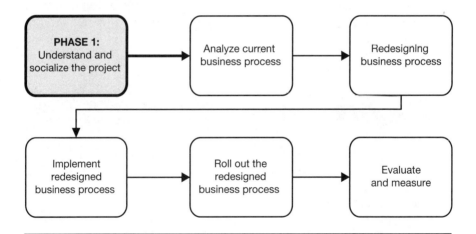

Phase 1 High-level Tasks

- Learn about the BPI project assigned – objectives, vision – why do this project
- Develop early planning documents (scope, high-level schedule)
- Begin to communicate to socialize and set expectations about the project
  – value/benefits
- Begin to communicate to engage stakeholders who are impacted by the project

Figure 4.1   Phase 1 of the six-step process

These tasks were discussed in previous chapters and are all necessary to fully understand the project. Until the project is understood—both from the perspective of the value to the organization and the value to individual stakeholders—it is not possible to socialize it effectively. Fully understanding the purpose and vision of the project—why the BPI project is being launched and what the future goal or objective of the BPI project is—helps when making the business case to get buy-in and support for the BPI project.

Once the project manager and the team have achieved a complete understanding of the project, it is essential to begin to socialize the BPI project with others whose support and commitment will be required, to ensure a successful project end result. It cannot be assumed that the project sponsor has socialized the project with other stakeholders, or that it is a responsibility the project sponsor will even take on. It is the responsibility of the project manager and his team to develop the plan for socializing the project and get the support he and his team needs from the sponsor.

Let's define *socializing the project* so that there is a common understanding of the term that is being used in this chapter and throughout the book. *Socialization*: The art and process of getting stakeholders comfortable with a particular BPI project in order to gain their support and commitment to achieving success on the project.

Socializing does not mean that if stakeholders decide they are not happy with a decision to launch a BPI project that it will not move forward, rather, socialization provides a way to increase the confidence in the BPI initiative and an understanding of why the BPI project is being launched.

THE VALUE OF SOCIALIZING EARLY AND OFTEN

Socializing the BPI project *prior* to beginning the actual work on project tasks enables the project manager and his team to more effectively manage the project and drive it to a successful conclusion. Too often project teams jump into a BPI project without taking the time to socialize the initiative throughout the organization. There may be a number of reasons for this, including:

- Lack of understanding about how to socialize the BPI project
- Lack of interest in socializing the BPI project
- Lack of understanding about the value in investing the time and energy to socialize the BPI project
- False belief that socializing is not actually considered as *working* on the BPI projects:

Personal experience has shown Gina, one of the authors, that socializing BPI projects increases the likelihood of success of the initiative. When she has taken the time, in collaboration with the BPI project team, to discuss with stakeholders the value of the project, she is better able to influence those stakeholders in helping her and the team to achieve project success. Undoubtedly, as the project progresses she will need to rely on stakeholders for any number of tasks (for example, providing information, running reports, or testing new processes); by socializing the project with the stakeholders before she needs their support, however, Gina notes she is more likely to increase their commitment to the project.

Socializing the project, however, is not once and done. Socializing the BPI project should be done just before work begins on the project's tasks and should continue throughout the project—for example, by continuing to talk of the value of the BPI project during stakeholder meetings or via a project portal. Failure to continue socializing and discussing the value of the BPI project could result in those who were initially on board and committed to become resisters—no longer interested in the BPI project or its value to the organization.

While, certainly, socialization is essential for *any* project, it is most essential for BPI projects, given that BPI initiatives have such a large change management component. Change management initiatives often fail when they are not effectively or sufficiently socialized prior to implementation. The larger the BPI project, the more likely the project manager would want to assign a team specifically for the purpose of socializing the BPI project and being the point of contact for all stakeholder inquiries. If the project manager has not developed strong relationships throughout the organization, attempting to socialize the BPI project by sharing benefits will be quite difficult, if not impossible. In such situations, since the project can't be put on hold to build relationships, assign a team member and/or request a key stakeholder with strong relationships within the organization to take the lead on socializing the BPI project.

Benefits of Socializing BPI Projects

Benefits in taking the time to socialize BPI projects are many and include:

- Increased commitment to the BPI project
- Increased likelihood of stakeholder participation in the BPI project
- Increased likelihood of BPI project success after implementation (the project *sticks*)

- Identification of champions (those who support the BPI effort) and resisters (those who are unsupportive and may try to derail the BPI project)
- Increased ability to convert those who may be negative or neutral about the project into *champions* who support the BPI project

Spending time up front to socialize the BPI project to achieve increased buy-in, commitment, and support for the initiative reduces the amount of work on the back end in trying to get the project to *stick* after implementation.

Challenges with Socializing BPI Projects

There are a number of challenges associated with socializing BPI projects. In Chapter 2 we discussed challenges in securing leadership support for the BPI initiative; here we'll discuss challenges specifically with getting support to socialize the initiative and getting stakeholders to commit to supporting the BPI project.

Past experiences with BPI projects—whether within the current organization or in another organization—will impact how supportive stakeholders will be of the BPI project being launched. This is certainly a challenge for a project manager who is trying to get buy-in for the BPI project. How can a project manager know the past experiences of the stakeholders? Ask! Consider this story:

Gina was working with a client specifically to help them socialize an upcoming BPI project. More than half of the employees were not engaged in the BPI project and, in fact, openly opposed it. It seemed odd to her that so many people were so negative about the BPI project. Further research, including asking a few of the more talkative employees, indicated that a little over two years ago the organization acquired a similar sized organization and, per the folks who were acquired (Gina's resisters to the BPI project), the acquisition was done so poorly that they had limited faith in the success of any BPI projects being launched. Gina convinced the CEO to push the start date of the initiative out by another two weeks in order to spend more time socializing the project to reduce the number of resisters. This required acknowledging past failures and explaining how the BPI project team would ensure that this project wouldn't repeat the failures of past projects.

When encountering individuals who are resistant to the project, the project manager should ask questions in order to gain an understanding of the reasons for their resistance. For example, the project manager may ask:

- Why do you think this project will not be successful?
- What worries you the most about this project being launched?
- What would you do instead if you were leading the effort?

The project manager might also inquire about past BPI initiatives in which the stakeholder was involved. This initiates a more open and honest conversation, which increases understanding of resistance and, therefore, encourages more resisters to be converted to champions of the BPI initiative.

In addition to challenges with past experiences related to BPI projects, challenges exist around finding time to socialize the project. Too often BPI projects are under tight deadlines; frequently because they are being launched in *reaction* to something happening within the organization. And, in some organizations, socialization is akin to doing nothing. For project managers who work in organizations where socialization is not valued because of tight deadlines or the impression that socialization is equal to not working on the project, it is essential to make the business case to allow for time to socialize. This is best done by highlighting the successes associated with socializing BPI projects to increase buy-in and support, which leads to an increased likelihood that the BPI project result will be long lasting.

One client linked socializing BPI projects to "having a party." In his opinion, it was a waste of time and delayed the project. In order to make the business case to move forward, a bit of research into the success rate of past BPI projects was performed. The research showed that projects that had been launched had very little support throughout the organization. While they may have come to what appeared to be a successful conclusion—the new process was rolled out organization-wide—in reality the new process was not being used consistently. The client was convinced to "give it a try" so that he could compare this project with past projects that were not socialized. He agreed to this and, after only two weeks of socializing, saw that more employees were engaged in the BPI initiative than had been on past BPI initiatives.

And, yet another challenge often encountered is the challenge around *how* to socialize the initiative. This frequently comes up in organizations that are uncertain about how to socialize initiatives, but also in situations where project managers feel like they have to push through socializing to get the project work begun as quickly as possible. In such situations, limited channels are used to socialize BPI initiatives, which reduces the number of stakeholders reached.

SOCIALIZATION CHANNELS

Similar to utilizing a number of channels for general BPI project communications, it is essential to utilize a number of channels for socializing your BPI project. Utilizing a number of channels allows you to reach the greatest number of stakeholders and increases the comfort level of stakeholders, as they have a number of options to communicate in return on the project. Not every stakeholder will be comfortable communicating in a group environment—such as during an all staff meeting—but may be more comfortable providing feedback one-on-one or in a small group meeting or via a survey.

Table 4.1 shows a number of channels to use to socialize the BPI initiative.

Figure 4.2 is an example of a poster displayed throughout the hallways of one of the author's clients.

Table 4.1   Channels to socialize BPI initiatives

• One-on-one conversations	• Small group meetings (multi-department)
• Department/business unit meetings	• E-mails and E-newsletters
• All staff or all hands meetings	• Posters in the hallways
• Breakfast, lunch & learns, or after-hours events	• Intranet sites/company portals
• Surveys	• Hallway conversations/conversations in company cafeteria

Free food! I'm there!

Thanks for Your Feedback!
Things Have to Get Better Around Here!
We Heard You and Have a Plan!

But We Need Your Help to Reach the End Goal!

Join us next Wednesday at noon in the cafeteria where we'll share with you:
- Our plan to improve how the work gets done in the office (based on your feedback)
- Our timeline to get started

Things are Looking up!

Lunch will be provided!

Figure 4.2   Example of socialization poster

After reading the feedback from an employee engagement survey, the executives realized that while the company has grown and is doing well overall, the system used to get the work done had to change to improve morale among the employees. Growth in the organization never took into account the changes needed to the processes and procedures for getting work done; and in trying to adapt, processes and procedures were becoming increasingly onerous. This poster was one of the first steps in getting employees socialized and engaged around the upcoming initiative.

Some methods work better than others in certain organizations. It is essential to keep in mind the goal of socializing the BPI project—to engage stakeholders in conversations about change early on and to keep them engaged throughout the initiative, thereby increasing the number of champions to the project and the likelihood of a successful launch of the BPI project.

> *The authors particularly like to keep their ears open at the water cooler or the coffee machine in an office or break room. They often hear things about the BPI initiative that they may not otherwise hear because some individuals aren't comfortable with sharing the information in a formal setting.*

Choosing the Right Socialization Channel for Your Project

Choosing the right socialization channel is based on four factors:

- Project complexity
- What works within the organization, given the culture and environment
- What works for the stakeholders
- What works for the BPI project team

Table 4.2 includes what to consider when evaluating the four factors involved in determining channels to socialize the BPI project.

Consider also past BPI initiatives that have occurred within the organization. What worked in socializing the initiative? What did not work well? Use lessons learned from past initiatives to determine how best to socialize the current BPI project. Reach out to other project managers within the organization to determine where they have had success in getting buy-in for their BPI projects. Ask project team members to share their ideas and best practices for getting buy-in.

Table 4.2   Factors to consider in socializing

Factor	Consider the following
Project complexity	The more complex the project, the more channels that should be used to reach a large group of stakeholders. Certainly for less complex BPI initiatives—for example, a project that impacts only one or two departments—a department meeting may suffice for socialization of the initiative, or even one-on-one meetings.
Organization culture/ environment	More formal organizational environments might react better to socialization via meetings or e-mail. In such cultures where blue suits are common, refer to socialization as "getting commitment" to increase buy-in. Organizations with a "fun" or relaxed environment may be engaged by posters in hallways. Certainly an organization that frequently has external visitors to the office would not want posters hung that visitors might see passing through the hallway.
Stakeholders	Getting to know the stakeholders enables selecting ways to socialize the BPI initiative that will work for the stakeholders. The project manager who has developed relationships with stakeholders understands how to best engage them—whether that means one-on-one meetings with quieter and more reserved stakeholders or via survey for those who prefer to remain anonymous. Certainly the more resisters to the initiative the more channels needed to get more stakeholders engaged.
BPI project team	Don't forget the BPI project team! Select channels for socialization that make sense given resources available, number of stakeholders, timelines, budgets, and what the team is trying to accomplish; as well as what is comfortable for the team.

DEVELOPING YOUR COMPREHENSIVE COMMUNICATION PLAN

In Chapter 3 we discussed preliminary communication planning. In this chapter the focus will be on further developing the communication plan that will be used to communicate and report on status throughout the BPI project.

While the comprehensive communication plan starts with socializing the BPI project, it also includes information on how project communications will occur, and when they will occur, throughout project implementation. Undoubtedly, adjustments will be made to the comprehensive communication plan as more information is gathered from socialization efforts. Comprehensive communication planning provides a number of benefits, including:

- Improving the effectiveness of communications overall (frequency and quality)
- Getting team members involved in, and responsible for, specific stakeholder communications
- Keeping stakeholders engaged in the BPI project through regular updates
- Getting stakeholders involved in communications through initiating more effective two-way conversations

Download a template and sample file for both an overview communication management plan and a more detailed communication management plan from the WAV™ section of the J. Ross website. The more complex the BPI initiative, the more likely the communication plan will be more robust with information beyond how the project will be communicated—including requirements or processes for distributing project information, an issue escalation process, as well as team member responsibilities for communications.

The project manager should work in collaboration with project team members to develop a comprehensive communication plan, ensuring commitment to the communication process. The more complex the BPI project, the more likely the project manager will need to rely on project team members' expertise to understand what should be communicated and when it should be communicated. Additionally, why should the project manager take on all responsibility for project communications? Share the leadership role with the team and provide exposure for team members by giving them responsibility for project communications, especially where they have expertise.

When developing communication plans, consider the following:

- What information will stakeholders need and want?
  - ◊ What are the key messages to be conveyed to stakeholders? (e.g., Why is this project being done? What are the benefits of the project? How will the organization support the project?)
- What questions or objections will stakeholders have and how might those questions or objections be addressed?

Selecting Appropriate Communication Channels

The process for selecting communication channels to provide ongoing and regular communications to stakeholders is very similar to how socialization channels are selected. The more options available—the better chance to capture the interest of the greatest number of stakeholders. Table 4.3 shows a variety of options for communicating with stakeholders and when/how those channels might be used.

Table 4.3   Options for communicating with stakeholders

Channel	When to Use
Meetings—small group, department/division, or all staff, virtual, or a combination	• To provide initial information about the project to stakeholders • To review and/or gather needed information from stakeholders (small group meeting or virtual meeting) • For regularly scheduled status updates on progress to stakeholders (not sponsor)
E-mails, e-newsletter or project portal (internal site)	• For sharing information • To provide updates between regularly scheduled stakeholder meetings
Surveys or interviews	• To gather information • To verify information gathered • To validate current documented processes and get feedback on proposed processes
One-on-one meetings	• To manage resisters to the BPI project • To engage stakeholders who are uncertain about the project • To engage quieter stakeholders

Utilize a variety of options for particular situations. For example, if the project manager needs to arrange for a stakeholder problem-solving session, either a face-to-face meeting or virtual meeting should be arranged rather than trying to accomplish problem solving via e-mail or conference call.

James was arranging for the initial stakeholder meeting to share project information and discuss the proposed timeline for implementation of new processes that would impact three departments in the organization. Given the large group he had to communicate with, he utilized the following channels to get out information to stakeholders in each of the three departments:

- *Scheduled two in-person meetings for those who were able to attend in person and needed options*
- *Scheduled two virtual meetings for those unable to attend in person or for whom in-person dates did not work*
- *Recorded the in-person and virtual meetings for those unable to attend either in-person meetings or virtual meetings*
- *Included all information about the project that was being shared via a project portal for access by all stakeholders*

By using a variety of channels for communicating with the stakeholders in the three departments, and providing a couple of options for each channel, James was able to reach over 90% of the stakeholders. The balance of stakeholders he reached out to one-on-one.

A Phased Communication Approach

A phased communication approach simply refers to managing communications based on the project life cycle. As noted earlier, communications early on are focused on socializing the initiative and are more inclusive of all stakeholders. The focus in early communications is mainly about the reason for the project moving forward and the value of the BPI project to the organization and individual stakeholders. Later on in the project, communications will change based on the current status or life-cycle stage of the project and the particular need for the communication. Later on in the project, communications are less about trying to *sell* the project and more about keeping stakeholders apprised of progress or asking for input on newly designed processes.

Figure 4.3 provides a partial snapshot of a phased communications plan specifically for the Human Resources (HR) department. This is a partially completed overview communication plan for HR based on what the group will need to know about the project from start to finish. (Recall this communication plan was started as part of Figure 3.13.)

As can be seen in Figure 4.3, the project team has determined communication needs (in this example through Phase 2) with the HR department, a key stakeholder in this example project. By developing the communication plan in detail, the project team increases the likelihood that communications will happen when they need to happen. Trying to remember to communicate *when something important happens on the project* is a bad idea and simply sets up the possibility of under-communicating with stakeholders or not sharing the right information at the right time. As a best practice, if team members are assigned to communicate, or be a point of contact, with specific groups, those team members should be the ones developing the communication plan.

Figure 4.4 provides an example of the types of communications that may be involved in the different phases of a BPI project. As a best practice, in the early project planning stages, determine what needs to be communicated from a major task or milestone perspective to begin to build your communication plan.

Table 4.4 shows the results of poor communications and the impact on the BPI project.

Human Resources Department Communication Plan (PARTIAL PLAN)				
PROJECT PHASE	**WHO**	**WHAT**	**WHEN**	**HOW**
Phase 1	Human Resources	Overview of the project charter, scope statement, schedule, and overall plan; involvement necessary in project	At project start (January)	Presentation and discussion at HR department meeting (1 hour allocated for presentation and discussion)
Phase 1		Follow-up meeting to respond to any questions based on overview meeting	(mid-January)	Via in-person meeting with department –2 meetings scheduled to accommodate all (1 hour per meeting allocated
Phase 1		Train HR in use of project portal to find information and communicate with project team	(mid-January)	Provide training via virtual platform, provide reference sheet for using portal (30 minutes)
Phase 2		Document current process	(end-January start)	Via one-on-one and small group meetings (1.5 hours per meeting)
Phase 2		E-mail with documented process to ensure valid/accuracy	(early-February)	E-mail to go with survey link to provide feedback

Figure 4.3   Phased communications snapshot

Special Considerations for Stakeholder Communications

Communications, in general, can be challenging. Certainly, adding the fact that the project is a business-process-focused initiative increases the challenges of communicating sufficiently, efficiently, and effectively with stakeholders. Not all stakeholders prefer the same types of communication—some are more visual and prefer to see charts and graphs; others prefer to read the information at their leisure—diving into details as they see fit; and yet others prefer to have a one-on-one conversation to learn more.

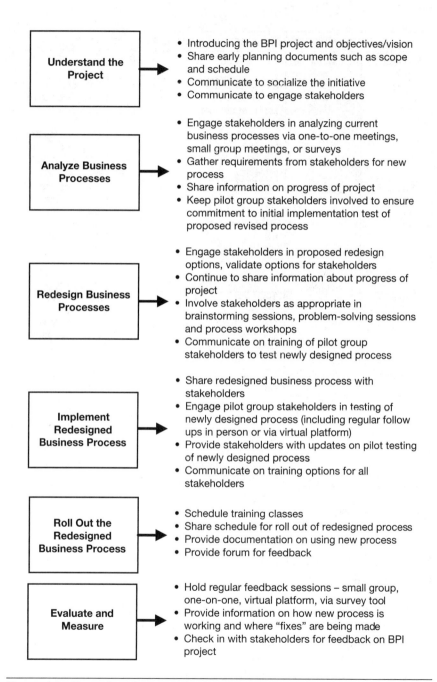

Figure 4.4   Examples of communication types

Table 4.4   Results of poor communications

Poor Team Communications	Poor Stakeholder Communications
• Misunderstanding around BPI project goals and objectives • Missed deadlines • Conflicts between team members • Individual team members moving in different directions • Decreased productivity on the BPI project leading to increased timelines, going out of scope or over budget • Lack of commitment on the part of project team members in accomplishing the goals of the BPI project • Failure to move the project forward	• Lack of or limited buy-in and commitment to the BPI project • Failure to provide input to requirements or other necessary information on documenting or designing processes • Misunderstanding around expectations on what is considered project success • Conflicts between the project team and stakeholders, or between stakeholder groups • Stakeholders who actively work against the BPI project • Failed projects

In an ideal world, project managers would communicate with each stakeholder *exactly* as the stakeholder wants to be communicated with. However, this is not practical to attempt and still accomplish the work of the project.

Gina has learned over the years that in order to better manage how she will communicate with stakeholders, and still leave the perception of options, she uses this approach: "I'd like to provide you and your team status on the BPI project via a brief update at your monthly department meeting. I would also like to provide you and your team access to the project portal where you'll be able to find information on the project and its progress at your convenience. Will that work for you?" In all her years taking this approach, Gina notes that she has yet to have an argument!

Consider these best practices for communicating effectively with stakeholders to both achieve your goals and provide the stakeholders information they need to stay committed to the BPI project:

- Ensure effective listening skills
- Initiate two-way conversations
- Be candid and nonconfrontational in communications
- Be aware of nonverbal cues from stakeholders

These simple best practices will enable better, more effective communications overall with stakeholders.

Additionally, on a regular basis, check in with stakeholders to ensure that what is being communicated about the BPI project *and* how it is being communicated is working for them. Simply ask the stakeholders the following question: Is the team communicating effectively and sufficiently about the BPI project—providing you information needed, in a way that works for you? If not, what else might the team do to support your needs?

Team Communications

Too often the assumption is made that communications between BPI project team members will come naturally; but this is not an accurate assumption. Team communications must be planned and nurtured to be effective, just as stakeholder communications must be.

As a starting point, relationships must be built among team members to allow for improved communications. In Chapter 3 best practices and ideas were shared regarding the team kick-off meeting—encouraging strong relationships between team members, which certainly begins to move the BPI team members toward effective communications with each other. In this section, the focus will be on working with the BPI project team to develop a team communication strategy.

During the initial kick-off meeting with the BPI project team, one of the areas of discussion should be about communication between team members. The strategies presented in this section will work whether the team is co-located or the team includes virtual or remote members. The communication plan developed for communications among project team members should include the information shown in Table 4.5. There is a downloadable example of a communication plan available on the J. Ross website.

When the BPI project team is involved in setting processes and procedures for how they will communicate among themselves, they are more likely to stay committed to those communications.

In addition to planning for communications relevant to the project, the project manager should also plan for regular social communications. This may be done quite simply. For example, by designating one team member at each meeting to be responsible for initiating the meeting with a question, which is to be answered by each team member, that encourages them to get to know each other on a personal level.

A team calendar enables tracking of upcoming vacation or holiday plans and other paid time off for employees. Additionally, consider including information in the calendar about team members who have called in ill to work and a point of contact in their place. In fact, as part of developing the team communication

Table 4.5 Communication plan components

Communication Plan Component	Description
Communication needs	What needs to be communicated and when?
Communication paths	From whom to whom do communications need to occur?
Communication channels	What channels will be used—e-mail, phone, virtual meetings?
Communication response times	When are team members required to respond to e-mails, phone calls, or other communications received by team members (turn-around time)?
Communication status	Is the communication a priority, routine, for information only? Tag the communication in the "subject" field with a status tag in order to manage communications.
Timing of communications	What is the timing of different communications? For example, will status be shared weekly? Will sub-teams communicate monthly or more frequently?

- If I could have dinner and spend time talking with one famous person (alive or dead), it would be _____.
- My dream holiday/vacation would be _____.
- When I retire I am going to _____.
- The one movie I can watch repeatedly is _____ because _____.
- You are starting your own band. What is the band's name and what kind of music do you play?
- If I didn't have to work for a living, I would do the following: _____.
- The most favorite way to spend my days off is to _____.

Figure 4.5 Questions to engage BPI project teams

plan, it is essential to include backup for vacation time off, holiday time off, and for team members who are out because of illness.

Figure 4.5 provides some examples of questions that might be asked at the start of each team meeting to engage the team and continue to enable them to get to know each other.

Figure 4.6 provides an example of a team resource directory, which provides a quick reference sheet for team members on how to reach others on the team.

BPI Project Team Resource Directory (partially complete example)

Team Member Name	Role on Team	Business Unit/Dept Affiliation	E-Mail	Phone Numbers	Work Location/ Hours/ Time Zone	Expertise/ Special Skills	Hobbies/ Personal Interests
Jasmine Alphonso	Sub-Team Lead	Sales	jalphonso@coname.com	+1 555 555-5555	San Diego 10:00 AM – 6:00 PM PST TIME ZONE GM - 7	Contract negotiation	Married with 3 children, 2 dogs, 2 cats and a frog! Loves hiking and bicycling
Johan Eberstark	IT Team Lead	Info Tech	jeberstark@coname.com	+011 49 89 55.55 5555	Munich 8:00 AM – 4:00 PM TIME ZONE GM + 1/2	App dev. IT security	Avid mystery reader, writes poetry Married with 2 children
Celeste Badeau	Team Member	Human Resources/Admin	cbadeau@coname.com	+011 33 1 55.55 5555	Paris 9:00 AM – 5:00 PM TIME ZONE GM + 1/2	Training	Single, 2 dogs, motorcyclist and avid gardener
Jack Samson	Sub-Team Lead	Info Tech	jsamson@coname.com	+1 555 555-5555	New York 9:00 AM – 5:00 PM EST TIME ZONE GM - 5	Infrastructure Networking	Single Bicycles all over the city Has visited every museum in NY at least twice!

Figure 4.6   Example of team resource directory

The category on *hobbies/personal interests* provides a bit of personal information about the team members that enables others to get to know them.

Store a team resource directory and other documents related to the BPI project team on a shared project portal/database.

WORKING WITH STAKEHOLDERS

While it has been covered earlier, it is important to reiterate that it is not possible to engage stakeholders if strong relationships do not exist between the BPI project, the team members, and the stakeholders. Working effectively with stakeholders requires an upfront investment in time and energy to understand the stakeholders and their needs and expectations around the BPI project. While some stakeholders will support the BPI project, many will not; and if leadership supports it alone, the project cannot be a success. It is important for individual contributors to also support the initiative.

Stakeholders will make or break the BPI project. As part of upfront planning of the BPI project, include time for socializing the initiative with stakeholders, getting to know the stakeholders, and learning their expectations around the project initiative.

Identifying the Right Stakeholders

There are always more stakeholders than expected for BPI projects. Too often, many BPI project managers and their teams tend to focus on those stakeholders who are in leadership roles within the organization. They mistakenly believe that if the focus is on the leaders, everyone else will follow along. Given that BPI projects are about change to *how work gets done* within the organization, it is essential to involve the individuals who are actually *doing* the work, and this is rarely the leaders.

Figure 4.7 provides a number of questions to consider for assistance in identifying the right stakeholders for the BPI project.

As part of preliminary project discussions and during the initial team meeting, consider the questions in Figure 4.7 to determine if the right stakeholders have been identified for the BPI project.

Selling the Need for New or Refined Processes

The assumption cannot be made that stakeholders—regardless of their role within the organization—are on board regarding the need to develop new or refined current processes. Each stakeholder must be sold on the need for the BPI project.

Identifying the Right Stakeholders for the BPI Project

Which key leaders' departments or divisions are impacted by the BPI project?
Who are the staff members of the departments/divisions impacted by the BPI project?
Which supervisors or mid-level managers will need to manage staff members utilizing the outcome of the BPI project?
Who will need to contribute to the BPI project—whether to ask questions of, provide information, run a report, or otherwise will need to engage with the project team?
Who has been involved in BPI projects in the past that may be able to provide guidance and advice for this project?
What external vendors will be involved in the initiative?
Who may be joining the organization within the next few months that may need to be engaged in the BPI initiative?
Are there any transitions planned that may bring current employees into new departments or divisions being impacted by the BPI project?

Figure 4.7   Questions to consider in identifying stakeholders

Once the right stakeholders are identified for the initiative, through initial communications and establishing relationships with stakeholders, the project manager can begin to convince them of the business need for moving forward with the BPI project. Earlier in this book we discussed the need for the BPI project manager to ensure he understands *exactly* why the BPI project is happening: How is it aligned to the organization's long-term strategic goals? What does it hope to accomplish when implemented? How does it benefit the individuals who use the process? This information is absolutely essential toward understanding how to sell the need for a new or refined process to the stakeholders.

Sally, a project manager in a pharmaceutical company, recalls that the time she spent attending all-staff meetings and meetings of other departments within the organization really paid off. When she was assigned a major BPI initiative within the organization, she was able to sell the initiative to a number of leaders and mid-level managers by linking back the benefits to how it would help them achieve goals and address challenges that were discussed during their department meetings.

GETTING STAKEHOLDERS INVOLVED AND KEEPING THEM ENGAGED

Throughout this chapter I have shared a number of ideas on how to socialize the initiative to keep stakeholders involved and engaged within the BPI project. It is essential for the project manager to ensure regular communications prior to the actual start of the work of the BPI initiative on through organization-wide implementation of the final process.

Stakeholders are also involved and engaged when they have responsibilities associated with the BPI project. While many of the stakeholders, especially at the mid-management or leadership level, are not going to be working on tasks associated with the project, the project manager can keep them engaged in any of the following ways:

- Request feedback on project documentation
- Participate in requirements gathering sessions
- Ask stakeholders to share their stories of what is working with the current process and where adjustments might exist to improve the work being done
- Invite stakeholders to status reporting meetings with the team

Throughout the BPI project implementation, the project manager should regularly reach out to stakeholders—via face-to-face meetings, conference calls, virtual meetings and/or a project portal—to check in on how the project is progressing from the stakeholders' perspectives.

Certainly some stakeholders may have specific tasks associated with the BPI project, such as:

- Providing information to document the current process
- Validating current process documentation
- Answering questionnaires and attending focus group meetings
- Testing proposed or *could-be* processes
- Testing *to-be* processes

Establishing Trust and Getting Buy-in

Of course, the need to establish trust and get buy-in from stakeholders to keep them engaged and committed throughout the BPI project implementation can't be emphasized enough. Trust does not happen overnight—nor does it occur by magic. BPI project managers are not automatically given trust simply because a senior leader has authorized them to lead a major BPI initiative within the organization. They are going to have to earn it.

Table 4.6 shows just a few ways in which the building of trust between the BPI project manager and the stakeholders is inhibited, along with key ideas on how to build trust from the start of the BPI project.

Table 4.6   Inhibitors of trust and building trust

What Inhibits Building Trust	How to Build Trust Right from the Start
Providing limited or infrequent communications to stakeholders	• Develop a communication plan early on in collaboration with stakeholders. • Even when there is nothing to report on, check in with stakeholders. • Regularly evaluate the communication plan and make adjustments based on the project's progress.
Withholding, or appearing to withhold, information from stakeholders	• If you don't know an answer, say so and find the answer. Don't just make up the answer. • When you can't share information immediately, explain that and let the stakeholders know when you can share it. • When issues arise, notify stakeholders immediately as well as letting them know how you'll resolve the issue.
Not listening to stakeholders' needs	• Actively listen to stakeholder needs; give them the time and attention needed to convey their thoughts, ideas, and comments. • Use techniques such as reflecting back what they have said and asking questions to clarify.
Ignoring issues that have occurred on previous BPI projects	• In initial communications with stakeholders, listen for references to past BPI projects that have been less than successful and explain how this initiative will be different (lessons learned). • Be upfront and honest about why past BPI initiatives have failed and what will be done to increase the chances for success of the current BPI project. • If you have failed at leading a past BPI project, acknowledge the failure and explain what will be different.
Not knowing or sharing the vision and business case for the BPI project	• Be clear prior to communications with stakeholders about the business case for the BPI project and share that information with stakeholders. • Discuss the BPI project from the perspective of the value to the organization as well as the value to the individual stakeholders.

When the BPI project manager and his team communicate openly, honestly, and regularly with stakeholders, trust is built. When just starting a BPI project and planning early communications with stakeholders, the BPI project team should consider the following questions:

- What communication activities have been most successful on past BPI projects?
- What communication activities have been least successful on past BPI projects?
- What communication activities would help to reach the largest stakeholder group?
- What communication activities are most important when the BPI project team needs to convert a large number of resisters to the BPI project?

Considering responses to these questions assists the BPI project team in developing a more effective communication and socialization plan.

Managing Champions and Resisters

Champions and resisters to the BPI project should be identified early on in the project initiative and a plan should be put in place to accomplish two goals:

1. Keep champions engaged and interested in the BPI project
2. Convert resisters to champions of the BPI project

Champions are the easier group to manage, obviously; they are excited about the BPI initiative and are engaged and committed. The BPI project team has their buy-in. However, don't think that because they are champions they don't need attention. Champions can easily turn out to be resisters or become indifferent about the BPI initiative, if the project team does not keep them engaged throughout the initiative.

Individuals may start off as champions of the BPI project if any or all of the following occurs because of the BPI project:

- There are personal or professional opportunities and benefits tied to the BPI project, such as new challenges to master, the ability to take on more responsibilities, a more visible role within the organization, interactions cross-department/across divisions.
- There is a clear vision and understanding of the need and business case for the BPI project. For example, it is apparent that processes are defective, or that customers are demanding more from the organization or that revenue is being impacted.

- There have been previous successful BPI projects launched within the organization that have enabled greater success in individual roles.
- There had been discussions about the BPI project that occurred *before* it was officially launched, thereby engaging stakeholders early on.

Resisters, on the other hand, need far more attention and communication to change them into champions. Note, however, that not every resister can become a champion of the BPI project; the goal of the BPI project manager should be to convert as many as possible to champions and to keep those who remain resistant in the communication loop to ensure that they don't work to derail the project.

Any of the following things may cause stakeholders to resist the BPI project right from the start:

- Failed past BPI projects
- Lack of understanding of why the BPI project is being launched, or no understanding of the benefits to the individual of the BPI project
- Fear that the BPI project will create additional work for the individual or will take away perceived benefits from the individual
- The BPI project is launched and work has begun without any early communications with stakeholders

As a best practice, when developing the initial socialization and communication plan, develop a plan for communicating and socializing with champions and another plan for communicating and socializing with resisters or stakeholders who are indifferent.

Learning How to Influence without Control

A challenge for BPI project managers is that they have no control over the stakeholders. The project manager can't tell a stakeholder what to do and when to do it—there is no official authority granted when charged with leading a BPI project. Thus, the ability to influence others without having formal authority is an essential skill for BPI project managers.

In order to influence others to accomplish the goals of the BPI project, the following must occur:

- First, the BPI project manager must have built strong relationships with stakeholders which will establish trust and confidence in the project manager and the work of the BPI project team.
- Second, the BPI project manager must communicate openly, honestly, and frequently about the project—sharing information such as the goals

of the BPI project and the link to both organizational strategy *as well as* how the BPI project will benefit the individual stakeholders.

Additionally, in order to get commitment from stakeholders concerning completing tasks and assignments, or providing information for the BPI project, it is essential to be clear about what is needed by when, and how it fits into accomplishing the project goals.

Dawn was managing her first BPI project. The project started in early June and was expected to wrap up in late October. She knew she needed information from a number of stakeholders to understand the current process and would need them again to validate the documented process and evaluate "could-be" processes. However, rather than understanding specifically when she needed stakeholder support, Dawn simply told the stakeholders the project starts in early June and wraps up in late October and she would need their support on the project and expected that they would be available. Three of the stakeholders were concerned and asked why she needed them the entire five months. The other two stakeholders asked specifically what was needed and by when as they were working on other major initiatives. Dawn was not able to provide additional information. Had Dawn done a better job of understanding exactly when the stakeholders would be needed—whether specific days of a particular month or even within a 2 to 3 week time frame—she would have had less resistance.

As can be seen in the story, Dawn is going to have difficulty engaging these stakeholders in meeting the needs of the BPI project. They do not have enough information, and have not been influenced to participate. Had Dawn approached this situation correctly, she would have been clearer about what was needed and when, shared information about how they were contributing to the project, and *asked* for their support rather than expected it.

PLANNING EARLY FOR TRAINING NEEDS

Even the simplest BPI projects will require some form of training or knowledge transfer to educate individuals about how to utilize the new process. Planning early for required training is essential to help engage stakeholders in the initiative. One of the biggest fears that causes resistance to BPI projects is stakeholders who are unsure of how they will be impacted by the BPI project—Will they need to develop new skills? Will someone teach them how to do the job differently? Will they be able to do what is required of them? and etc.

While the BPI project team likely will not have a fully developed training plan for the stakeholders, especially since the process has not yet been defined, it is important to ensure the stakeholders that training will be provided and that it will be provided *prior* to the stakeholders being expected to work with the new process.

Figure 4.8 provides a checklist of what to consider when planning early for training needs as a result of the BPI project. Of the most importance on the checklist is ensuring that someone on the BPI project team is assigned to the task of *training* so that it doesn't get forgotten. An assessment might be done as part of the analysis of training needs to help answer the questions in Figure 4.8.

During information sessions, when the BPI project team is gathering data about the current process, information may come to light that will indicate training needs. Additionally, a gap analysis between current skills and behaviors required to perform the *as-is* process compared to skills and behaviors required to perform the *to-be* process will indicate training needs.

A survey, similar to the one shown in Figure 4.9, may also be sent to determine training needs.

BUILDING SOCIALIZATION INTO YOUR SCHEDULE AND PROJECT PLAN

As a best practice, build the task of *socializing the BPI project* into the schedule to ensure that it is visible and seen as a *must do* by the BPI project team.

Checklist: Planning Early for Training Needs

YES	NO	
☐	☐	Is it known which individuals, workgroups, departments, and/or divisions will need training?
☐	☐	Will Human Resources (training department and/or learning and development) need to be involved in training?
☐	☐	Will an outside vendor need to participate in developing training?
☐	☐	Has it been announced that training will be provided as needed *before* the release of new processes?
☐	☐	Has someone on the team been assigned to lead the task on "Training?"
☐	☐	Does training need to be provided in a variety of formats (face-to-face, virtual, webinar, reference documents)?

Figure 4.8　Planning early for training needs

Name:	
Role:	
Years Performing Role:	
What are your responsibilities performing the process?	
What tools or equipment do you use to perform the process? (e.g., telephone, computer, specific software)	
What skills and abilities do you utilize to accomplish your responsibilities related to the process?	
What critical success factors are important for you in accomplishing the process?	
What do you find most challenging about using the process?	
How do you learn most effectively? (e.g., reading, seeing and then trying, listening)	
What other information would you like to share that would assist in determining training and other needs related to updating the current process?	

Figure 4.9   Survey to determine training needs

Similarly, include socializing the BPI project in the communication plan as part of risk planning, and be sure to assign team members who will be responsible for this important task.

> For every BPI project Gina has led, one of the first tasks on the schedule was "socialize BPI project." Gina assigned a team member (or even herself as the project manager for particularly complex BPI projects) as the lead person for the task. If it is on the schedule and in the communication plan—it will get done!

The project manager may need to sell the idea of socializing the BPI project to both key stakeholders and to the BPI project team. In Figure 4.10, the *Socialize BPI Project* task shows the methods that are planned to be used for socializing the BPI project.

Socialize BPI Project (partially developed)

1. Develop initial stakeholder list
    1.1.   List of champions
    1.2.   List of resisters
    1.3.   List of indifferent stakeholders
2. Socialization plans
    2.1.   E-mail communications
        2.1.1.   Develop content for initial e-mail from sponsor (first week of February)
            2.1.1.1.   Send to sponsor for review
            2.1.1.2.   Finalize initial e-mail content based on sponsor review
            2.1.1.3.   Send out initial e-mail from sponsor
        2.1.2.   Develop content for e-mail from BPI project team (third week of February)
            2.1.2.1.   Send out e-mail from BPI project team
        2.1.3.   Develop schedule for future e-mails on BPI project
    2.2.   Internal newsletter
        2.2.1.   Develop article for internal newsletter
            2.2.1.1.   Send to sponsor for review and input
            2.2.1.2.   Finalize based on sponsor review and additional input
            2.2.1.3.   Send to internal communications for inclusion into newsletter
        2.2.2.   Work with internal communications to develop a schedule for future articles on BPI Project
    2.3.   Department meetings
    2.4.   "Lunch & Learn" sharing sessions
    2.5.   Webinars

Figure 4.10   Socialize BPI project task

Adding the task *Socialize BPI Project* to the project schedule increases the likelihood that the task will happen and be completed, as it will be provided a timeline for completion and have resources assigned to it.

This chapter focused on efforts around socializing BPI projects and the benefits in doing so. It is, really, a simple two-step process:

1. Ensure a thorough understanding of the project: why it is being launched; how it is beneficial to the organization; why it will be of value to stakeholders; how it will be implemented to ensure as small an impact on the stakeholder as possible; etc.

2. Share that information and knowledge with the stakeholders.

Sometimes, this step of socializing the BPI project cannot happen until the sponsor and other key leadership are sold on the value of it. The word *socialize* may not always be the best choice. Other terms to use are *engage, get buy-in, ensure support,* and *share information.* Use whatever terminology works in the organization where you work.

> *Gina was working with an engineering client for the first time. She met with the CEO about launching a large BPI initiative. Gina suggested to the CEO that some time should be spent up front "socializing" the initiative to ensure that the stakeholders understand what was happening and why. The CEO asked the following, "What is socializing? Are you having a party? Do we need party hats? We just want this project to get done!" Obviously "socializing" was the wrong word to use with the CEO. Gina clarified what she intended to do and it still took convincing. To this day, every time Gina goes in to assist in managing a BPI initiative, the CEO takes two party hats out of his desk and puts them on the table. It is their little joke—but he does see the value!*

5

ANALYZING CURRENT
BUSINESS PROCESSES

Analyzing the current business process is mapping out the *as-is* model of the process to enable the business process improvement (BPI) project team to understand where the gaps exist and where improvement opportunities lie. Effectively, the BPI team is looking for the root cause of the problem with the current process to understand how to fix it. Root causes of a problem, when resolved, eliminate that problem from occurring again. By asking *why*, something occurs, a root cause is identified. Asking *why* a problem is occurring is a Japanese quality technique that clarifies explanations for a problem until the root cause is determined. The challenge for BPI project managers is in distinguishing between the symptoms and the real cause of the problem. Let's look at an example.

A project manager is asked to determine why a product being manufactured is not getting to the customer in a timely manner. The late delivery of the product cost the organization over $150,000 in penalties last year. When the project manager asks the manufacturing group why the product is late getting out to customers, he learns the following:

Root Cause 1: Procurement (vendor) issue

- Products manufactured sometimes have to be reworked because they fail testing. WHY?
  - ◊ Quality is poor. WHY?
    - ♣ The materials are not always the right ones or are faulty. WHY?
      - ♦ There is a new supplier. WHY?
        - The new supplier is lower cost and budgets were cut requiring a move away from the previous supplier.

When the project manager probes for other symptoms of the late product, he learns the following:

Root Cause 2: Older, failing equipment

- The machines break down frequently. WHY?
  - ◊ The machines have not been maintained in a number of years. WHY?
    - ♣ The maintenance contract expired and was not renewed. WHY?
      - ♦ New machines were supposed to be purchased but it never happened.

By diving deeper into the problem—products being shipped late to customers—the project manager finds there are two main issues, or root causes, that are causing the delay in shipment. If the project manager focuses his efforts on those two areas, he can correct the issue and get shipments of products back on track.

While BPI project teams may be tempted to shortchange analyzing current business processes, by simply reviewing a process mapped out by the process owners, this often results in failed BPI projects. While the currently documented business process may be used as a guide, it should not be taken at face value.

PHASE 2 OVERVIEW

Figure 5.1 depicts the second phase of the six-phased approach to managing BPI projects—*Analyze Business Process.*

In Phase 2 of the BPI project, the project manager and his team are looking closely at the current process that is to be changed or modified in some way as part of the project. This phase includes gathering information from a variety of stakeholders via a variety of methods, evaluating current documentation on the process, and understanding how the business has changed since the process was initially developed and implemented, as well as future business needs.

Individuals necessary to have on the BPI project team in this phase include a process analyst, a process modeler, a facilitator to lead focus group workshops, and process advisory team members.

Mapping out the process as it currently works is essential to understanding where gaps exist and where improvements can be made in the process. When a

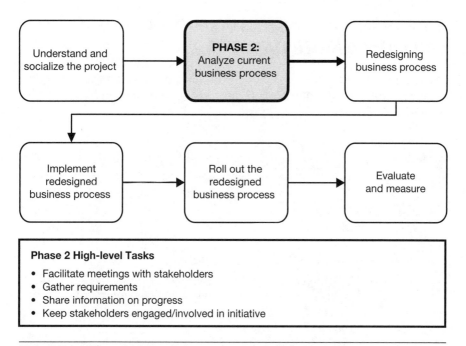

Figure 5.1   Phase 2 of the six-step process

process is mapped out, it is clear what steps are involved in getting the process completed, as well as responsibility for each part of the process. When a process is mapped out and analyzed, the BPI project team begins to see those activities that add value (are necessary and contribute to the process) and those activities that are non-value added.

Mapping out the process enables the BPI project team to understand the process from the perspective of those using the process as well as those impacted by the process—the customer.

Once the *as-is* process is documented, it should be validated with those individuals utilizing the process to ensure that nothing was missed or misrepresented. A properly documented *as-is* process is essential to moving the BPI project forward. Any issues in this phase of the BPI project will impact future phases and decrease the chances of BPI project success. At the end of Phase 2, the BPI project team presents its findings of the challenges/issues with the current, *as-is* process to the sponsor and key stakeholders. Prior to doing so, however, agreement needs to be reached by all involved stakeholders on what problem needs to be solved by redesigning the business process.

IDENTIFYING THE RIGHT STAKEHOLDERS FROM WHOM TO GATHER DATA

More important than the *number* of stakeholders from whom the BPI project team will gather information about the process, is the *background and relevancy* of those stakeholders.

> Jamie was tasked with gathering data on a sales process that required salespeople who were on the road to input customer data into a Customer Relationship Management program. The process did not seem to be working as well as it could be and, while some of the salespeople used it just fine, others had great difficulty inputting their data while on the road. Jamie was asked to document the current process for discussion at the next BPI project team meeting. Jamie decided that she needed to reach out to a variety of salespeople—including individuals who were working well with the process along with individuals who found the process cumbersome and had difficulty inputting customer data while on the road. These salespeople would also represent a variety of years with the organization as well as sales experience. Additionally, Jamie decided to meet with the sales manager to understand his challenges in getting the salespeople to input data on the road and how sales used the data that was entered; she also met with marketing to understand how they used the data that was input.

While it is always easier to work with individuals who are interested in the BPI initiative and support it, BPI project teams will get much more significantly valuable information from individuals who are *not* supportive of the effort and either do not want the process to change or prefer no process in place at all. A combination of data from supporters and nonsupporters—those using the process and those who refuse to do so—results in a much better understanding of what is working and what is not. Include in the list of stakeholders with whom to meet those individuals who use the process frequently and those who may only use it on occasion. Additionally, ensure that a combination of management and individual contributors are involved in providing feedback. Sometimes it is a challenge to get managers to allow individual contributors to provide information on the process. However, keep in mind that rarely are the managers the ones doing the work; rather it is the individual contributors who are likely using the process day in and day out. While management perspective is necessary to understand how they control and are responsible for processes, to fully understand the problems with the process, it is essential to talk with those individuals actually working with that process.

> *Yusuf, one of the authors, once spent a few hours convincing a manager that it was essential that his staff was involved in helping him to document the current "as-is" process, since they were the ones who worked with the process on a daily basis. The manager, however, believed that since he was the boss, he could tell Yusuf what was working and what was not with the process and there was no need to bother the employees. Yusuf shared a number of client stories of successful process improvement projects, all of which included meeting with individual contributors and not solely the management staff.*

Getting the right people from throughout the organization, at a variety of levels and experience, working with the process being documented ensures that the *as-is* process is documented accurately. When this phase of the BPI project is well performed, the rest of the BPI project goes much more smoothly. While it is essential that modeling the *as-is* process doesn't take up too much of the overall BPI project time, it is important that it is done well and includes the right stakeholders.

ENSURING A VARIETY OF METHODS TO GATHER DATA

There are a variety of ways to gather information and data about the process being documented as part of the BPI project. Let's look at these ways in more detail.

Document Reviews

It is likely that there is already documentation such as policies and procedures about the current process, as well as the templates that are used to do the work related to the process being examined. This information should be sought out and reviewed as it is a starting point for understanding the current process.

> *Often companies have mapped out a process early on, when the process was initially developed. Certainly, as time goes on and employees find better ways of getting work done, or managers formally change the process, these process maps may not have been updated. However, they provide an excellent starting point for understanding the process as it was intended to be used.*

One-on-one Interviews

One-on-one interviews are most effective for understanding a process in-depth. They are best done in person, however, they can be effective via conference call if necessary. One-on-one interviews enable the BPI project team, in most cases, to get more detailed, honest feedback on the business process being evaluated. Individuals are more apt to share information when their coworkers and manager are not also in the room.

Interviews should be structured with specific questions asked about the process in order to ensure that there is consistency from interview to interview. Open-ended questions will bring about a better conversation between the BPI project team member and the stakeholder.

Figure 5.2 provides a list of open-ended questions that might be asked during interviews with stakeholders to gather information about a current process.

While tallying up the results of open-ended questions is not an easy task, these types of questions will lead to more detailed responses that will be more valuable in documenting the *as-is* process.

Recently a colleague of the authors told us that he was tasked with managing a large multi-project to replace an antiquated phone system with a digital, IP-based one. He describes the transition as akin to going from a campfire for cooking a meal to using a microwave. The customer is a large paper product company with multiple buildings, each with their own management structure and mission at hand. For example, he noted that in some buildings they manufacture the paper products, while others house the executives, administrative staff, etc. Needless to say, this topology has led to strong silos within the company where, essentially, the left hand has no clue as to what the right hand is doing. The challenges encountered with strong silos within a company often take months to resolve, so asking the right questions of the stakeholder is crucial to making progress.

1. What about the current process has been most effective for you, enabling success in your role?
2. What about the current process is challenging or hinders your ability to be completely effective in your role?
3. Have you made changes to the process, as it is documented currently, to enable increased efficiencies and effectiveness? If yes, please detail changes you have made.
4. If you were given the opportunity to change the process, what changes would you recommend that would enable increased effectiveness in getting the work done?
5. What else would you like to share about the business process?

Figure 5.2 Open-ended questions for stakeholder interviews

Focus Groups

Focus groups enable a group of stakeholders, ideally from throughout the organization, to share their perspectives about a business process. Questions are asked in a group setting and participants share their challenges and successes about the business process with the facilitator and others and are free to talk with each other. Focus groups *must* be well facilitated or they can get out of control quickly! The facilitator must be able to keep the discussion on track, avoid stakeholders monopolizing the conversation, and ensure that everyone participates.

The authors have used focus groups successfully to gather information about a process from large groups of stakeholders. If they find that some folks in the meeting are quieter, they will arrange for one-on-one interviews with those individuals to be sure they have the opportunity to share their ideas and perspectives. Sometimes the focus groups require follow up to probe further into ideas, suggestions, and comments that arose during the focus group meeting, but are better handled outside of the meeting.

Division/Department Meetings

Division and department meetings are most effective when the BPI project impacts only a particular division or department. The BPI project team will use division/department meetings to gather from the group of stakeholders what's working and what's not, regarding the process to be changed. The group format—similar to a focus group—enables the group to react to each other and share their ideas. Similar to focus group sessions, division and department meetings must be well facilitated to ensure that the conversation is managed, everyone is contributing, and the BPI project team is getting the information needed to move forward with the project.

Yusuf was working with a technology company to lead a meeting to map out a current process that was being evaluated as part of a large BPI initiative. There was a mixture of managers (process owners) and the users of the process (subject matter experts). Yusuf noticed during the meeting that the users and managers disagreed over what was being done on a day-to-day basis. Additionally, the users of the process would often defer to the managers, changing their statements when a manager contradicted them. In order to get the information needed, Yusuf separated the groups into two, so that he could better understand from the users of the process, exactly how they performed the process—and from the managers of the process, how they managed or oversaw the process.

Surveys

Surveys can be used in two ways. The first is as a supplement to focus groups or division/department meetings with stakeholders about the current process. Secondly, surveys provide a way to capture information about current processes when the BPI project team is unable to meet in person with stakeholders, or there is difficulty in scheduling a meeting to gather data about a process. Surveys can be used to understand stakeholders' experiences with using a particular process, as well as their successes (what's working) and challenges (where is there room for improvement in the process).

Gina has used surveys successfully to expand the list of stakeholders from whom the BPI project team is gathering data about the process. For example, if there are 5 to 8 key stakeholders from whom data must be gathered, but a number of other stakeholders who are either interested in sharing their ideas or who have used the process on rare occasions, then Gina might use surveys to gather some additional information that may be of value to the BPI project.

Gina notes that only in rare cases does she allow an "anonymous" response to surveys. She often needs to follow up with respondents to get more information and needs a name to do so. However, Gina has worked with organizations where there are penalties for not following processes to the letter. In such cases, when she knows that it is likely that the stakeholders have made changes to processes to make it possible to get the work done more easily, she will permit anonymous responses to ensure she gets the information needed.

The open-ended questions used during interviews (see Figure 5.2) also work effectively in surveys. Naturally, if surveys are being used to reach out to stakeholders where one-on-one meetings are not possible, the same questions should be used in the surveys as was used in the interviews, for consistency.

Observation

Observation entails watching the stakeholder perform the particular process that is part of the BPI project. Through observation, the BPI project team can see exactly *how* the process is performed and can document how it is being performed.

The challenge with observation is that if stakeholders don't normally follow the process as they should, they will likely follow it *exactly* when they are being observed. This does not help in documenting how the process is being utilized currently.

When analyzing current business processes, focus on analyzing the process *as it is actually happening* and not on how it should be happening.

> *During observation of processes, Gina reminds stakeholders that she is not their boss and wants to work with them to improve the process. To that end, she asks them to show her how they currently use the process and not how their boss wants them to use it. This enables Gina to create a level of comfort and the stakeholder is more likely to share with her information needed so she can accurately document how the process is currently working.*

Figure 3.13 showed a partially completed communication plan that was initially developed at the start of a BPI project. Figure 5.3 continues this plan, but with a focus on how data will be gathered for documenting the current *as-is* process.

As can be seen in Figure 5.3, the BPI project team is spending more time with the Human Resources group in gathering information about their current process. This is done because the process is owned, and primarily utilized by, the HR group. However, information on the process is also being gathered by Accounting/Finance (via a department meeting) and by the training vendors (via a survey). The training vendors will provide input primarily on the challenges, or difficulties, from their perspective in the process (how it impacts them in particular).

When gathering information to map out the current process, be prepared to change the strategy if needed to ensure accurate information is gathered. If

Communication Plan: Document "As-Is" Process			
WHO	**WHAT**	**WHEN**	**HOW**
Human Resources	Analysis of current process in use	Over 3 week time period From <date, 20xx – date, 20xx>	Via one-on-one interviews – 45 minutes per meeting Follow up survey based on data gathered
Accounting/Finance	Analysis of current process in use	On <date, 20xx>	Via Department meeting – 2 hour meeting scheduled
Training vendors	Challenges seen with process	Over 1 week time period <date, 20xx>	Via survey

Figure 5.3 Partial communication plan

there are conflicts in information being gathered or if it is believed that accurate information is not being shared because of management staff in the room with users of the process, hold smaller group sessions by separating staff from management, utilize surveying tools, or meet one-on-one with users.

MAPPING OUT THE CURRENT PROCESS

When mapping out the current process that is part of the BPI project, it is absolutely essential to include as many of the *right* stakeholders as possible. *Right* means stakeholders who are involved in using that process as well as stakeholders who oversee the process. In mapping out the process, the BPI project team needs to be sure the following is considered:

- All inputs to the process
- Business rules or guides pertaining to decision making within the process
- Enablers to the process
- Outputs of the process
- Value-added activities and non-value-added activities

Additionally, the BPI project team may determine that other processes will need to be included in the scope of the project because those processes are so intertwined with the process being evaluated as part of the project.

If the scope of the project must change to include other processes, then it is necessary for the BPI project manager to update the relevant project documentation and request approval for a scope change from the sponsor. Certainly a scope change will impact any number of areas on the project, such as the budget, timeline, and stakeholders involved.

When working with stakeholders to analyze a current process, it is essential to capture the roles and responsibilities of those stakeholders as it relates to the process. How much involvement do they have with the process? How often do they utilize the process?

Figure 5.4 provides an example of a workflow for a current process and shows the responsibility of each stakeholder interviewed.

In Figure 5.4, not only is the process mapped out, but it is clear where responsibility lies for each part of the process (swim lane). In mapping out the process, the BPI project team members who are gathering information want to look at what business rules impact decision making for the process. For example, in Figure 5.4, what are the business rules around *review invoice for all necessary data*? Figure 5.5 provides an example of the business decision rules for the process.

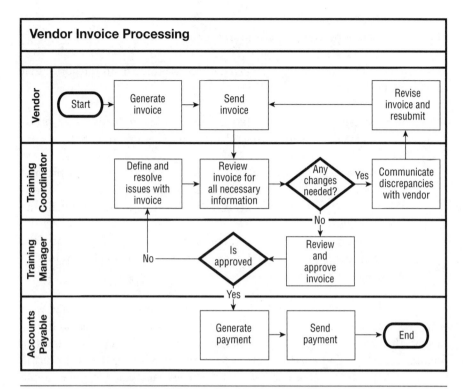

Figure 5.4   Example of workflow

Example: Business Decision Rules

If this happens...	Then take this action...
Vendor does not supply invoice after training event	Training coordinator contacts vendor within three days after completion of training event to receive invoice
Information is missing from the invoice	Training coordinator to reach out to vendor to get corrected information

Figure 5.5   Example of business decision rules

Determining the Root Cause

Root cause analysis looks for the origin of a particular problem. It looks beyond the symptoms of the problem to determine exactly why the problem occurred in the first place. When looking at the root cause of a problem, the BPI project team answers the following three questions:

1. What happened?

2. Why did it happen?
3. How can it be prevented from happening again?

When looking at *why* a problem occurred, there are three main categories that the cause may fall under:

- Physical—for example, defects may be high in production of a product because the machinery keeps breaking down or raw materials are defective
- People—for example, defects may be high in production of a product because the machinery is not being maintained or the person responsible for securing raw materials is insufficiently trained to evaluate the quality of those materials
- Organizational—for example, there is no regular procedure or time allocated for maintaining the machinery or the process for evaluating the quality of raw materials is lacking

A problem statement analysis provides a way to track problems associated with a process and provides examples of those problems to better understand how to solve the problems. Figure 5.6 is a snapshot of a problem statement analysis document that would be used in order to summarize data gathered from the various stakeholder sessions and through root cause analysis. For the example document in Figure 5.6, refer back to the example project discussed in earlier chapters, *Improvement in HR A/R Processes*.

In this figure we see three main issues, the specific examples brought up during stakeholder data gathering sessions, the impact on the process when these issues arise, as well as what success looks like for the stakeholder. This information provides information for the BPI project team when designing the *could-be* process to develop options that will enable stakeholders to achieve goals (or success).

Documenting the problems in the process, as shown in Figure 5.6, enables the BPI project team to determine gaps in the process and highlights the areas where improvement is needed when modeling the *could-be* process. These problems will come to light during conversations with stakeholders.

Consider the issue in Figure 5.6, *Delay in review of invoices by HR manager*. There is no business decision rule (see Figure 5.5) that delineates what is to happen if the HR manager is out of town and unreachable. Any new process developed will need to include a business decision rule delineating what to do if this issue occurs in order to improve the process.

Utilize brainstorming techniques to determine the root cause of problems with a process, in combination with cause and effect diagrams. Figure 5.7 is an example of a cause and effect (also called a fishbone) diagram.

Example: Problem Statement Analysis

Project: Improvement in HR A/R Processes			
Problem Detected	**Example of Problem**	**Impact**	**Success Measurement**
Process problems (input)	• Delay in receipt of invoices for processing	H	Invoices sent to HR by vendors in a timely manner (within 24 hours of service being provided).
Process problems (output)	• Invoices not paid timely (on average 5–8 days late) • Delay in review of invoices by HR manager (especially when out of town and unreachable)	H	Invoices approved by HR manager within 2 days of receipt from training coordinator and sent to A/P for processing.
Vendor problems	• Interest being paid on late invoices • Vendor dissatisfaction – cancellation of vendor contracts	H	Vendor satisfaction increases (no cancelled contracts due to consistent late payments) Interest not paid on late invoices (expected savings of $800-$1,000 per year)

Figure 5.6   Snapshot: problem statement analysis document

Figure 5.7 shows that *Poor Customer Support* is the symptom of the following problems: long hold times on the phone, unfriendly customer support staff, and unsatisfactory resolution of customer problems. In this example, the effect is *Low Customer Satisfaction*.

Let's define a few terms used in the cause and effect diagram example in Figure 5.7:

- **Category**—the category that causes fall into, (e.g., training, processes/ procedures, resources, etc.)
- **Cause**—the reason behind the problem, for example, lack of necessary skills, outdated processes, etc. (solutions should not be included in the *cause* area, save them on a list for evaluation later)
- **Effect**—the problem

Figure 5.8 is a checklist of best practices for building cause and effect diagrams to determine the root causes of a problem with a process.

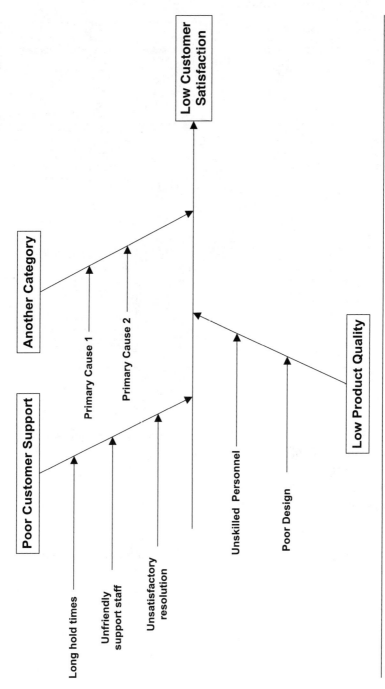

Figure 5.7   Example of a cause and effect diagram

Checklist: Building a Cause and Effect Diagram

☐	Through brainstorming–identify all possible causes of the problem. What are the possible causes of this problem? Why is it happening? Verify that the causes are actually related to the problem.
☐	Develop categories for the causes. Group the causes into categories so they are more easily managed (keep in mind that some causes may fit into multiple categories)
☐	Construct the cause and effect (fishbone) diagram
☐	Select the root causes (most essential to the problem). Identify the root causes by looking for those that appear repeatedly.
☐	Verify the root causes with data

Figure 5.8   Checklist for building cause and effect diagrams

A cause and effect diagram enables BPI project teams to create an image of the possible causes behind a particular problem in order to see how those causes might be related and why the problem is occurring, then more easily arrive at a solution to the problem (the *could-be* process).

When looking at possible areas for improvement in the process, consider using the Pareto Principle, also called the 80:20 Rule. When reviewing complaints or errors about a process, the Pareto Principle states that 80% of the complaints or errors are derived from 20% of the causes.

> At a local hospital, in a review of the processes within the Radiology Department, it was determined that 80% of the requests for services came from 20% of the departments within the hospital. In examining the processes within Radiology, stakeholders were primarily selected from those specific departments that used the services of Radiology.

As-is Modeling

To develop the *as-is* model of the current process, utilize the information obtained from stakeholder sessions and from observation of the process in use. Review also how the process is *supposed* to be utilized and compare to how it is *actually* utilized.

The BPI project team will discover the problems with the process, suggestions for improvements, as well as opportunities to make changes by asking stakeholders these specific questions during the information gathering sessions as well as during the process mapping workshop. If a process impacts a third party (customer or vendor, for example), review and walk through the process as if the BPI project team is the third party. This enables the BPI project team to see the process in action from the third party's point of view and can develop recommendations on improving or changing the process to better accommodate the needs of the third party.

To develop the *as-is* model, the BPI project team should include a process analyst and a process modeler on the team who can utilize the information gathered from stakeholders to ensure a well-documented *as-is* model of the process.

Having stated the need for a well-documented *as-is* model of the process, don't get hung up on perfection in this stage of the project. While it is important that the BPI project team does a solid job of documenting the process, remember the process *will* be refined or changed in some way. Be sure that all relevant information is captured and documented, but reviewing the process over and over to achieve perfection is not necessary and will only impact the overall project timeline.

VALIDATING THE CURRENT PROCESS

As a best practice, after the current process has been modeled, the BPI project team should meet with key stakeholders of the process—those utilizing the process as well as those who manage the process—to ensure that what has been documented is accurate.

Validate the current process through any or all of the following methods, depending on the complexity of the project documented:

- Face-to-face group meetings
- A virtual platform
- An e-mail
- The project portal

Part of the validation of the documented process includes validating the root causes that have been identified. Make any corrections necessary to the process before finalizing it for review with the sponsor. Work with the stakeholders to identify process improvement areas.

THE VALUE OF *QUICK WINS* TO ENABLE BUY-IN

Look for potential quick wins—some change that might be implemented immediately to improve the current process. Criteria should be developed to help the BPI project team determine quick wins for the BPI project. Criteria may include:

- Number of departments or division impacted
- Time to implement the change
- Budget needed to implement the change
- Support from management and those using the process

Refer back to Figure 5.5. Recall there is no business decision rule that delineates what is to happen if the HR manager is out of town and unreachable. A quick win might be to recommend adding a business decision rule for such a situation, as shown in Figure 5.9.

This change should meet a number of criteria including being quick to implement, having no impact on the budget, and garnering support from management and those using the process.

Ideas for quick wins often come from those individuals being interviewed about the *as-is* process. Recall that those implementing a current process are already finding *work-arounds*, when needed, to make the process a success. Only rarely are processes followed to the letter. Even if a quick win does not result in a great benefit, if it is recommended by a user of the process—implement it! What better way to gain champions who will continue to improve upon the process. Once it is implemented, measure the success of the quick win, to show how it improved the process.

Example: Business Decision Rules

If this happens...	Then take this action...
Vendor does not supply invoice after training event	Training coordinator contacts vendor within three days after completion of training event to receive invoice.
Information is missing from the invoice	Training coordinator to reach out to vendor to get corrected information
Below are two new business rules to address one problem with the current process, which may enable for a quick win...	
HR manager is unreachable to sign off on invoice	Send invoice to peer of HR manager for signature, along with all supporting documentation
Peer HR manager is unreachable to sign off on invoice	Send invoice to VP of HR for signature, along with all supporting documentaton

Figure 5.9   Example of business decision rules quick win

PRESENT YOUR FINDINGS TO THE SPONSOR AND OTHER KEY STAKEHOLDERS

Present the documented *as-is* process—as well as findings around root causes and quick wins that could be implemented—to the sponsor and other key leadership stakeholders, including managers of the process. Share also ideas presented to improve upon or fix the process based on the information gathered during stakeholder sessions.

If the scope of the project has changed based on findings in Phase 2 of the BPI project, then update the scope document and other relevant project documentation, such as the budget and timeline; then present it to the sponsor for approval to move forward with Phase 3 of the project. As with any project change, make the business case to get approval to expand the scope of the project. It is not uncommon, as the process is documented and problems with the process are brought to light, that the BPI project scope must change to accommodate the needs of the BPI project. The better a job is performed in Phase 2 of the BPI project, the more likely that necessary scope changes will be captured early on in the BPI project.

PREPARING TO MOVE TO PHASE 3

Once the BPI project team has achieved validation of the documented *as-is* process, they are ready to move to Phase 3—redesigning of the business process. Preparation for Phase 3 includes doing the following:

- Documenting all possible quick wins that can be achieved for refining or enhancing the process
- Reaching out to stakeholders to prepare them for upcoming meetings and conversations regarding redesigning of the process
- Preparing for how stakeholders will continue to be engaged in Phase 3 activities so that they continue to support the BPI project efforts

As a best practice, the authors prefer to develop a communication plan for each phase of the project. For Phase 3 of the BPI project, the communication plan includes how the authors will communicate what happens during Phase 3 to prepare stakeholders, what the BPI project team will need from stakeholders to ensure a redesigned process that meets their needs, and how and when the team will communicate with the stakeholders throughout Phase 3 of the project.

This chapter shares a number of ways to get information from stakeholders (process users and their managers) about the current, *as-is* process. Additionally, the importance and necessity of understanding exactly what the problem is (the root cause) was shared, along with a few ways to determine the root cause.

The value of *quick wins* in the BPI project enables the BPI project team to show the benefits of changes made to a process in order to solve a problem. These *quick wins* enable stakeholders to begin to see value in the BPI project long before it is fully implemented and rolled out to the organization. Quick wins drive engagement in the BPI project. Quick wins are especially important for complex BPI projects to keep stakeholders from feeling overwhelmed.

REDESIGNING BUSINESS PROCESSES

Redesigning business processes is where significant work on the business process improvement (BPI) project starts. Certainly, if Phase 2 went smoothly—meaning that stakeholders were engaged and readily shared information about the process for documenting—Phase 3 moves forward a bit more easily. The project manager should *not* assume that because he has socialized and engaged the stakeholders early on at the start of the project that the work is done. Socializing and engaging stakeholders is a continuous effort in BPI projects.

If Phase 2 did not go smoothly, however, before Phase 3 begins, more time must be invested in understanding the issues that arose during Phase 2 and how those same issues may be resolved (if they haven't been already) and avoided in Phase 3.

> *Allison did a brief lessons-learned session with her project team after Phase 2 of the BPI project. This was such a difficult phase because many of the stakeholders who actually use the process that was part of the project were not very forthcoming with information. The management staff however had many ideas on how to improve the process. After talking with a few of the stakeholders who use the process, Allison learned that they just didn't get enough of a "heads up" about the project early on. She wanted to be sure that they were well aware of what was ahead and wanted to be sure that she had their buy-in and support. She needed it to design a process that would work for them.*

PHASE 3 OVERVIEW

Figure 6.1 depicts the third phase of the six-phased approach to managing BPI projects: *Redesigning Business Processes.*

In Phase 3 of the BPI project, the project team works in collaboration with key stakeholders who are using the process, or will use the process, to redesign their current process in a way that brings about increased effectiveness and efficiencies for the users of the process and improves upon the current process—certainly, in a way that meets the objectives of the BPI project. This might include reducing costs, improving customer service, or any other number of goals for the redesign of the business process.

While the BPI project team will use information gathered in Phase 2 to begin to develop the *could-be* process, additional research is needed before the team will begin to develop could-be options. This includes research of best practices within the industry and through facilitated workshops to map out potential could-be processes for evaluating.

The redesign phase is sure to be one that will be wrought with challenges for the BPI project team. Inevitably a variety of stakeholders will have their own ideas on how to best redesign the process, and often these ideas are in conflict

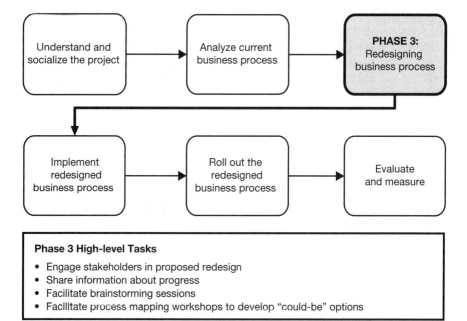

Figure 6.1 Phase 3 of six-step process

and may not help the BPI team achieve the goals of the project. Additionally, the BPI team will still be managing those individuals who were resisting the BPI project from the beginning. Since it is unlikely that everyone who was a resister was converted to a champion, those resisters still must be managed.

As a best practice, the BPI project team is well advised to conduct another all-stakeholder meeting to discuss moving into Phase 3, and, particularly, the involvement needed by stakeholders during this phase.

The outcome of Phase 3 is a formal proposal and business case describing the *to-be* process for the sponsor and other senior key stakeholders. Approval will be needed by these senior individuals in order to move forward with implementing the redesigned process as part of a pilot test.

KEEPING STAKEHOLDERS ENGAGED AND INVOLVED IN PHASE 3

The author's last large BPI project required so many meetings with stakeholders that by the time they got to Phase 3, the stakeholders were exhausted and completely uninterested in the project. Re-engaging them in the project was essential to keep it moving forward.

The communication/engagement plan developed at the beginning of the project often needs to be revised and updated once Phase 3 begins. At this point, new stakeholders may join in and the current stakeholders need to be assured that the project still requires their attention.

Review Figure 4.4—showing the types of communications that might occur in each phase of the BPI project. As is apparent, there is significant engagement that is necessary with stakeholders in Phase 3.

Figure 4.3 showed a partial plan for communicating with Human Resources (HR) in Phase 1 and Phase 2. Figure 6.2 continues that example for Phase 3 of the project.

In addition to the communication points noted, as a best practice the BPI project manager will build on this communication plan with additional information for the BPI project team specifically. Table 6.1 shows two specific communications that are for *team eyes only*.

In this example in Table 6.1, two separate communications are planned early on for both resisters and champions (or supporters) of the initiative. As discussed earlier, it is essential to engage resisters separately from champions. Each group has different needs and expectations from the others. Resisters need to

Human Resources Department Communication Plan (PARTIAL PLAN)				
PROJECT PHASE	WHO	WHAT	WHEN	HOW
Phase 3		Overview of Phase 3 of project – "what's next" on the project	(late February)	Via stakeholder meeting (2 options provided)
Phase 3		Schedule attendance at process mapping workshop	(early March)	Via e-mail, invitation to entire department (4 options provided– 2 in-person, 2 virtual)
Phase 3	Human Resources	Process mapping workshops	(mid to late March)	In-person and virtual options provided for workshops
Phase 3		Send "could-be" options for review	(early April)	Via e-mail and portal
Phase 3		Feedback on "could-be" options	(early to mid-April)	Via a variety of forums: e-mail, portal, in-person, virtual

Figure 6.2   Example of partial communication plan

Table 6.1   Example of specific team communications

Type of Communication	To Whom	Forum	Due Date
Detailed information about Phase 3—specifics around benefits to individuals within HR and Accounting/Finance	HR and Accounting/ Finance resisters	One-on-one meetings; small group meetings; casual conversations	Mid-February
Request for assistance in developing "could-be" processes—reaching out to peers, sharing information at process mapping workshops (specifically—assistance in helping out with resisters)	Select members of HR and Accounting/ Finance departments who are champions	One-on-one conversation	Mid-February

understand how the project will help them individually—basically, what's in it for them. For every BPI project there are champions who seem to be really engaged and interested in the change that is happening. These are usually the individuals who have been pushing for a change for a while. These individuals can be invited to help with the project by engaging with resisters to bring them along.

> *Gina, one of the authors, has found that it is of value to have a "team eyes only" communication plan. She has used this type of plan successfully on BPI projects to manage resisters to the project and even specific stakeholders who need special attention due to being demanding or requiring "hand holding" to understand the project and therefore being able to participate in providing information to the team.*

RESEARCH CURRENT BEST PRACTICES

Look in a variety of places for inspiration on redesigning the process—internal and external to the organization.

Step one in determining could-be processes is to look internally into the organization because, undoubtedly, there are individuals who are doing the job well. These individuals have developed their own best practices for getting the work done. Learn what they are doing that is making them successful. Then research current industry best practices to find ideas that will work within the organization.

Best practices can be gathered from within and *outside* the industry. When the BPI project team expands their research to what is happening outside the specific industry, they expand their ideas for improving upon the current process that is part of the BPI project.

Implementing best practices will improve how the business functions overall and, in the case of the BPI project, how that particular process will be refined and improved to promote increased efficiencies and effectiveness in getting work done.

What Are Your Competitors Doing?

When it can be determined, understanding how competitors are getting work done allows the BPI project team to benchmark the current process against similar companies' processes and practices. This is not always easy information to gather, however, as many companies keep processes and procedures close to the vest. These are, after all, the core of their business. The BPI project team might benchmark performance in a variety of ways, including: surveying current customers, getting information from sales and marketing, or surveying members of an industry association to which the organization belongs.

Using Others' Best Practices

Every company has best practices, some of which may be of value in helping to refine the process. However, best practices gathered from others cannot be used *as-is*—they must be adjusted or changed in some way. Even within the same industry, companies need to adjust best practices for how work gets done to suit their specific, unique needs. This is a company's distinctive or unique benefit to their customer base. Best practices gathered from others are simply a baseline or starting point for refining the current process. Combine the best ideas in new ways to develop an innovative redesign that works for the organization.

Table 6.2 is a snapshot of how the BPI project manager might assign responsibilities for doing internal and external research prior to developing the could-be process options.

Table 6.2   Snapshot: assigning responsibilities

What	Research Type	Responsible Team Member	Report by Date
Develop a list of and reach out to internal stakeholders to determine current personal best practices.	Internal	John	Month/day
Review data gathered from stakeholders on current process/ documented current process	Internal	Alison	Month/day
Research industry best practices (associations)	External	Sam, Jack	Month/day
Research competitor best practices	External	Sarah, Abigail	Month/day

REQUIRED CRITERIA FOR NEW PROCESSES

Early on in the BPI project, the project sponsor would have shared objectives, from a leadership perspective, for refining the process. Objectives will likely be linked to a strategic initiative or challenge. Examples of strategic objectives include:

- Reduction in manufacturing time
- Reduction in processing time
- Address customer complaints
- Reduction in costs
- Reduction in time to get services delivered to customers

These objectives help to drive the criteria used to evaluate options for the could-be process. For example, potential criteria might include:

- Time to implement redesign
- Number of organizational units impacted
- Cost of implementation
- Risk introduced
- Expected support by staff
- Expected support by executive management

Consider the project used as an example in earlier chapters, *Improvement in H/R Processes*. Figure 6.3 shows the objectives for this example BPI project with

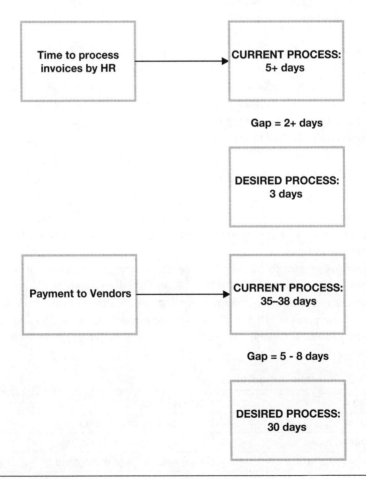

Figure 6.3 Example of objectives of a BPI project

a focus on the current process and desired future process end state—showing the gap between the current and desired process.

These objectives first appeared in the project charter and then in the project scope statement (downloadable files referenced in Chapter 2).

Any redesign of the process for the BPI project, *Improvement in H/R Processes*, must meet these objectives. In this example, the time to process invoices should be no longer than three days after receipt from vendor. The ultimate goal is to increase vendor satisfaction with the organization by paying vendors within the 30-day time frame established in an agreement with vendors. Criteria relevant for this project may include:

- Expected HR staff support
- Meets vendor needs/expectations
- Ease of processing by A/P

Certainly, as the BPI project team goes through analyzing the current process as part of the project, they may find a number of other objectives or goals that are raised by stakeholders that should be considered in developing could-be options. Improvements in the process will certainly decrease time involvements for HR personnel in processing invoices and in following up with vendors who call in to inquire about late payments.

Weighing Criteria

Determining weight for each criteria is essential to evaluating potential could-be options that are put forth by the BPI project team. Develop weight criteria as well as a scale for whether or not the criteria are met. A common scale is shown in Table 6.3.

Figure 6.4 provides a snapshot of an example of a could-be evaluation worksheet for one possible redesign of the BPI project using weighted criteria.

A worksheet should be developed for each alternative option for a could-be design of the process. This information is utilized to make a decision on the could-be process with which to move forward for implementation with a pilot

Table 6.3   Example: weight and criteria

Weight	Criteria Met
3 = must have	2 = meets all of the criteria
2 = should have	1 = meets some of the criteria
1 = nice to have	0 = meets none of the criteria

"Could-Be" Process Evaluation Worksheet Project: Improvement in H/R Processes			
Process Component: Improve time to process invoice			Option: 1
Description of changes proposed: • Eliminate approval by Training coordinator and have invoice sent directly to Training Manager • Require vendor to submit invoice on day of event • Change contract to note that incorrect invoices will result in late payment of up to 5 days			
Criteria	**Weight**	**Criteria Met**	**Score (Weight x Criteria Met)**
Reduces time to process to 3 days or less	3	2	6
Improves vendor satisfaction	3	1	3
Makes process easier to follow	2	2	4
Reduces number of individuals involved	2	2	4
Enables approvals at lowest level of organization	3	0	3
		TOTAL SCORE:	20
Scale use:			
Weight: 3 = must have 2 = should have 1 = nice to have		Criteria Met: 2 = meets all of the criteria 1 = meets some of the criteria 0 = meets none of the criteria	

Figure 6.4   Snapshot: example *could-be* evaluation worksheet

group. Team members involved in this process of evaluating potential redesigns against set criteria include:

- Process redesign team members
- Process advisory team members

PROCESS MAPPING WORKSHOPS

In Chapter 5 we discussed a variety of ways to determine the validity of the current mapped process with stakeholders (*Validating the Current Process*). One of those methods was through face-to-face group meetings—also called process mapping workshops. In this chapter, we'll share more information on process mapping workshops with a focus on specifically capturing ideas for could-be options for the process.

Process mapping workshops to develop could-be options for the process require a number of roles available to lead and assist in the workshop, including:

- Process redesign team members
- Workshop facilitator
- BPI project manager
- Key stakeholder representatives (internal and external)
- Process advisory team members

The workshops should be held *after* research has been done on possible options and after analysis of possible redesign options (see Figure 6.4 as an example).

Use this process mapping workshop to review possible options and expand upon the options presented to enable better evaluation of the could-be options, eliminating those options that are not practical or feasible. However, a good facilitator may also be able to draw out additional options from participants in the workshop, and such ideas brought up during the process mapping workshop should not be discounted.

The ideal outcome of the workshop would be two or three could-be options to be modeled and evaluated further to develop the to-be model which will be presented to the sponsor and other key stakeholders for review and approval.

Preparing for the Workshop

Depending on the number of stakeholders who need to be involved in the discussions around could-be options for the process, it may be necessary to hold more than one meeting.

> *Given how siloed each department is at one university client, it was absolutely essential to hold workshops separately for each department because together it would be too contentious and nothing would be accomplished. Once the workshops for considering "could-be" options were completed, two representatives from each department (selected by the department head) were invited to attend a final "to-be" process development meeting, utilizing the options developed in the individual process workshops.*

Prior to the workshop session, ensure the following is in place:

- A list of key participants who are attending
- The process map of the current process

- Gaps in the current process that will need to be addressed in a could-be process option
- A room large enough to accommodate all stakeholders participating in the workshop
- A room setup that enables interaction and participation—round or oval tables work well
- Flip charts, white boards, and plenty of sticky notes to capture ideas

Developing Your Agenda

Develop a detailed and timed agenda for the process mapping workshop. Table 6.4 provides an example agenda for a process mapping workshop.

Figure 6.5 provides a checklist of what to send to participants in the process mapping workshop, at least one to one and a half weeks prior to the scheduled meeting date.

In the balance of this chapter, let's review the process mapping workshop in more detail. This is an important part of Phase 3 of the BPI project. These workshops must go well in order to keep stakeholders engaged and participating in the BPI project. Additionally, they are necessary to ensure development of a to-be process (from the could-be process options) that will meet the overall project goals, sponsor's objectives, and the needs of the stakeholders.

Facilitating the Workshop

The position of workshop facilitator is a *key role* and requires a strong coordinator who is able to pull ideas from stakeholders as they consider the alternatives presented for the redesign of the process. The facilitator *should not* be someone who expects to participate in the process mapping workshop; therefore an external facilitator is most desired. The workshop can be contentious, as everyone has ideas to share and wants to design a process that meets their own personal objectives. Additionally, keep in mind that some of the individuals who have initially developed the process may feel protective of the current process and may be hesitant to make changes.

Brainstorming Techniques

Even though ideas for a redesign are already being presented, it is often of value to hold a brainstorming session to generate any new ideas. When done properly, brainstorming produces creativity and innovation in redesigning the process. For process improvement initiatives, consider asking the following questions to spark creativity in redesigning the process:

- If the organization was number one in the industry, how would we be working differently?

Table 6.4 Example agenda: process mapping workshop

Task	Timing	Key Participants	Desired Outcome
Introductions and ice breaker	45 minutes	All	Understanding of roles and responsibilities of each participant
Objectives/goals for the workshop session, ground rules to be agreed upon	20 minutes	BPI Project Manager (goals) Facilitator/All (ground rules)	Common understanding of goals for session, collaboration and agreement on ground rules
Review of project progress to date, background information, review of current process, documentation to be referenced, Q&A on information previously provided	45 minutes	Project Manager (status update on project) Facilitator/All (review of documentation, Q&A)	Understanding of documentation distributed and currently mapped process
BREAK	15 minutes	All	n/a
Discussion of "could-be" process options to meet project requirements, stakeholder needs	75 minutes	Facilitator/All	Presentation of "could-be" options researched, additional "could-be" option ideas, further development/refinement of options.
BREAK	15 minutes	All	n/a
Narrow down "could-be" options to 2-3 viable options	60 minutes	Facilitator/All	Agreement on 2-3 options to share with larger stakeholder pool
Further refinement/ development of the 2-3 "could be" options	75 minutes	Facilitator/All	Further development/refinement of "could-be" options.
Next steps and evaluation of process mapping workshop	30 minutes	Facilitator/All	Agreement on next steps, determine effectiveness of workshop, lessons learned

- If the organization was the best in customer service, how would we be interacting and engaging the customer?
- What could the organization be doing differently today that would enable us to meet our long-term strategic goals more easily?

Process Mapping Workshop Documentation

☐	Detailed agenda along with list of participants, meeting location and whether or not food & beverages will be provided
☐	Documentation that will need to be reviewed prior to the workshop–such as the currently mapped process, information on gaps in the process, any "quick wins" implemented or to be implemented, "could-be" process evaluation worksheets
☐	Objectives of redesigning the process–what needs to be achieved to meet BPI project goals (the business case for the BPI project)
☐	Potential "could-be" options to discuss based on prior research and prior discussions with stakeholders.
☐	Contact information for the project manager and other BPI project team members including a point of contact for any questions regarding the workshop
☐	Any other information that may be relevant or of interest to the participants

Figure 6.5   Checklist for process mapping workshop participants

These questions also prompt the participants to think carefully about the could-be process options that are already being proposed. Does the potential option for a refined process answer these key questions? If not, the process being proposed needs to be developed further. Refer back to Figure 6.4—in the workshop, this evaluation worksheet would be distributed to all participants for discussion. The goal of the facilitator is to achieve consensus around the weighted criteria and the viability of this could-be option. Use the workshop time to make updates/changes as needed to the worksheet based on stakeholder feedback and input.

The authors have worked with clients where the "could-be" process evaluation worksheets are completed during this workshop. They have found from personal experiences that having relevant and key BPI project team members work directly with a handful of key stakeholders to develop the worksheets, then sharing that information and validating it during Phase 3, seems to be most effective and efficient. It provides a broader group of stakeholders who are involved in Phase 3 and in this process mapping workshop with a straw model from which to work.

Just because options are presented during the process mapping workshop doesn't mean that those are necessarily the only options to consider. Potentially a completely new process, from scratch, or a radically different approach to the current process may be a possibility. Use brainstorming to generate innovative ideas. During brainstorming the facilitator should be guiding the discussion by encouraging participants to build on others' ideas to create new ideas.

There are a number of approaches for brainstorming that might be tried depending on the group. Some examples include:

- Post-its™: Use of sticky notes in order to capture ideas from each individual and then have them categorized and shared on a wall for all to view. This works well in cases where the stakeholder pool is a quieter group that prefers to share ideas anonymously.
- Online brainstorming: Through the use of a collaborative tool, stakeholders who are not co-located may share ideas online. The tools are many and include GlobalMeet®, Stormboard, and Glinkr®, to name just a few. Search Google for a list of many other free online brainstorming tools.
- Charette Procedure: This approach is used with larger groups of stakeholders (usually over 10). Stakeholders are divided into smaller groups to brainstorm ideas. Then, those ideas are passed around to the other groups to be built upon and refined. The Charette Procedure is also of value when a number of issues need to be brainstormed. Each group can take a particular issue and brainstorm ideas around solving that issue and then share with the other stakeholder groups for input.

Using Round Robins to Enable Participation

Gina was facilitating a virtual process mapping workshop with over 20 participants. Shouting out ideas for "could-be" processes during the brainstorming session was not going to work! In order to allow participation by all 20 workshop attendees and ensure that everyone was heard, Gina used a "round robin" approach that entailed calling on each participant in turn in order to share ideas.

Round robin brainstorming utilizes an approach where stakeholders take turns sharing their ideas. This works well if brainstorming is being done virtually or in large groups or in situations where stakeholders are quieter and would not share ideas easily. In this case, the facilitator calls on stakeholders, one by one, to share their ideas. Stakeholders may share a new idea when it is their turn or build on an idea presented earlier. A round robin approach might also be utilized to provide feedback on any proposed could-be process options brought to the process mapping workshop based on previous data gathering and interviewing sessions with stakeholders.

Effective Listening Skills

Effective listening skills are definitely necessary for leading process mapping workshops, but frankly, are needed for success in all phases of BPI projects. *Effective listening* refers to ensuring understanding of what the other person is saying through asking clarifying questions and paying attention to body language as well as the words being spoken.

Consider this statement from a stakeholder and the response from the project team member:

> *Stakeholder: "The process really works fine as it is. Well, maybe it is not great, but we have been using it for so long and really it is going okay. I have never heard anyone complain about it."*
>
> *A BPI project team member who is practicing effective listening knows that this stakeholder does likely see the need for process improvement overall, but may be hesitant because he is a bit worried. A proper response that utilizes effective listening skills might go something like this:*
>
> *BPI project team member: "You are correct that there have been no complaints, and I can see how you might feel it is fine overall, but as the company changes, we'll have to make changes as to how we get the work done so we can keep meeting the needs of customers. And it would be better to make small tweaks now, while all is going well, rather than having to do it completely differently in the future. If you were going to change one or two things about the process to make your job easier overall, what would you change? Remember that you will have time to learn the process and get training on the new process before you have to implement it officially."*

In the example conversation, the project team member is reducing fears on the part of the stakeholder but enabling him to feel as if he has some control over the project and can participate in making decisions on changes to the process. The stakeholder will leave the conversation feeling as if his input is welcome and he will be able to contribute to designing the process. The stakeholder will be more comfortable with the BPI project overall.

Consider this next example of a conversation between a stakeholder and a project manager about a current BPI project.

> *Stakeholder: "Nothing is going right with this process improvement project. It should be stopped immediately!"*

> *Project manager:* "*I can tell you are frustrated. Please help me to understand what is not going well with the project from your perspective?*"
>
> *Stakeholder:* "*All of these changes are going to happen and who knows if they will work. What if the process gets worse?*"
>
> *Project manager:* "*I can see how that would be a problem and we wouldn't want to do anything untested. We are going to be holding a stakeholder meeting to discuss changes associated with the process improvement initiative and ask for volunteers to pilot test any changes to the process. In this way, we can see what is working and what is not, prior to rolling out the final "to-be" process.*"
>
> *Stakeholder:* "*Oh, that makes sense. I didn't realize we were going to pilot test the process before full implementation. I'd like to be involved in that.*"

Similarly, in this example, the project manager is drawing out the stakeholder and calming him down by getting him to express his real problems with the project and providing ideas on how those problems will be addressed. Review the checklist in Figure 6.6 of best practices for effective listening skills.

Organizing Ideas Presented in the Process Workshop

As a best practice, and to ensure capturing of all ideas presented at the process mapping workshop, be sure to include a scribe in the workshop. This individual should not be one of the participants in the workshop and certainly not the facilitator.

Table 6.5 provides a number of best practices for organizing ideas presented in the process workshop.

Best practices for effective listening skills

☐	Make eye contact with the stakeholder sharing ideas
☐	Nod to demonstrate understanding and attention to what is being said
☐	Encourage the stakeholder to share his ideas with verbal and nonverbal support
☐	Ask clarifying and genuine questions to ensure understanding and support for ideas presented
☐	Reflect back/summarize what the stakeholder has said

Figure 6.6   Checklist for effective listening skills

Table 6.5 Organizing ideas presented in the process workshop

Consider ...	Value/Benefit
Utilizing sticky (Post-it™) notes to capture ideas presented	Enables viewing ideas more easily when placed on a wall and easily categorizing and moving ideas around.
Using an interactive whiteboard to capture information	Enables easily transferring to a computer (without having to type up from flip charts) and distributing notes to participants.
Using a "parking lot"	Keep ideas that don't help to achieve the goals or objectives on a parking lot list so they don't get lost.
Using large rolls of paper to map out "could-be" process ideas	Large rolls of paper enable the "could-be" processes to be mapped and easily viewed. Sticky notes may be used initially and, when the process is fairly well finalized, the information might be transferred to a large sheet of paper for easier viewing.
Using mapping software	Business process mapping software takes the place of large rolls of paper and enables mapping the "could-be" process options for sharing with others.

Designing Could-be Options

In designing could-be options consider the criteria established for the new or refined process as well as ensuring that any could-be options meet the objectives of both the BPI project scope as well as stakeholder's needs. This can be tricky as, undoubtedly, each stakeholder will have personal objectives that they would like to achieve in a redesign of the process.

Figure 6.7 provides a checklist to utilize when considering could-be options for the process. The items to consider in the checklist in Figure 6.7 enable the participants in the process mapping workshop to be sure that they have considered key requirements when developing could-be options to improve the process. For example, the first item on the checklist asks if non-value-added activities have been eliminated. If we consider our example used previously in this book, *Improvement in H/R Processes*, a non-value-added activity may be a vendor sending an invoice for approval, H/R processing the invoice by adding a PO number, the invoice then going back to the vendor to add the PO number to the invoice, and the vendor then resending the invoice back to H/R for another approval.

Figure 6.8 shows a potential could-be option for the *Improvement in H/R Processes* project discussed previously.

Considerations when developing "could-be" options

☐	Are non-value-added activities eliminated?
☐	Has a roles/responsibilities worksheet been developed so it is clear where responsibilities lie for implementing the process?
☐	Are any changes in reporting relationships required or suggested to increase efficiencies in completing the process?
☐	Will training be needed around the "could-be" process? If so, has a high-level training plan been developed?
☐	What resources are needed to implement the "could-be" process and are those resources available or can they be sourced?
☐	What is the budget requirement for implementing the "could-be" process?
☐	What is the expected timeline for implementing the "could-be" process?

Figure 6.7   Checklist for *could-be* options

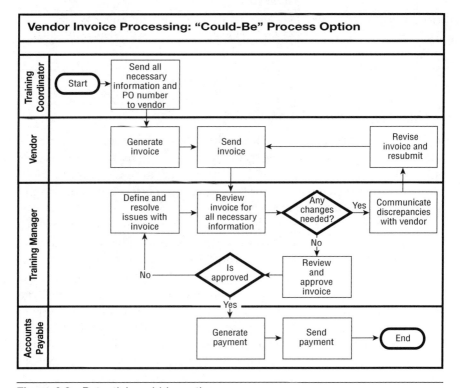

Figure 6.8   Potential *could-be* options

Recall that Figure 6.4 shared a potential could-be option via the could-be option evaluation worksheet. Figure 6.8 builds on that worksheet by mapping out the process as detailed in the worksheet and also eliminating the non-value-added activity (which adds significant time to the process) of having the invoice initially reviewed by the training coordinator and, instead, sending the invoice directly to the manager for approval. The training coordinator, being involved up front in the process, before the invoice is even generated, eliminates multiple people from reviewing an invoice after it is submitted. In this scenario, the BPI project team would have worked with a group of stakeholders during a process mapping workshop in order to evaluate and fine tune the worksheet (see Figure 6.4).

Evaluating and Wrapping Up the Workshop

When the BPI project team and stakeholders have produced 2 to 3 viable could-be options, the process mapping workshop has been successful in accomplishing its goal.

Figure 6.9 provides a checklist for wrapping up the process mapping workshop. If the process mapping workshop is really over—the project manager has checked off each item in the checklist in Figure 6.9—the BPI project team is ready to move toward validating the design with others, getting feedback, and designing the to-be process.

But first, any good project manager knows that it is essential to evaluate the effectiveness of the session (lessons learned). Even if the goal was accomplished of achieving 2 to 3 feasible designs for the process, was the process mapping workshop a satisfactory experience for participants overall? Ask the following

Is the Process Mapping Workshop really over?

☐	Have 2–3 feasible "could-be" options been developed?
☐	Has consensus been reached on the "could-be" options to be put forth for review?
☐	Have all relevant stakeholders participated in the process?
☐	Have all criteria been met in development of 2–3 "could-be" options?
☐	Do the "could-be" options developed meet the objectives of the BPI project?
☐	Have non-value-added activities been eliminated in development of "could-be" options?
☐	Has necessary additional information to support the "could-be" options been developed at a high level, including: necessary budget, resources required, training needs, roles, and responsibilities?
☐	Are the "could-be" options developed fully enough in order to move forward to get further review and input by others?

Figure 6.9 Checklist for wrapping up process mapping workshop

questions of participants in the process mapping workshop to gauge the level of satisfaction with the workshop:

- What worked well from your perspective?
- Was your voice heard and were your ideas fairly discussed?
- What improvements would you like to see in how process mapping workshops are conducted?
- What else would you like to share about the process of designing could-be options?

VALIDATING YOUR DESIGN

It is unlikely that every stakeholder attended the process mapping workshop but, hopefully, a number of key stakeholders did. The next step after the process mapping workshop has been completed is to ensure accurate mapping of the could-be processes developed during the workshop and getting that information out to the sponsor and any other key stakeholders.

At this point, the process may need to be professionally and more formally mapped (especially if sticky notes were used). Formally mapped could-be processes will be presented to the stakeholders for feedback. This feedback will drive selection of a could-be process option for further development, leading to a to-be process.

Getting Feedback

When presenting the two or three could-be options for formal feedback from key stakeholders (such as management level staff who have not participated in the process mapping workshop), include the following information for each could-be process option:

- How option maps achieve, or help to achieve, the objectives of the BPI project
- Budget necessary to implement the option
- Timeline to implement the option
- Resources required to implement (as part of the BPI implementation team), as well as resources needed for pilot testing

Feedback for selection of a could-be option to be developed into a to-be option should come from:

- Management staff who will be responsible for overseeing the process when released

- Individual contributors who will need to use the process as part of their job (a combination of those who will use the process regularly and individual contributors who may have to use the process only on occasion)
- Vendors who may need to utilize the process
- Change management experts
- Individuals responsible for training on the process
- Relevant subject matter experts—such as finance, HR, sales and marketing (business units with expertise on the process; individual contributors listed above may fall under this category also)
- Quality assurance team members
- Risk management team members

Evaluate each option to determine the one could-be option that should be moved forward for presentation and approval by the sponsor.

Some examples of questions to be asked to gather feedback include:

- Does the could-be process option include all necessary activities?
- Are there activities depicted that may not add value?
- Are there roles and responsibilities that are missing, or that are depicted but unnecessary?
- How will the could-be process option impact the customer (vendor, another department)?
- Is there any part of the could-be process option that you believe will not work or be effective?
- For managers—do you see any part of the process that would be difficult to manage/oversee?

Narrowing Down Could-be Options to a To-be Process

After the feedback is gathered, the BPI project team will select the could-be process that will become the proposed to-be process. Of the two or three could-be options that were initially developed during the process mapping workshop and then shared with a broader group of stakeholders, the one selected as the to-be process should be the process that meets all of the criteria established, as well as the one that garners the most support from all stakeholders, at all levels of the organization. Certainly some adjustments, or tweaks, may have been made to the final to-be process to be shared based on the feedback received. When reviewing could-be options, consider each option from the perspective of the:

- Technical feasibility of implementing the could-be option
- The high-level costs and benefits of the could-be option

On a BPI project engagement a few years back, the BPI process team, after gathering feedback from a number of key stakeholders from throughout the organization, took the two "could-be" processes and further refined them to create a "to-be" process that captured the ideas and suggestions of all stakeholders and further built upon the two "could-be" processes to make them even more effective and efficient.

A high-level overview of the feedback that was gathered and the selection of the to-be process should be shared with all stakeholders prior to reviewing with the sponsor of the BPI project. This keeps stakeholders engaged and feeling as if they have contributed to the development of a to-be process. When stakeholders feel as if they have had a strong say in determining how they will get the work done, they are more accepting of the change overall.

Consider also the need for incentives for stakeholders who will be using the new process as well as receiving on-going training (especially for more complex BPI projects). Upon roll out of the new process organization-wide, evaluation systems will need to be put in place in order to ensure the process is working as expected and meeting the objectives and measures determined of importance. Incentive programs, training, and evaluation will be discussed further in Chapter 8.

PRESENTING TO THE SPONSOR

A key skill of BPI project managers is the ability to present information clearly and concisely to the sponsor. Naturally, this applies to status reports and other regular communications with the sponsor and/or key leaders in the organization; but it is an absolute necessity when presenting the to-be process. The goal here is to sell the sponsor and other key leaders on the to-be process in order to move forward. The focus in the presentation to the sponsors and others should be in these key areas:

- An overview of the to-be process specifically focusing on how it meets the criteria and objectives outlined for the BPI project
- The divisions/departments that were involved in the process up to this point
- How the to-be process will increase effectiveness and efficiency
- Time required, as well as budget and resources, to roll out the to-be process—initially as a pilot and then full implementation

- Other cost considerations: salary and overhead, technology needs, communications, equipment, policy and procedure development, organizational change components, business disruption impact, and training needs
- Who would be involved in pilot testing and why—as well as expectations around pilot testing

The goal of this presentation to the sponsor and other key leaders is to get approval to move forward with pilot testing the to-be process. This includes getting commitment for funding and resources needed.

The BPI project manager and other key BPI team members should prepare for the meeting with the sponsor and other key leaders by considering all possible questions and challenges to the process that may arise during the meeting. As a best practice, prepare possible answers to all questions and challenges that may arise so that the team is prepared to respond and decisions are not delayed.

Best Practices for Getting Decisions Made by the Sponsor

Gina was working with a BPI project team at a manufacturing company. The "to-be" process had been designed and more than met the objectives set forth in the project scope. Additionally, the process, as mapped, would likely be even more efficient than previously expected. It seemed a "no brainer." However, during discussions with the sponsor and other senior leaders, they just couldn't seem to make a decision to move forward and approve pilot testing of the "to-be" process. Reasons included being unsure of timing needed to test the process—given so much else going on—and whether it made sense to change the process now. Undoubtedly, the proposed "to-be" process was going to help manage everything that was going on and would directly impact a number of upcoming key initiatives.

Figure 6.10 provides a checklist of best practice steps for driving decision making from sponsors and other key leaders.

If a decision must be made at a later time, for example, to get more details from the BPI project team or for the stakeholders to get others involved, the BPI project manager should schedule a date for follow up with the sponsor and key leaders. The responsibility resides with the project manager to follow up with the stakeholder group. As with any executive group in any organization, the

Best Practices Steps to Drive Strategic Decision Making

	Steps to Drive Strategic Decision Making from Sponsors
☐	Provide overview of "to-be" process–share a graphic of the process that displays roles and responsibilities for all involved in the process.
☐	Highlight how the "to-be" process meets the objectives/goals set forth by the sponsors as well as how it will solve problem(s) being addressed by the BPI project.
☐	Provide background information on how the "to-be" process was developed: • Stakeholders involved • Factors considered
☐	Include a "do-nothing" option–what happens if the process is not changed.
☐	Cost of implementing the "to-be" process as well as required timeline and required resources (including costs such as salary and overhead, technology, communications, equipment needs, policy and procedure development costs, organizational change impact, disruption to the business, training needs).
☐	What is needed for a decision to move forward with approving and implementing the "to-be" process (e.g., budget allocated, timeline approved, resources committed).
☐	Have handy, in case requested, other options ("could-be" processes) considered.

Figure 6.10 Steps to drive decision making

project team has significant responsibilities, and without follow up, the project manager is likely to find that the decision is not reached quickly enough to meet project deadlines and keep the project moving forward.

FINALIZING THE TO-BE PROCESS

Once approved by the sponsor and any other key leaders, finalize the to-be process by doing the following:

- Formalize the to-be process map (it may need *tweaks* based on discussions in the executive meeting) depicting roles and responsibilities and highlighting the changes in the process from the current process
- Develop a plan for the pilot group roll out including timing and expectations around testing the new to-be process
- Highlight the benefits of the new to-be process, such as improved customer service, reduced error rate, improved quality, and/or reduced costs

Sharing with Extended Stakeholders

For BPI projects concerning significant numbers of stakeholders, this is a good communication point at which to reach out to those extended stakeholders who may not have been involved in the development of could-be processes or the to-be process. Extended stakeholders may include individuals who work with the process on occasion (possibly as a backup when another employee is out of the office) or who are impacted in some way by the process (such as the stakeholder who now might receive a report from Bob rather than Sally because of the process change). To engage extended stakeholders, consider a virtual meeting or a face-to-face meeting option to update the stakeholders on the approved to-be process. E-mail or the project portal would be another way to interact with extended stakeholders; but if there is a possibility of interacting more personally—such as via a virtual meeting or face-to-face meeting—choose this path, instead, to engage the stakeholders.

In sharing the to-be process with the extended stakeholder pool, be sure to cover the benefits of the newly refined process—not solely for the organization, but also for the stakeholders: How will they personally benefit or find value in the changed process? Why does the change matter to them?

PREPARING TO MOVE TO PHASE 4

Now that the to-be process has been defined, mapped, and approved, the BPI project team is ready to move to Phase 4—implementing the redesigned business process (pilot testing). Preparation for Phase 4 includes the following:

- Communicating with the pilot group members who will test the to-be process
- Develop overall stakeholder communication plans for Phase 4 communications
- Setting up a sub-team to help with pilot testing through answering questions and providing support to pilot testers
- Developing a change management plan for Phase 4 to manage any required or suggested changes to be made to the to-be process

This chapter shared a number of ways to keep stakeholders engaged and to get their support and assistance in developing could-be process options. The more involved stakeholders are in developing options for the newly designed process, the more likely they will follow that process once it is implemented. Key considerations for facilitating workshops to design could-be process options were shared. Ensuring well-facilitated process mapping workshops is essential to getting information needed from a potentially large group of stakeholders in as efficient and effective manner as possible. It is not always easy to *go back to the well* to get more information after having a process mapping workshop that was chaotic and uncontrolled.

IMPLEMENTING REDESIGNED BUSINESS PROCESSES

What a distance the business process improvement (BPI) project team has come! A *to-be* process is now designed and ready for initial pilot testing with key stakeholders who will be using the process as well as those managing the process being used. There is still some *heavy lifting* ahead, however, as pilot testing must be carefully overseen in order to ensure that those who are participating are committed to a serious review of the process.

As a best practice, a brief *lessons-learned* session with the BPI project team and key stakeholders will provide a chance for correcting issues and moving in to Phase 4 better prepared.

For every BPI project the authors manage, they hold a brief lessons-learned session with the BPI project team and sponsor and/or other key stakeholders just to check in on the successes and challenges to date. For one BPI project, the lessons-learned session following Phase 3 resulted in making changes to the authors' communication plan to better engage stakeholders moving forward. The BPI project team noted that there were a number of comments from stakeholders that communications were so frequent that they tended to ignore them. This explained why so many stakeholders seemed unaware of upcoming meetings. With this feedback, the BPI project team changed to a less-frequent communication plan.

This chapter will focus on pilot testing of the process and using sub-teams reporting to the BPI team in order to keep pilot testers engaged and enable a point of contact when questions or concerns arise.

PHASE 4 OVERVIEW

Figure 7.1 depicts the fourth phase of the six-phased approach to managing BPI projects, *Implement Redesigned Business Process*.

In this phase of the BPI project, the BPI project team works in collaboration with a number of stakeholders who were selected to implement the new to-be process via a pilot test. Basically, they will be the only ones in the organization utilizing the new process while others continue to use the current process. Pilot groups will be discussed further, later on in this chapter.

The goal of Phase 4 of the BPI project is to ensure the to-be process will be ready for roll out throughout the organization. In Phase 4 any issues with the to-be process should be discovered and resolved prior to official full roll

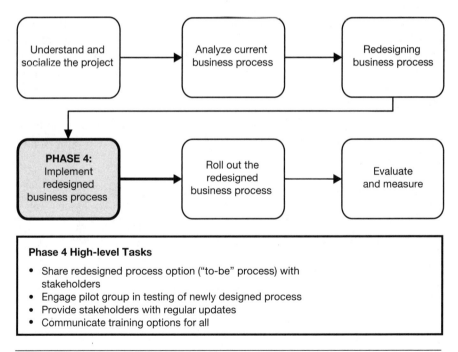

Phase 4 High-level Tasks

- Share redesigned process option ("to-be" process) with stakeholders
- Engage pilot group in testing of newly designed process
- Provide stakeholders with regular updates
- Communicate training options for all

Figure 7.1   Phase 4 of the six-step process

out. Processes rolled out organization-wide should be nearly perfect. Failure to determine issues via a pilot test will only complicate an organization-wide roll out, with the possibility of stakeholders refusing to move to the new process or increasing organizational risk that could have a bottom-line impact.

UNDERSTANDING THE RISKS OF IMPLEMENTATION

In Chapters 2 and 3, risk planning was discussed. During Phase 4 of the BPI project, it is important to consider risks involved in this particular phase of the project.

> *The authors have learned that just because stakeholders were initially excited about the process change, doesn't mean they will stay excited. On one BPI project being completed for a university, nearly all of the stakeholders who would be impacted by the process change were thrilled that steps were finally being taken to improve the way they supported first year students. They were engaged in the early planning stages and in development of a variety of "could-be" options. There was consensus in developing a "to-be" process. However, once the pilot group started to use the "to-be" process, the whole project began to fall apart! Although people were excited about changes, when it actually came time to use the new process they were not as excited and engaged. This was a risk the authors just did not foresee in the BPI project team.*

Risks involved in Phase 4 of the BPI project could include any or all of the following:

- Lack of interest in utilizing the new process due to fear of failure or fear of falling behind in getting other priority work accomplished
- Lack of resources available to test the new process or resources pulled for other initiatives
- Lack of management support for a process change
- Lack of management support for enabling pilot testers to utilize the new process
- Insufficient training of pilot testers
- Insufficient or ineffective communications with pilot testers

Risks that are not identified or managed in this phase of the project will delay the overall project and potentially reduce the use of the new process once it is rolled out organization-wide.

Revisiting Your Risk Management Plan

As a best practice in project management in general, the project team should be reviewing the risk management plan on a regular basis. In the case of BPI projects, review the risk management plan at least at the start of each phase of the project. This review will entail determining which risks on the plan are still active, which are no longer relevant, and where new risks have arisen—given any number of circumstances. For example, Figure 7.2 is a completed risk register for an identified risk in Phase 4 of the BPI project: *Improvement in HR A/P Processes*.

In Figure 7.2, a new risk that is identified is the loss of three individuals who were members of the pilot testing group due to changing circumstances in the organization. In this example, the BPI project team has determined to address the risk by moving forward without these three individuals participating in the pilot testing and will add one other individual, a new Human Resources (HR) employee, to join the pilot testing team. It can be assumed that the BPI project

Risk Register Example – Phase 4

Project Name: Improvement in HR A/P Processes		Date: April 20xx	
Risk ID/WBS Number WBS Number: XIX	**Risk Description:** Three of the individuals selected for pilot testing of "to-be" process have limited time available due to the fact that there was a high turnover rate in the organization last month and these individuals within HR are in the middle of hiring new employees.		
Risk Category: Stakeholders			
Probability: 5 (it has occurred)	**Impact** 4		**Overall Rating:** 20
Priority Ranking: High			
How will risk be addressed? Will move forward with testing by other individuals and eliminate these individuals from the pilot test group. Will add one more tester from HR– a new administrator recently hired within the group. This will require Allison, one of the members of the BPI project team, to spend more time with the new individual who has not been involved in the project.			
Team member responsibility (name and role) Allison Jackson, BPI Project Team Member			

Figure 7.2   Completed risk register

team decided that the other pilot testers are sufficient to accomplish the goal of testing the viability of the to-be process.

USING PILOT GROUPS

As noted earlier in this book, the goal of a pilot test is to enable testing out the process in *real time*, in order to understand how effectively and efficiently it really will work *prior* to rolling it out organization-wide. In addition, BPI project teams use pilot testing in order to:

- Ensure the process will work as mapped
- Reduce the risk of the process failing during full roll out
- Enable increased buy-in for the use of the process once it is rolled out because peers of future users have already worked with it

There are a number of advantages to using pilot groups to test potential new or refined business processes, including:

- Reducing risk during organization-wide roll out
- Testing the process in a controlled live environment
- Understanding where changes may be needed to further improve upon the to-be process

While it could be argued that in the example used in this book—*Improvement in HR A/P Processes*—a pilot test is unnecessary given the limited reach of the process, some form of pilot testing is actually of value in any size of BPI project.

Undoubtedly, pilot testing should be utilized for complex BPI projects that cross a number of divisions or departments, may be expensive to roll out and implement, and could cause significant negative bottom-line impact if it fails.

Develop a role and responsibility document for pilot testers similar to the one shown in Figure 7.3. Using a roles and responsibilities document sets expectations for pilot testers so they understand exactly what is expected of anyone performing the role of a tester of the to-be process.

Engaging the Pilot Group

Recall that Chapter 3 discussed the selection of pilot group members. These individuals were not contacted and then ignored until they were ready to start their work; throughout the entire BPI project they had been involved in the project either through participating in sharing information about the current

Process Tester: Role & Responsibilities

ROLE	"To-be" Process Pilot Group Member (Tester)	
RESPONSIBILITIES	**PROJECT STAGE**	**SPECIFIC RESPONSIBILITIES**
	Before Testing	Engage in the BPI project overall by: • Ensuring understanding of vision and business case for process change • Contributing ideas and suggestions for improving process • Offering insight into current process • Asking questions and challenging assumptions
	During Testing	Contribute to the success of the BPI project by: • Utilizing the methodology, tools, processes and procedures developed for testing the process • Reporting regularly on progress in testing • Reporting issues as encountered, providing sufficient details • Responding to online surveys and other requests for feedback/information • Meeting the milestones set for testing
	After Testing	Contribute to the success of the roll out of the new process organization-wide by: • Supporting the roll out of the process with peers, colleagues, and co-workers • Answering questions posed by peers, colleagues, and co-workers about the process

Figure 7.3   Role and responsibility document

process, helping to design could-be processes, or just via communications about updates on project status. They should have an understanding of the project overall and how the to-be process was developed. They understand the benefits of the new to-be process, but also understand where challenges may arise in utilizing the process.

Prior to the start of Phase 4, engage the pilot group through a face-to-face or virtual meeting that covers the following agenda items:

- Review of the to-be process, including roles and responsibilities associated with the process
- Testing process/methodology to be used for pilot testing the to-be process
- Testing schedule plus dates/times of check-in meetings
- Evaluation plan and how evaluation of to-be process testing will be conducted (e.g., meetings, surveys, etc.)
- Points of contact on the BPI project team to respond to questions (if the pilot testing team includes virtual team members, be sure that there are project team members available at remote locations, or close to remote locations, in order to allow for more effective support of virtual pilot testers)
- Use of a portal (or some other forum) for logging issues that arise during the testing process

Training the Pilot Group

Earlier on when planning the BPI project, the BPI project team should have included a plan for training the pilot group in the to-be process. And, as a best practice, the team should have communicated that training will be provided to pilot group testers *prior* to the start of testing.

Training should entail explaining the new proposed (to-be) process, how it differs from the current process, roles and responsibilities associated with the new process, and the expected benefits—as well as any challenges of the new process. Each pilot tester should walk through the entire process as part of training and have access to documentation, as well as a point of contact on the BPI project team should questions arise.

Plans need to be made to ensure a safe environment for testing the to-be process; the work of the business must still go on as the new process is being tested. For more complex to-be process projects, a safe environment might be established by having testing done in an environment that does not impact customers or financials of the business. In such a situation, pilot testers may be provided sample client information or other data relevant to the process that would lead to effective testing of the process but would not use actual, real client information. Whenever the process has a big impact on the bottom line, it is necessary to have a safe environment that will not allow a negative financial or customer impact, or risk to the tester.

Training should also cover topics such as:

- Contact information for points of contact on the BPI project team to assist with questions about the process during testing
- How to log issues in a database or via the portal (or any other forum utilized)
- Testing schedule and expectations around testing

Ensuring Effective Testing of the New Process

As noted earlier, it is imperative to have a testing process and methodology; a plan for what is being tested and how it is being tested. The goal is to ensure that each tester performs their role and responsibility around the process in the same way and exactly as documented. However, before testing can even begin, everything must be in place to ensure the pilot group can actually use the to-be process. This includes:

- Complete and accurate documentation and instructions on using the process
- Ensuring technology is available and pilot groups being tested have been trained on its use
- Any other updates or changes have been made to accommodate the new process and enable effective testing

As part of the plan for testing, ensure that there are regular feedback sessions scheduled—whether face-to-face, virtually, or via conference call—to gather information about how testing is progressing. For larger test groups, schedule small group sessions. Consider also dividing testers based on their role and responsibility for testing. This enables those testers performing the same role to discuss their particular experiences with the process.

Figure 7.4 provides one potential checklist for ensuring that pilot group test members are ready to move forward with testing.

Is the pilot group ready to begin testing the "to-be" process

☐	Pilot group members have been trained on what is required to work with the new process
☐	Communication plan for testing has been developed
☐	Pilot test group members understand the vision and the business case for the new process
☐	Evaluation criteria is developed
☐	Methods for gathering feedback on the testing has been developed
☐	Step-by-step documented instructions have been provided to testers
☐	Roles and responsibilities for testing have been developed
☐	Managers of pilot group testers have been educated on the importance of testing and the time commitment required from the testers. They support their employees' involvement in testing.
☐	Back-up pilot group testers (in case needed) have been trained and are ready to step in if necessary to complete testing

Figure 7.4   Checklist for pilot group testing

Setting Up Feedback Mechanisms

Earlier in this chapter we briefly mentioned using a portal or database or some other system to capture how effectively the process is working and issues that arise during testing. Feedback may also be provided via online survey tools. The most effective surveys will include open-ended questions to allow for sufficient commentary from the testers. In fact, a combination of methods for collecting feedback on the process is optimal and allows for more effective sharing of information between testers and the BPI project team. Consider any or all of these options for collecting feedback on the testing of the to-be process:

- Online survey
- BPI project portal
- Database to capture issues
- Face-to-face or virtual meetings
- Regular conference calls
- One-on-one check-ins with testers

While pilot testing a "to-be" process for a marketing firm, we enabled testers to provide feedback via the project portal, e-mail, or via biweekly conference calls. If testers were not able to join in on a conference call, expectations were set that they would need to provide feedback via the portal or by sending an e-mail to their point of contact on the BPI project team. Since we provided several options for sharing feedback, it reduced the need of the BPI project team to track down testers who could not attend the conference calls. Only on rare occasions, because expectations were set and agreed to ahead of time, did the BPI project team have to chase after testers to get feedback.

Especially for larger pilot test groups, a variety of options should be provided for capturing information from the testers in any number of ways that work. The easier it is to provide feedback, the more likely feedback will be provided by testers.

DETERMINING AND SELECTING SUB-TEAMS

Sub-teams and sub-team leads would be a necessity for any large, complex BPI project and most certainly for a project that includes remote or virtual team members and/or stakeholders. Sub-teams may be used for a BPI project that has a number of key components or *mini* projects. For example, let's assume that a BPI project has three different processes impacted by the project, each of which is tied to a specific division within the company. Each of the processes for each of the divisions should be managed as a sub-project under the main project (or program), with sub-team leads and their sub-teams heading up each sub-project.

The purpose of sub-teams in this phase of the BPI project is to generate improved support of larger pilot test groups and also to bring about points of contact for pilot test teams—especially teams that are remote or virtual.

Figure 7.5 depicts an organization chart for using sub-teams in Phase 4 of the BPI project. As can be seen in the figure, there are two sub-teams with sub-teams leads. In this example, the sub-teams are responsible for particular pilot test groups—one team is responsible for pilot testing by management staff and the other is responsible for pilot testing by process users.

Figure 7.6 shows responsibility for remote or virtual testers where sub-team members are not responsible for specific pilot test groups, but rather, are set up to respond to questions/inquiries and be a main point of contact for remote or virtual testers. For example, in Figure 7.6, Sarah, located in Oregon, is responsible for interacting with and engaging pilot group members in Oregon, Washington, California, and Mexico. Jackson, located in Chicago, is the sub-team lead responsible for overseeing the work of the BPI team members: Jack, Sarah, and Siraj.

If pilot group testers span a number of locations of the business, they should be provided with a point of contact that is *convenient* for them should questions or concerns arise during testing.

For one client that had just one or two testers throughout a number of offices in the Midwest and West Coast of the United States (for a total of 10 testers), the BPI project team found it worked well to have just one BPI project team member as a point of contact for all 10 testers. However, in their Utah office, there were 12 testers. To accommodate this group, the project manager assigned a BPI project team member located in Arizona to be the point of contact for them.

Figure 7.7 provides a checklist of desired experiences, skills, and competencies for both sub-team members and sub-team leads.

Over all else, sub-team members should be customer-focused and very patient. They will undoubtedly have their patience tried throughout the testing period. Additionally, they must be well-versed in the new to-be process—including how it is expected to impact the organization overall, the individuals who utilize or manage the process, and customers. The ability to set expectations with stakeholders

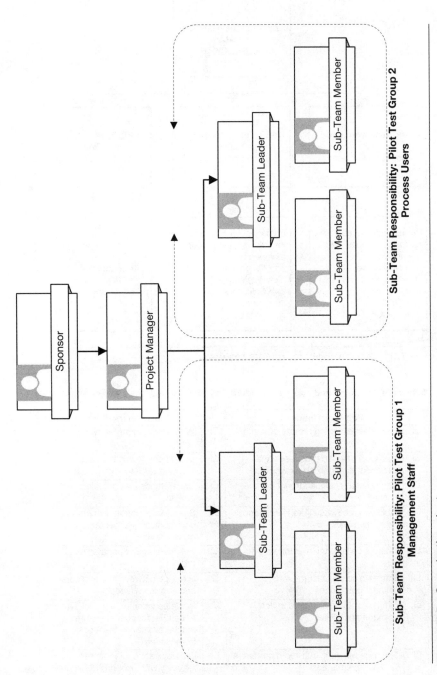

Figure 7.5 Organization chart

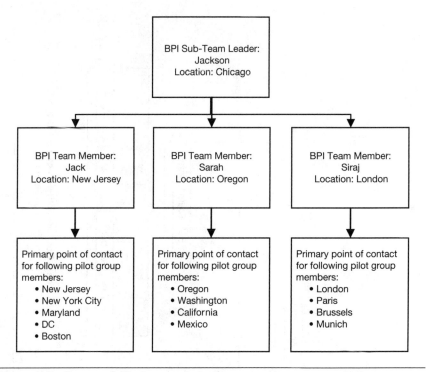

Figure 7.6   Responsibility for remote testers

Sub-team members' and sub-team leaders' key experiences, skills and competencies

	Sub-team leader		Sub-team member
☐	Experience leading remote or virtual teams	☐	Works collaboratively with others
☐	Ability to develop processes and procedures, establish expectations	☐	Strong communication and listening skills to engage others
☐	Strong relationships throughout the company	☐	Understands vision/goals of BPI project
☐	Ability to motivate stakeholders and team members	☐	Shares information with others, communicates expectations of pilot testers
☐	Fosters collaboration among others	☐	Provides regular updates on BPI project
☐	Effective communicator across cultural boundaries	☐	Is bridge between stakeholders and sub-team leader
☐	Strong problem solving/conflict management skills	☐	Provides training on use of systems to capture feedback, ensures regular evaluation feedback from testers
☐	Is bridge between sub-team members and project manager	☐	Develops schedule to meet regularly with pilot group testers

Figure 7.7   Checklist of skills, experiences, and competencies

is also a necessary skill; especially when managing those stakeholders who expect every change they suggest for the to-be process to be utilized.

Enabling Sub-team Success

In order for sub-teams to be successful, the BPI project manager should ensure that processes and procedures have been developed in collaboration with sub-team leads. Regardless of the size of the pilot testing group, processes and procedures for how the sub-teams will work with the core BPI project team, as well as with the pilot group members, must be established. Certainly, the more complex the pilot group—such as those groups that encompass members from remote or virtual locations or in situations where there are a number of processes being tested or a number of stakeholders performing testing—the more imperative it is that the processes and procedures establish consistency among testers and in documenting and reporting test results.

Table 7.1 shows a number of processes and procedures that should be developed for success of sub-teams engaged with the pilot test group.

More information on processes and procedures for implementation will be discussed later in this chapter.

Setting up Roles and Responsibilities of Sub-teams

Ensuring that there are clear roles and responsibilities for sub-teams is necessary so that the sub-team members understand what they need to do and when it needs to be done. It also keeps the remote sub-team members from stepping on each other's toes or from confusing the pilot group testers with too many connection points.

One client brought Gina into their BPI project during Phase 4 in order to get them "unstuck." During interviews to understand the issue, it was apparent that the sub-teams that were put in place to manage pilot group testers were unsure about what they were supposed to be doing and when. For example, one pilot group tester (stakeholder) told Gina that she had three team members—from three different sub-teams—reach out to her regarding her portion of the testing. They all gave her different instructions! Yet another pilot group tester told Gina that she had reached out for help regarding a few questions she had on the process she was testing and didn't hear back from anyone. She sent the e-mail to four different people because she was unsure as to whom she should communicate with.

Table 7.1 Processes and procedures for sub-teams

Process/Procedure	Description
Problem solving/managing conflicts	Inevitably problems and conflicts will arise during testing and certainly conflicts will arise between testers; therefore, having processes in place to manage through problems and resolve conflicts will enable sub-teams to not have to rely on the core BPI project team to get involved.
Collecting feedback from pilot group testers including managing requests for changes to the "to-be" process	Especially for cases where there are multiple sub-teams managing a larger pilot group, processes should be developed on how feedback will be collected (informal and formal methods) and how individual pilot group member requests for changes will be managed. Specifically, the BPI project manager would not want promises being made to pilot group testers that any and all changes they request to the process will be made.
Interactions and communications between: • Pilot group testers and sub-team members • Sub-team and BPI core team • Remote/virtual sub-teams	Channels for formal communications between various groups involved in the BPI project as well as paths (whom communicates to whom and when) are essential for larger BPI projects in order to ensure information is shared as needed and regularly between groups/teams.
Formal channels for reporting on work of the sub-teams as well as reporting relationships	In addition to procedures on how sub-teams will report on their work, there needs to be communication channels and paths developed as well as responsibilities outlined for reporting on work progress.

Refer back to Figure 7.6; Jack, Sarah, and Siraj are three team members with responsibility for being the primary point of contact for pilot group members in specific locations. Figure 7.6 simply provides an overview of responsibility for specific pilot group members. However, the BPI project manager may break this chart down further to show specific *point of contact* responsibilities, as shown in Figure 7.8. This figure not only indicates specific responsibilities for the sub-team member as it relates to being a *point of contact* for the pilot group testers, but also includes timings for meetings, phone calls, and other related events.

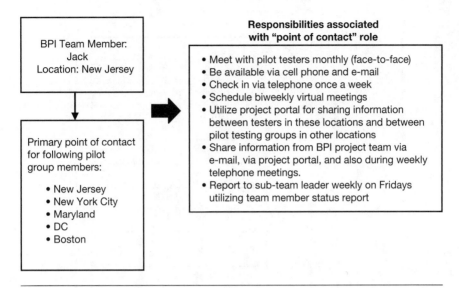

Figure 7.8   Point of contact responsibilities

Certainly, there may also be roles for technical support, process mappers, the process designers, and others on the team who are likely involved during this phase of the BPI project. For example, a process mapper may be needed to provide an overview of the process to pilot group testers early on in the launch of this phase of the BPI project, or a technical expert may be needed to provide training in the use of technology used as part of the process.

Regular Meetings

Scheduling regular meetings early on in the testing phase and throughout this phase is necessary to ensure that the BPI project keeps moving forward. When multiple sub-teams are involved, it is likely that the sub-team lead and not the sub-team members, will be meeting regularly with the BPI project manager and other BPI core team members. Naturally, the sub-team lead will need to get information from his sub-teams to report back to the BPI project manager. Figure 7.9 displays how reporting may flow from stakeholders to sub-team members to the sub-team lead to the BPI project manager/BPI core team.

As can be seen in Figure 7.9, sub-team members collect information from the pilot group stakeholders and submit it to the sub-team lead. The sub-team leader compiles information gathered from all sub-team members and sends that information to the BPI project manager. The BPI project manager then takes that information, compiles it with other required information and reports back to the project sponsor.

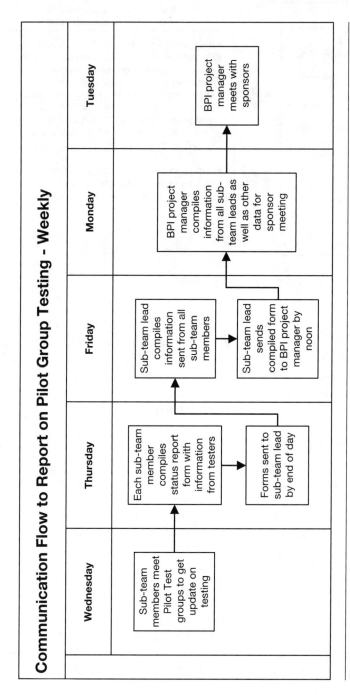

Figure 7.9   Reporting flow

In addition, regular communications and meetings should be set up for outside of this particular reporting requirement. Recall that Figure 7.8 includes required meetings with pilot group members. This information should be compiled into a formal communications and reporting template to be used in Phase 4 of the BPI project.

Regular meetings may also include:

- Training sessions for pilot group members
- General information sessions for all stakeholders
- Decision-making sessions
- Brainstorming or problem-solving sessions

The Necessity of Processes and Procedures for Implementation

Processes and procedures for how the to-be process will be implemented during pilot testing are necessary to make sure that all testers are performing the process in the same way, and under the same conditions. This ensures consistency in testing and ensures that the to-be process is implemented just as it will be when it is rolled out organization-wide.

Processes and procedures will assist in making sure that:

- Regular communications happen between the BPI project team and pilot group testers
- The to-be process is implemented the same way for each tester
- There are documentation and instructions to be followed for utilizing the to-be process
- Regular feedback is gathered on the effectiveness of the to-be process

It is likely that some processes, procedures, and guidelines that were in place for the as-is process are no longer viable or necessary for the to-be process. As a best practice, include a comparison chart for pilot group testers that clearly differentiates the differences between the as-is and the to-be processes.

Check in and Status Reporting

Checking in with pilot group testers as well as status reporting has been discussed earlier in this section. In Phase 4 it is absolutely necessary to ensure regular check-ins on how effective the process is working for the pilot group testers as well as reporting on status to the BPI project manager, sponsor, and other key individuals. It is very easy to fall back to the *old way of doing things*—and this is certainly not an exception for the pilot group!

Expectations around reporting on status, including what needs to be reported, should be set early on in Phase 4 and should be updated as needed.

Jeremy, the project manager, has requested that the sub-team leads update him every other week on status for testing. However, he started to notice that, from report to report, there were many issues that seemed to be arising in testing of the "to-be" process. In some situations it was apparent that testers were getting frustrated with having to wait until the next status report meeting for an answer. To ensure that issues were addressed sooner, rather than later, Jeremy asked the sub-team leads to give him a progress report on a weekly basis and to bring issues on the use of the process immediately to his attention, so that a special meeting could be called to address the issue if needed.

Table 7.2 provides a partially completed example of a communication plan worksheet for use in ensuring regular reporting on the BPI project.

A copy of the communication plan worksheet template is available via download from the Web Added Value™ (WAV) Download Resource Center at the publisher's website: www.jrosspub.com/wav (hereafter referred to as the J. Ross website).

Ensuring Regular Feedback

Regular feedback is essential to the success of Phase 4. Through regular feedback, the BPI project team learns what is working and what is not as it relates to the to-be process. Regular feedback, however, can only be assured through careful planning of communications and by setting up expectations. Simply asking pilot group testers "How's it going?" will not suffice. Formal forms to gather feedback

Table 7.2 Partially completed communication plan worksheet

Project Role	Communication Need	Communication Method	Frequency of Communication
Sub-team leads	Report on status from sub-teams	Meeting with BPI project team	Weekly (every Friday morning at 9:00 AM)
Project manager	Update on testing of "to-be" process to sponsor	Leadership meeting	Monthly (first Monday of each month)
Process trainers	Updates on available face-to-face training sessions and webinars	Project portal and e-mail	As needed

should be used and expectations should be set that pilot group testers must complete the feedback forms on a specific basis and submit to their point of contact.

Consider the following questions that may be asked to gather information on the testing of the to-be process:

- Did the testers have what they needed to be successful?
- Were the testers sufficiently and effectively trained in the to-be process?
- Were the documentation and instructions that were provided clear, concise, and easy to follow?
- What additional information would have been of value to ensure the successful testing of the to-be process?
- What challenges were encountered?
- Was the process followed exactly or were deviations made? If deviations were made, where were they made, what were the deviations from the to-be process, and why were they made?

Let's look at the last question in particular—"*Was the process followed exactly or were deviations made?*" While expectations should be set to follow the process to be tested *exactly* as documented, instructed, and trained on, it should be expected that pilot testers may deviate from the documented process. Deviations often occur because the tester is either having difficulty with a component of the process, was not sufficiently or effectively trained on using the to-be process, or has found a better way (improved upon) of using the process. By making accomodations for and setting the expectations around regular feedback, deviations can be avoided, improvements can be considered, and if implemented, distributed to *all* pilot group members to test.

> One of the more successful BPI project managers set the stage for testing the "to-be" process by asking the pilot group members to "find a better way of doing it if you can!" She effectively challenged the testers to fine-tune the designed process prior to rolling it out organization-wide. She asked only that once they believed they could improve upon it, to immediately notify their point of contact on the BPI project team and a meeting would be scheduled to evaluate the opportunity to further enhance the designed "to-be" process. She asked that a form be submitted to the point of contact that contained the following information:
> - What was the original component or step of the process
> - How can it be changed?
> - How will that be better? (e.g., shorter time frame to complete the process, increased accuracy, less risk of failure, etc.)

USING THE COLLABORATION PORTAL TO GATHER DATA AND FEEDBACK AND SHARE INFORMATION

While feedback on the testing of the to-be process can certainly be provided via forms, meetings, and conference call updates, a project portal may just make the task easier. Using a portal, such as Microsoft SharePoint™, Zoho, Basecamp, or any other number of project and collaboration software available, the BPI project team, sub-teams, and pilot group testers, as well as other stakeholders, can more easily share information with each other. Additionally, collaboration portals provide access to a variety of benefits in Phase 4 (and the entire BPI project frankly), including:

- Access to templates used during the BPI project
- Current project status information
- A place to ask questions and reach out to BPI project team members/ experts
- Testing and other relevant schedules
- Contact information for project team members, stakeholders, and others
- Training and other relevant documentation for the to-be process
- Process maps (as-is process, to-be process)

If a portal is to be used on the BPI project, ensure that individuals who will be using the portal are trained on how to use it and access the information in the portal.

MANAGING NEEDED CHANGES TO THE PROCESS

The whole point of Phase 4 of the BPI project is to test the to-be process *before* it is rolled out organization-wide. The process may look perfectly fine and workable on paper, but until it is tested, the BPI project team really is unsure as to how successful it will be. Inevitably, changes will be suggested, requested, and required based on the testing. Changes may even be demanded by stakeholders! Capture all requested changes, regardless of how small they are, in a form or via the project portal.

Figure 7.10 is an example of a completed template utilized to capture a requested change to a process. As can be seen in the figure, there is a request for a change to accommodate alignment to a department strategy—in this case, the Marketing Department. Once the top section of the template is completed, it would be submitted to the BPI project team via the appropriate channels and a decision would be made whether or not to make the requested change. In such a case as this one, the change would likely be approved to accomplish alignment

Example: Recommended Change to "To-be" Process

BPI Project Team Point of Contact Sandra White	Stakeholder Requesting Change: Jim Smart, Social Media Administrator (Pilot Group Tester)
Description of Change to "To-be" Process There is no auto-submission of company blog posts to LinkedIn and to GooglePlus; submissions go to Pinterest, Twitter, and Facebook only.	
Reason for Change to Process (be specific in explanation) There needs to be auto-submission to LinkedIn and GooglePlus in addition to the other social media channels as our marketing strategy includes increased use of these two channels in the coming year.	
Impact on Process if Change Does Not Occur/Is Not Approved We will need to manually submit blog posts to LinkedIn and GooglePlus and we run the risk of it not getting done if it is not auto-submitted and must be done manually.	
Decision Made (Approve, Reject)	
Justification for Decision	
Approved by:	**Date:**

Figure 7.10   Example of requested change to process

to the strategic goal of the department. This change request template is downloadable from the J. Ross website.

As a best practice, there should be a plan in place to capture all requested changes during the testing process, as well as ensuring there are individuals on the BPI project team along with key stakeholders who are tasked with reviewing and making a final decision on all change requests.

By setting expectations early on during Phase 4, the BPI project manager can make sure that it is clear to pilot group testers and any other stakeholders that changes will go through a formal request and approval process to ensure that the project stays on track and that only those changes which serve to enhance and better the process are considered and incorporated.

During one process improvement project that involved a significant number of executives, leaders, and mid-management stakeholders, the authors spent time upfront, prior to actual testing, to explain that it was important that any change requests went through the appropriate channels, regardless of who initiated the change and even if the change was something that clearly would have to happen. This helped to make it clear to senior staff that simple changes would not just be made if requested and even changes that executives required would have to go through a formal process. In order to "sell" this to senior leaders, the authors simply explained that not following the change management process put the entire project at risk and this was a project that would impact their customers directly.

MAKING ADJUSTMENTS AND FINALIZING THE PROCESS

Once changes to the to-be process have been evaluated and necessary changes have been implemented, the process should be run through, at least one more time, in order to test the changes. At times, depending on the change, the testing may be interrupted for the change to be made and then restarted. Of course, if a process is just not working in testing, the testing process should be halted until changes can be made, and then testing should start again from scratch. For major changes—such as changes to a number of steps within the to-be process—testing should be halted while the process is redesigned. Testing will then start from the very beginning, after training has been provided to pilot group members on the redesigned process. It is essential, even for minor changes, to ensure the modified process is stable and will work with the change that is being made.

The to be process, with any necessary changes determined through pilot group testing, should then be finalized for wider implementation within the organization.

Getting Buy-in from the Pilot Group

The final meeting with the pilot group participants should be to accomplish the following tasks:

- Discuss the final, to-be process and specifically highlight accepted changes, as well as changes that were not accepted
- Capture lessons learned from the testing process
- Finalize the to-be process with the pilot group

A simple table highlighting each requested change, in priority order (based on impact to the process) and whether or not it was accepted and applied should suffice to share the information with the pilot group. As a best practice, if a pilot group participant suggested a change that was not implemented, the BPI project manager or a representative team member might reach out to the individual to personally thank them for their input and explain why the change was not implemented.

As a best practice, the authors always allocate some additional time in the schedule for continued testing of a "to-be" process, based on changes that may be required. Certainly, the more complex the "to-be" process, the more groups impacted by it, and the more "moving parts" it has, the longer the time set aside for further testing.

Presenting to the Sponsor and Key Stakeholders

The presentation to the sponsor and any other key stakeholders is specifically to get approval to roll out the final to-be process organization-wide. Before roll out, the following details must be finalized and should be reported as *ready* to the sponsor and any other key stakeholders:

- Ensuring technology and equipment is being updated as needed to support the new process
- Training plans and curriculum are finalized (this will be discussed further later in this chapter)
- BPI project team members have been trained on implementation of the new process organization-wide
- Any new organizational structure has been put in place to support the roll out (changes in reporting structures, roles, and responsibilities)
- New policies, procedures, and business rules have been developed
- Measurement and evaluation systems have been put in place as well as any necessary incentive programs
- A plan for roll out (department by department, for example) has been developed and key leadership of impacted divisions and departments have been notified and are on board

Present the plan and schedule (including budget and resource needs) for roll out to the sponsors and get approval (go/no-go decision) to move forward.

FINALIZING TRAINING PLANS

The more complex the process—the more robust the training plans will need to be. Once the *final* process is ready to go, training should be started. Figure 7.11 provides a checklist to use for ensuring effective training of the new final process.

Is training ready to be rolled out?

☐	Quick reference step-by-step documentation and instruction is available for users of the new process
☐	More robust (if necessary) training guides are available
☐	Training is offered in a number of formats (face-to-face, virtual, webinars)
☐	Training has been scheduled at a variety of times to accommodate users' work schedules
☐	Trainers have been trained in the process and are ready to be deployed
☐	Support for after training is available for those using the process
☐	Follow up training via webinars or via a project portal where Q&A is available and is complete and ready to be implemented
☐	Invitations have been sent out via Outlook or another scheduling tool to get users scheduled for training sessions

Figure 7.11 Checklist to ensure training

It should be noted that if all is going well during the testing phase, and only minor or no changes are being implemented, then training may begin early for users of the new process. However, if users have begun training and significant issues arise with the testing of the process, those users will need to be retrained. The move to train all users prior to testing being completed is not always an easy decision to make. It is difficult enough to get buy-in for process improvement initiatives from those impacted by a change in the process, but if training is started too early and the process needs rework/refinement, the BPI project team risks losing buy-in from stakeholders (end users of the process), which would significantly impact the success of the BPI project.

Training will be discussed in more detail in Chapter 8.

PREPARING TO MOVE TO PHASE 5

Once approval has been gained for rolling out the finalized process organization-wide, the following steps must be taken:

- A change management plan focused on managing stakeholder expectations around change must be implemented
- A variety of communication channels should be utilized to share information about the new process to the organization
- Sub-teams should be put in place to interact and be made available to users of the new process
- Training and incentive programs should be finalized and shared

- A schedule for regular *check-ins* on the use of the process should be implemented

The pilot group testers are champions of the new process. After all, they have been working with the process all along; they understand how it works and have seen the benefits and value of a change in processes for getting the work done. Rely on these individuals to help spread the word about the new process and its effectiveness and value. These individuals, if available, might also serve on sub-teams to help answer questions and interact with users of the process during roll out.

This chapter focused on utilizing pilot group testers to evaluate a proposed to-be process to ensure it will work as planned and as necessary to accomplish the goals of the BPI project. In this phase, the to-be process is implemented on a smaller scale in order to work out any issues *before* it is rolled out to everyone who will be using it. Collecting feedback from testers is essential in this phase, but not always an easy task. To improve the likelihood of getting the information/feedback needed from those stakeholders involved in pilot testing the process, share *what* is required from those in the pilot group role and *when* it is required. By setting expectations early on in the project—during the initial stakeholders meetings—and reiterating what is needed and expected from pilot group members, the BPI project team will spend less time chasing people down to get information that will demonstrate the success of the to-be process. Refer back to Figure 7.3 for a list of specific responsibilities for pilot group members.

ROLLING OUT THE REDESIGNED PROCESS ORGANIZATION-WIDE

Prior to this phase of the business process improvement (BPI) project, the BPI project team has pilot tested the *to-be* process, resolved any issues with the use of the process, and have received approval to finalize the process and roll out throughout the organization. As part of the roll out organization-wide, it is important to share the results of the pilot test of the process. Certainly, good news should be shared to get users engaged early on and excited about the change ahead. This will be discussed further in this chapter.

> *For one BPI project, the project team shared the good results from a pilot test of the "to-be" process including some comments from key pilot testers. One such comment shared with the users prior to full roll out came from a long-time respected employee in one of the divisions who noted, "Wow! Thanks for allowing me to participate in the pilot test of the new process. This is going to be fantastic! I cannot tell you how happy I am with these changes—you shortened the time I spend doing a number of tasks by more than 40%!" This kind of great news traveled fast throughout the organization and got others engaged in the changes that were about to be implemented with the new updated process.*

Throughout the BPI project, the project team should have been keeping the organization (especially those impacted by the BPI project) updated through regular communications. These communications would naturally begin to increase as the project nears the pilot testing phase (Phase 4). News should be shared about the success of the pilot testing or (in cases where changes were required to the to-be process) about the updates on changes that were happening to ensure a more effective process upon organizational roll out.

Too often BPI project teams think that once they have rolled out the new final process, their work is done. While others will be responsible for maintaining the process moving forward and promoting continuous improvement, the BPI project team should stay involved for a period of time in order to ensure all is working smoothly with the process. Transitioning to maintenance/operations will begin during this phase of the project.

Much of what is discussed in this chapter—communicating with stakeholders about the roll out, scheduling training, ensuring follow up—must all be planned and held *before* the actual roll out of the process. While there may be additional training in one form or another *after* initial training and roll out of the process, be sure that all users of the process are trained early on so they are comfortable using the new process. This is discussed further in this chapter.

PHASE 5 OVERVIEW

Figure 8.1 depicts the fifth phase of the six-phased approach to managing BPI projects: *Roll Out Redesigned Processes Organization-wide.*

In Phase 5, the focus is on the organization as a whole. The process is now finalized with feedback from the pilot group taken into account and the process updated based on that feedback as necessary. Some of the biggest areas of concern for the wider stakeholder group is whether the process:

- Will be easy to learn and if training will be provided
- Will enable them to do their job or perform their role more effectively
- Has been tried and validated by people they trust (peers and coworkers)

Certainly, questions will also arise around:

- The stability of the process
- Whether it will be used immediately or phased in
- What support is available should assistance be required

In this chapter, the focus will be on communicating with the wider stakeholder group ensuring the right questions are answered, even if they are never asked!

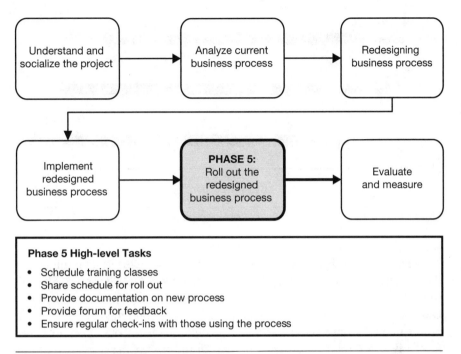

Figure 8.1   Phase 5 of the six-step process

A CONTROLLED APPROACH TO ROLL OUT

Although the process designed, tested, and now finalized is ready to be released throughout the organization, it still makes sense to control the roll out process. Let's assume, for example, that the BPI project team is rolling out a new process to three divisions: Sales, Marketing, and Operations. Sales will more heavily rely on the use of the process, followed by Operations, and then Marketing. In order to control the roll out and give each user group the attention they will need, the BPI project team has decided to roll out the process as shown in Figure 8.2.

As can be seen in Figure 8.2, roll out is staggered with the process being rolled out based on use of the process by department. Since Sales more heavily relies on the process, the process will first be rolled out to them. This gives them more time to work with the process before Operations and Marketing start to use it.

If the process will be rolled out to a significant number of users throughout the organization, control the roll out by focusing on specific departments or workgroups within divisions, as shown in Figure 8.3.

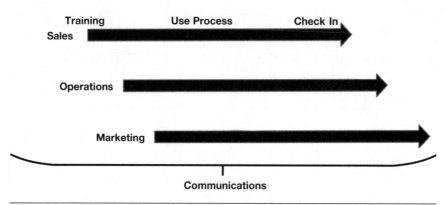

Figure 8.2   Example of high-level roll out of process

In Figure 8.3, BPI project team member Sara is taking the lead on rolling out the new process to the Learning & Development Group in Division A. She will roll out the new process first to Training Coordinators, then to the Instructional Designers and Course Developers, and finally to the Training Managers.

The more divisions and departments involved in the roll out, the more beneficial it is to control the process by rolling out the process in stages. This results in a variety of benefits including:

- More focused attention on the group to which the process is being rolled out
- Smaller training classes
- More focused communications
- An opportunity to correct any issues that may arise during roll out early on

Note that not all components of a process may be rolled out immediately. Large process improvement initiatives may have a staggered roll out—with easier to moderate components of the process being rolled out and implemented prior to the more difficult components, such as those with more resistance and higher cost associated with roll out.

For a manufacturing client, the authors were able to implement about two-thirds of the process improvement changes immediately. The other third required new facilities to be finalized and, therefore, could not be implemented until those facilities were complete and ready for employees to move into.

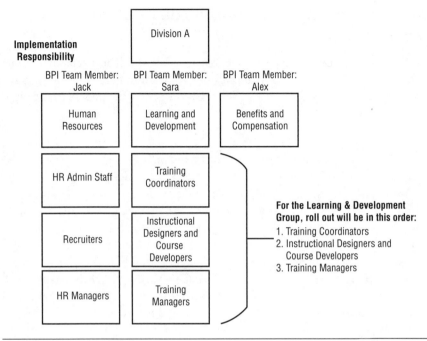

Figure 8.3   Example of roll out of process

PUTTING YOUR CHANGE MANAGEMENT PLAN INTO ACTION

Chapter 3 covered developing the change management plan. It is likely that after the pilot test of the to-be process, changes were made to the change management plan to accommodate the roll out of the finalized process. The same change management process utilized during the BPI project will remain in effect; however, changes here should be focused purely on situations where the process is *not* performing as designed and expected. These situations, if pilot group testing was done effectively, should not even be a concern. At this point there should be no reworking of the process. This was done after input from the pilot group.

The authors have seen only one project where the BPI project team needed to rework the process after it was tested by the pilot group—and that was because the members of the pilot group were not individuals who would be using the process regularly. Once the process was rolled out to the actual users, it didn't work as expected and actually required more effort on the part of the users than the original process did.

An Introduction to the People-side of Change Management

In Chapter 11, the people-side of change management will be discussed in more detail. Here, it is important for the BPI project team to keep in mind that any process change—regardless of its complexity—impacts the people in the organization.

> *The authors were leading a business process initiative for an organization that wanted to change the process for how a team of five individuals input customer data into a system. Under the current process, it took up to 15 minutes to input data for a new customer. The organization was growing and management wanted to reduce the time to input data for new customers from 15 minutes to no more than 8 minutes per customer. Sounds like a great idea— right? It will save those five employees time in getting their work done. But for the employees, it was not a great idea. Going through their heads were a number of worries: Will they be able to learn the new process? Will they still have jobs or is the company trying to get rid of some of them?*

The role of the BPI project team in the roll out of the finalized process organization-wide is to help the wider stakeholder pool adapt to the change that is about to occur. Inevitably there will be people on the project team who are skilled in areas that would be of value in helping others adapt to change. For example, a subject matter expert on the team can serve as the *go-to* person for stakeholders who have questions about the process. A team member who has strong relationships throughout the organization may serve well as someone who can join in conversations that are taking place or initiate conversations when needed.

Table 8.1 provides a few common methods to help others to adapt to change.

COMMUNICATING THE NEW PROCESS

The communication plan developed earlier will need to be updated to include communications that are specific to the launch of the finalized process organization-wide. In this phase, communications will focus on the following points:

- A schedule for launching the new process
- Transition period from the old process to the new process
- Training to be provided on the new process and formats for training

Table 8.1   Methods to adapt to change

How to Help Others Adapt to Change	What to Do
Join in conversations	Talk with stakeholders about the process change. This may entail joining in conversations already taking place where stakeholders seem frustrated, confused, or upset, or initiating conversations where necessary. Discuss the benefits of the process change for the individual as well as the organization and what is being done to ensure success in working with the new process.
Be the "go-to" person	Utilize subject matter expertise about the process and encourage stakeholders to reach out with questions about how to use the process. This project team member serves as the key resource for those who need extra support in using the process. For complex BPI projects, more than one subject matter expert will be needed to support a larger stakeholder group.
Encourage questions	Undoubtedly many stakeholders have questions they will not ask because they don't want to appear stupid or embarrass themselves. Have a few project team members who walk around to the various stakeholder groups who will use the new process to encourage them to ask questions they have—either in small groups or one-on-one. Alternatively be sure there is a place on the project portal where users of the new process can ask their questions. Also, include a Frequently Asked Questions (FAQ) document that covers many of the common questions that arise from BPI project implementations.

- Resources available to support stakeholders using the new process (people, documentation, online support, main points of contact, etc.)
- Meeting schedules for check-in on how things are going, as well as options for checking in (meeting, phone call, portal, etc.)
- New facilities opened up or new technologies to be used as part of the roll out of the process
- Roles and responsibilities of employees updated to reflect use or oversight of the new process

The goal of communications in Phase 5 of the project is to increase the success of implementation of the new process by engaging stakeholders in the change. This is done through providing the information that is necessary for adapting to the change, as well as alleviating concerns by ensuring that stakeholders understand that training will be provided to ensure they can utilize the new process successfully.

Socializing the New Process

While the BPI project has been socialized from the start and the successful BPI project team has kept stakeholders engaged in the initiative, it is essential to socialize the new process. This can effectively be done through sharing stories from pilot group testers about their success in utilizing the new process. These pilot group testers are champions of the new process! They will carry more credibility about the value and benefit of the new process than the leadership team—maybe even more than the BPI project team—because they have used the process to get the work accomplished. Don't discount the value of reaching out and securing pilot group testers to engage stakeholders in the implementation of the new process.

As a best practice, consider holding a meeting early at the start of Phase 5 via a format that will reach the widest stakeholder pool and use this time to share the following:

- Information about the roll out (implementation) of the new process (timeline)
- Main points of contact during implementation of the new process
- Information about upcoming training and other relevant documentation for users of the new process
- Feedback from pilot group testers about the process—this may take the form of case studies written up and shared during the meeting or asking a few pilot group testers to speak during the meeting and share their thoughts on the process

Developing Appropriate Communication Channels in Phase 5

Communication channels were discussed in Chapter 4. Many of the channels used throughout the BPI project will continue to be used in Phase 5 of the project. However, since the stakeholder pool has likely expanded because of the implementation of the new process, additional channels may be required. As a best practice, use the checklist provided in Figure 8.4 to determine what communication channels may be required to engage stakeholders in Phase 5.

As shared earlier in Chapter 4, a variety of channels are necessary to ensure the BPI project team reaches out to the widest stakeholder pool in ways that works for them to receive and process information.

What communication channels are needed?

Are your stakeholders...		Consider using these communication channels...
☐	Executives and senior leaders	• Presentations at leadership meetings • One-on-one meetings with leaders • E-mails
☐	Mid-level management	• E-mails • Project portal • Department or division meetings
☐	Individual contributors	• E-mails • Project portal • Lunch and learns • Small group meetings
☐	Remote individual contributors	• E-mails • Project portal • Virtual meetings • Conference calls
☐	External vendors/suppliers	• E-mail • Visits to vendor/supplier sites • Project portal • Meeting at company site

Figure 8.4   Checklist to determine communication channels

Part of communications will also include coordinating external communications about the new process. This may apply with processes that directly (and noticeably) impact customers, vendors, or suppliers. Separate communications may need to be developed to inform these external stakeholders about the new process. In these situations, the focus will be on the benefit *to the external stakeholder*, rather than the benefit to the individual or the organization.

Establishing Sub-communication Teams

Similar to sub-teams created during Phase 4 (pilot testing), it would be beneficial to utilize sub-teams for communicating with the larger stakeholder pool. Project team members who are assigned to be part of sub-communication teams should be individuals who have the following skills and display the following behaviors:

- Ability to communicate effectively—both verbally and in writing
- Strong listening skills
- Ability to engage others in conversation
- Strong relationships throughout the organization
- Ability to handle conflicts and individuals who are frustrated (remain calm in the face of adversity)

- Be available via a variety of ways (e-mail, phone, instant message, etc.)

These are many skills required for BPI project team members in general and are absolutely essential for implementation of the final to-be process.

The number of members who comprise the sub-communication teams will be based on the number of stakeholders and their locations. Ideally, team members will be available in every location in which a stakeholder is located, though this may not be practical when large groups of stakeholders are involved or when stakeholders are very scattered throughout a variety of locations or work from their homes.

Figure 8.5 provides a few examples of deploying sub-communication team members depending on the situation.

Examples of Deploying Sub-communication Teams

Stakeholders span three departments but are all co-located in one office.	Sub-communication team members should number at least 3, one for each department. Team members should provide backup to one another.
Stakeholders span multiple divisions that reach across the United States primarily on the East Coast, West Coast, and in the Midwest.	Sub-communication team members should be located in areas represented by stakeholders: East Coast, West Coast, and in the Midwest. The number of team members in each area should be 2–4 depending on the number of stakeholders in that area.
Stakeholders distributed throughout the United States and internationally, language issues exist.	Sub-communication team members should be located where the largest influx of stakeholders are located. For example, if there are a number of stakeholders in London, only a handful in Paris and a couple more in Belgium, locate sub-communication team members in London but ensure they are available for stakeholders in Paris and Belgium. Ensure teams members speak the language of the stakeholders.
Stakeholders are all remote workers, working from home offices within the United States.	Deploy at least 1 sub-communication team member for every 4 remote stakeholders. Ensure back up systems are in place and regular communications occur to ensure remote workers are engaged and do not feel left alone to fend for themselves.

Figure 8.5   Examples of deploying sub-communication teams

Ensure consistency in the support provided by sub-communication team members by having one or more team leads who coordinate among the sub-communication teams as well as by ensuring a standard communication plan is in place and used by all sub-communication teams. When external stakeholders are involved, it is a best practice to ensure they have a primary point of contact within the organization (a dedicated sub-communication team) to assist in answering questions and providing guidance as needed.

Utilizing Your Pilot Group Members

As mentioned previously, pilot group members are champions of the process who should be deployed among the rest of the stakeholders to discuss the benefits and value and share their experiences. Pilot group members might serve on the sub-communication teams or as subject matter experts available to respond to questions about the process.

SHARING TRAINING PLANS AND INCENTIVE PROGRAMS

Training was discussed in Chapters 3 and 4. As noted in these chapters, there is a need to share preliminary training plans early with stakeholders of the BPI project in order to alleviate concerns around learning the process.

> One BPI project team who hadn't developed or shared any preliminary training plans around a major BPI project learned quickly—that was a mistake! Over a period of two days, 50 stakeholders asked members of the BPI project team if they would be trained on the process or would need to learn it on their own!

Training should be provided for anyone using the process—whether they are a regular user of the process or may only use it on occasion (such as individuals who provide back-up support to their coworkers or, for example, individuals who may only run a report using the process once a quarter). Certainly the extent of the training will correlate to the complexity of the process. A minor process change that requires no new skills may not require more than a simple instruction sheet to follow or a webinar that walks users through the new process. More complex initiatives will likely require a formal training program accompanied by practice using the new process, as well as documentation/instruction sheets to keep for reference. If a variety of training options are used, such as handouts and webinars as well as face-to-face training sessions, the individuals should be allowed to partake of the option that best suits their needs. However, don't rely on the user choosing the right option—they will usually go for the easiest. Rather, develop the training plan and schedule and include stakeholder names where, based on their role, they should seek training. Figure 8.6 provides examples of a variety of training methods that might be used, depending on the stakeholders and their roles.

The information gathered earlier on training needs (refer to Figures 4.8 and 4.9) will assist with building a comprehensive training plan that will meet the needs of the stakeholder and ensure successful implementation of the new process. Undoubtedly, as the pilot group performs testing of the new process, additional information will arise that will require refinement of any previously developed training plans.

Incentive Programs

Incentive programs are often utilized to encourage stakeholders to switch to the new process quickly, rather than trying to stick with the old process. Incentive programs may include any variety of options, such as:

- Recognition by senior leadership
- Cash or gift certificates

Example Training Plan and Schedule

Training Method	Participants	Start Date; Duration
Handouts, webinar	Managers and others who will oversee the process	On demand; 15 minutes in duration (webinar)
Webinar	Admin support staff	On demand; 15 minutes in duration
Face-to-face training sessions and virtual training sessions	Individuals who use the process regularly as part of their role	Numerous start dates; 2 hours per session
Webinars and virtual sessions	Individuals who use only a part of the process, not a regular part of their role	On demand; 30 minutes in duration
Follow up materials: documentation, on demand webinar "how to's," quick reference guides on intranet	All users of the process and managers will have access to these materials	At end of all scheduled training sessions; provided for future reference

Figure 8.6 Examples of training methods

- Time off (extra vacation time)
- Bonus money
- T-shirts, plaques, or other such items

If incentive programs are to be used, be sure to include the cost of any incentive in the project budget.

SOCIALIZING AND IMPLEMENTING TRAINING

Although it would be expected that everyone would eagerly attend the training sessions to learn how to utilize the new process, socializing the value and benefits of training is of help in getting stakeholders to attend. To implement training, provide a number of options for any particular training session. For example, if the training is a two-hour session on how to use the process, schedule one session in the morning, one around mid-day and one later in the day on different days of the week. Consider a virtual two-hour session for those stakeholders who cannot attend the scheduled face-to-face sessions, and schedule a variety of those, also.

As a best practice, utilize sign-in sheets for training sessions and require sign-in for webinars. This enables the BPI project team to track who has attended training and who still needs to attend.

> *For one BPI project that Gina led at a consulting organization, she gave responsibility to one team administrator to follow up with stakeholders to ensure they were signed up for training sessions. Only a handful of stakeholders signed up via the portal when training dates were released and after a week, only a couple more had signed up. By having the team administrator reach out to each stakeholder individually, the team was able to get everyone who needed to be, signed up for training sessions.*

Especially for a complex BPI project, keep the number of training session participants at 10 to 12 per session. Smaller groups allow for more individualized attention. Individualized attention enables more effective learning of skills and behaviors required to utilize the new process and increases success of implementation.

Increasing End Users' Comfort Level and Confidence

Much of what has already been discussed within this chapter and in previous chapters will provide for increasing the comfort level and confidence of end users (the stakeholders) in using the new process. Insufficient time spent in determining the amount of training needed to utilize the new process successfully will only increase the risks of the BPI project and of possible failure over the long run in implementing the new process.

Table 8.2 provides a number of ideas and best practices to ensure stakeholders are comfortable and feel confident about their ability to utilize the new process successfully.

Table 8.2   Ideas and best practices to ensure stakeholder comfort and confidence

Idea/Best Practice	Description
Variety of formats for learning	As discussed earlier, a variety of formats for learning—workshop, virtual classroom, webinar, handouts, and other documentation —provide something that works for everyone. Since everyone learns and absorbs information differently, a variety of formats increases the chances of success in learning the process.
FAQs on a project portal	Regularly updated FAQs enable a place to go to get answers when the stakeholders begin to use the process. Include detailed answers with the FAQs as well as main points of contact for further information (support team, webinar, further documentation/how-to's, etc.). Update the FAQs frequently as new questions arise about the process.
Transition period	Providing a transition period, especially for complex processes that need to be rolled out, increases the comfort level of stakeholders. They feel as if they have more time to truly learn the process before they must use it. A word of caution however—limit transition time periods so that stakeholders can become familiar with the new process and don't just assume they can use the old process indefinitely.
Hands-on practice/ simulation	Regardless of the training format utilized, allow for practice in using the new process in a safe environment. This may entail setting up a testing platform that includes the systems and other tools used as part of the process so stakeholders can try out the process without worrying about a major impact on the systems or clients if they make a mistake.
Action planning	As part of any learning about the new process, include action planning which enables stakeholders to map out how they will utilize what they learned—in this case, how they will utilize the new process. Action planning may include information about: support needed, additional training desired or needed, timeline for additional training, timeline for moving over to using the new process, and when they will check-in to report on how they are doing using the process.

Making the Training *Stick*

When the BPI project team can help stakeholders retain what is learned in the training sessions, it is much more likely that the stakeholders will be able to successfully utilize the process when they attempt to do so back on the job site. Success in using the process leads to increased comfort in continuing to utilize the process.

Any of the methods noted in Table 8.2 will assist in making the training stick—as will ensuring that there is downloadable documentation or *how-tos* about the process or brief 10 to 15 minute webinars to review particularly complex process steps.

As a best practice, for particularly complex process improvement projects, consider providing a coach to assist stakeholders in using the process. Individuals from the pilot group pool will be great coaches since they have already been using the process. Consider also those stakeholders who have quickly grasped the use of the process and are utilizing it successfully; they may be able to function as coaches providing guidance to their peers and colleagues. And, certainly, BPI project team members will also make great coaches for new users of the process.

REGULAR CHECK-INS

Checking-in on the progress of the use of the new process is essential, regardless of the complexity of the process launched. However, let's focus on more complex BPI projects. The more complex and larger the project, the more check-ins that should be planned and facilitated for complex processes that cross a number of departments or divisions. Utilize a combination of formal and informal check-ins as shown in Table 8.3.

Formal check-ins are important; but the BPI project team will find that they will also get significant information by informally checking-in with stakeholders. Often times more information will be shared during one-on-one informal conversations than in a formal structured environment. Capture information where you can!

Table 8.3 Formal and informal check-ins

Formal Check-in Options	Informal Check-in Options
• Regularly scheduled meetings	• "Hallway" conversations
• Online surveys	• Stopping by stakeholders' desks/offices
• Project portal Q&A section	• Having coaches check in with stakeholders

At one manufacturing client, the authors received the most information by just asking stakeholders "How's it going?" in the cafeteria, at the coffee machine, and passing by in the hallways. Stakeholders seemed to be more willing to share their thoughts about the new process, and any challenges they were having, when they weren't surrounded by a group of other stakeholders.

SHARING YOUR EVALUATION AND MEASUREMENT PLAN

As part of the roll out of the new process, reiterate the purpose for the BPI project, specifically, how success of the new process will be measured—which traces back to why the project was launched in the first place. Was it to reduce costs of developing new products? Or did processes need to be updated to accommodate the use of new technology within a specific division? Or was there a need to change processes to improve the response time when customers call a help desk line?

The authors shared with a number of customer service reps at a software company that the process for changing how calls came in from customers was done to accommodate a number of requests. This included requests by both customers and the customer service reps to reduce the number of "buttons" that needed to be pushed to reach a customer service rep. As part of the process change, the authors were able to reduce the number of options required to finally reach a customer service rep from 7 options to 3 options. This would initiate increased customer satisfaction and less complaints to the customer service rep once the customer did reach someone on the phone. What would be measured was the success of reducing the number of options to reach a customer service rep from 7 to 3. Would that be satisfactory to reach the right customer service rep to address the issue? Based on feedback from the pilot group testers, it was believed that it was accurate. This would be tracked and measured over the next 2 months now that the new process had been rolled out to the entire customer service team.

The BPI implementation team will need to ensure that the new process is accomplishing what it is supposed to accomplish. To achieve this, there will need to be systems in place to ensure the new process is meeting expectations. This includes methods to capture feedback from stakeholders as well as methods for ensuring the process is effective upon roll out and is meeting the goals it was designed to achieve. Evaluation of the effectiveness of the process in meeting the outlined goals may be done through any variety of ways, including:

- Online surveys
- Tracking by stakeholders
- Regular meetings with stakeholders
- Observation
- Focus groups
- Reporting from financial, administrative, or other systems

As a best practice, use more than one method to gather the data on the effectiveness of the process. More on collecting feedback on the process will be discussed in Chapter 9.

Metrics to Measure Against

As discussed previously, BPI projects are launched to accomplish specific goals which are tied to long-term strategic initiatives of the organization. These goals might include, but are certainly not limited to:

- Reduction in time-to-market for new products and services
- Reduction in number of steps to complete a task to increase efficiencies
- Improved use of technology
- Reduction in turn-around time to respond to customer requests
- Reduction in time to ship orders
- Reduction in cost of unit production
- Reduction in shipping costs
- Improved percentage of on-time delivery

Revisit Figure 2.6 in Chapter 2—recall that the BPI project was launched to:

- Reduce the amount of time required to process invoices received by Human Resources (HR) from external training vendors
- Improve customer satisfaction with vendor interactions with the organization

Success of a new process would accomplish the following:

- Pay all vendor invoices within 30 days
- Reduce the amount of time for reviewing and approving invoices to no more than 3 days

In order to evaluate the effectiveness of the new process once it is implemented, the BPI project team might choose to track vendor payments made (to ensure payments are made within 30 days) and to track the amount of time it takes from when an invoice is received by HR to when it is sent to Accounts Payable for payment. Observation of HR using the process may not be the most effective method for evaluating the success of the new process. Rather, the BPI project team may schedule check-in meetings with stakeholders to ask questions about the use of the process and can track the invoices in the financial systems used by the organization. They may also ask those performing the process to track the process from start to finish in a journal.

The amount of time to measure the new process and whether it is meeting its goals is entirely based on the process. A simple process, such as the example discussed above, can be measured within a couple of months. A more complex project may take up to six, nine, or 12 months to measure.

Chapter 9 will go into more detail about evaluating and measuring the success of BPI projects implemented within the organization.

TRANSITIONING TO MAINTENANCE AND OPERATIONS

Once the process has been shown to be working as expected and designed, it is ready to be transitioned to maintenance and/or operations for ongoing use of the process. Consider the example process used throughout this book, *Improvement in HR A/P Processes*; once the process has been rolled out to all stakeholders who will use it and/or be impacted by it and it has been shown to work as designed, it is now ready to be turned over to HR and Accounts Payable—the two groups responsible for the process. If at some point the process needs to change again, it is then another BPI project and follows the same steps followed previously.

At one University where the authors were doing work to improve processes on managing construction projects, it became apparent that maintenance/ operations were not kept updated on the project progress. For example, when systems were changed within one building on campus, at the conclusion of the project, the systems were turned over to maintenance to manage and keep updated. Other than being involved at the very start of the project, maintenance/operations did not know the project was coming to an end and did not receive any training or documentation to facilitate maintenance of the systems. The project effectively had to remain with the BPI project team until maintenance/operations was comfortable with taking control of the process.

Those stakeholders who will ultimately be responsible for maintaining the process going forward should be involved at the onset of the BPI project. Unfortunately, this is not always the case. Too often organizations neglect to include those responsible for maintaining the process in the planning stages of the project. In some cases, training the stakeholders in using the process may be sufficient for those maintaining the process (as in the example of HR A/P processes), but in other situations there may need to be separate training scheduled for maintenance personnel if they are responsible for maintaining, but not necessarily using, the process. An example may include the installation of new systems where the stakeholders are trained on how to use the systems, but IT support (maintenance/operations) is trained on how to update the systems and keep them maintained.

CAPTURING LESSONS LEARNED

Capturing lessons learned from the BPI project lead the way for continuous improvement in how business process projects are managed in the future. It is important to capture lessons learned from as many stakeholders as possible, including:

- Sponsors and senior leadership
- Management staff
- Individual contributors
- BPI project team members

Plan to spend at least an hour to an hour and a half at the end of the BPI project to capture lessons learned. If face-to-face or virtual meetings are not possible, consider capturing lessons learned from the stakeholders via an online survey.

The authors have captured lessons learned after Phase 6 of the project (discussed in Chapter 9). However, they have found that in the majority of the cases, especially when the BPI project is more complex, capturing lessons learned sooner rather than later enables them to get more information from stakeholders and the team before it is forgotten. In certain cases, they have captured lessons learned after each major phase of the project as well as a comprehensive lessons-learned meeting at the end.

When meeting with the BPI project team, three simple questions will suffice to understand how effectively the team functioned:

- What worked well from each team member's perspective?
- What improvements would team members like to see?
- What else would team members like to share?

As part of lessons-learned discussions with stakeholders, the BPI project team will want to understand how effectively the team performed in a number of areas. Utilize the checklist in Figure 8.7 to ensure areas of importance are examined in lessons-learned meetings.

Summarize and share information that is captured in lessons-learned meetings with other BPI project teams and retain the information in a project portal where it is easily accessible by other BPI project teams. This information may be categorized to allow for easy search by other teams. Categories may include:

- Stakeholders
- Processes
- Technology
- Pilot test groups
- Resources

Have the following been discussed during the lessons-learned meeting?

How well did the BPI Project Team...	
☐	Engage stakeholders in understanding the value and benefits associated with the BPI project?
☐	Utilize a number of options to gather information on the "as-is" process from stakeholders?
☐	Document the current "as-is" process with the support of stakeholders?
☐	Share information about the schedule for the project, taking into account the need for stakeholder involvement (develop timelines that enable for stakeholder participation?)
☐	Engage stakeholders in redesigning the process ("could-be" process options) considering what's important for the stakeholders who use the process as well as what's important to meet project objectives?
☐	Build consensus in developing a "to-be" option for the process?
☐	Select appropriate pilot group testers and engage the pilot test group?
☐	Ensure feedback on the process at each phase of the project is gathered from stakeholders?
☐	Communicate throughout the BPI project life cycle?
☐	Provide sufficient training and a variety of options for training on the new process?
☐	Enable a comfortable environment in rolling out the process?
☐	Solve problems collaboratively with stakeholders and resolve conflicts that arose?

Figure 8.7   Checklist to ensure lessons learned are captured

Or any other labels for categories that make sense given the organization.

> *As a best practice, the authors utilize Microsoft SharePoint® to track all of their BPI project initiatives, including lessons learned. It enables them to effectively search through the information about past BPI projects by a variety of categories and keywords to ensure that lessons learned in the past are applied to future projects. In this way, the authors improve upon each BPI project they undertake.*

PREPARING TO MOVE TO PHASE 6

Phase 6—evaluate and measure—focuses on evaluating the success of the BPI project. Specifically, did it do what it was expected to do? Has it achieved the objectives established when the project was launched? This is the last phase of the BPI project and focuses on showing the business impact of the BPI project before it is turned over to maintenance/operations. While some of the BPI project team may remain on in this phase, not all team members may stay involved. Naturally, individuals with analytical expertise as well as the ability to engage stakeholders will be essential in Phase 6.

This chapter shared the importance of preparing the organization for a new process *before* it is rolled out for them to use. Strong communication through a variety of formal and informal channels as well as ensuring that stakeholders are trained in how to use the process is essential to ensuring they *will* use the process. Regular check-ins are required to answer questions as they arise and get stakeholders *unstuck* if they are having problems with the process. While evaluating the process and measuring against metrics was discussed in this chapter, the following chapter will provide more details on evaluating the success of BPI projects.

9

EVALUATING THE SUCCESS OF THE BPI PROJECT

The evaluation process for the business process improvement (BPI) project may be a simplified process or may be a much more detailed process that, effectively, becomes a new project. For smaller BPI projects that may impact only a work-group or one department, a simplified evaluation process to ensure the success of the final process may be satisfactory. This might be done through a survey or simple observation.

For more complex BPI initiatives, however, doing a more robust evaluation to determine the business impact will be beneficial to truly show the value of the process redesign to the bottom line.

Regardless of the type of BPI project, however, it should *always* be evaluated to determine the success of the initiative.

PHASE 6 OVERVIEW

Figure 9.1 depicts the final phase of the six-phased approach to managing BPI projects: *Evaluate and Measure*.

In this phase, the focus is on evaluating the success of the BPI project implementation as well as determining if the newly redesigned process accomplishes the objectives and goals set forth at the start of the initiative.

Feedback is gathered from stakeholders who are using the process, as well as from stakeholders who are managing or overseeing those who are using the process.

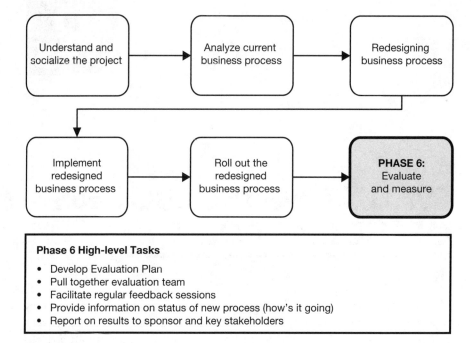

Figure 9.1   Phase 6 of the six-step process

Phase 6 accomplishes a number of goals:

- Ensures the BPI initiative is aligned to the organization's strategic business objectives
- Determines the business impact of the business process initiative on the bottom line
- Demonstrates to executives the benefits of BPI initiatives
- Can assist with decision making regarding the continued roll out of BPI initiatives to other parts of the organization

MEASURING SUCCESS: EVALUATION BASICS

In 1959 Donald Kirkpatrick developed the four levels of evaluation of programs. The model was updated in 1975 and for the last time in 1994. Evaluating BPI project initiatives is based on the four levels of evaluation developed by Kirkpatrick. Figure 9.2 is based on those four levels of evaluation.

While it could be argued that the first level—satisfaction with the training on the new process—is unnecessary, it is of value to the BPI project team. If

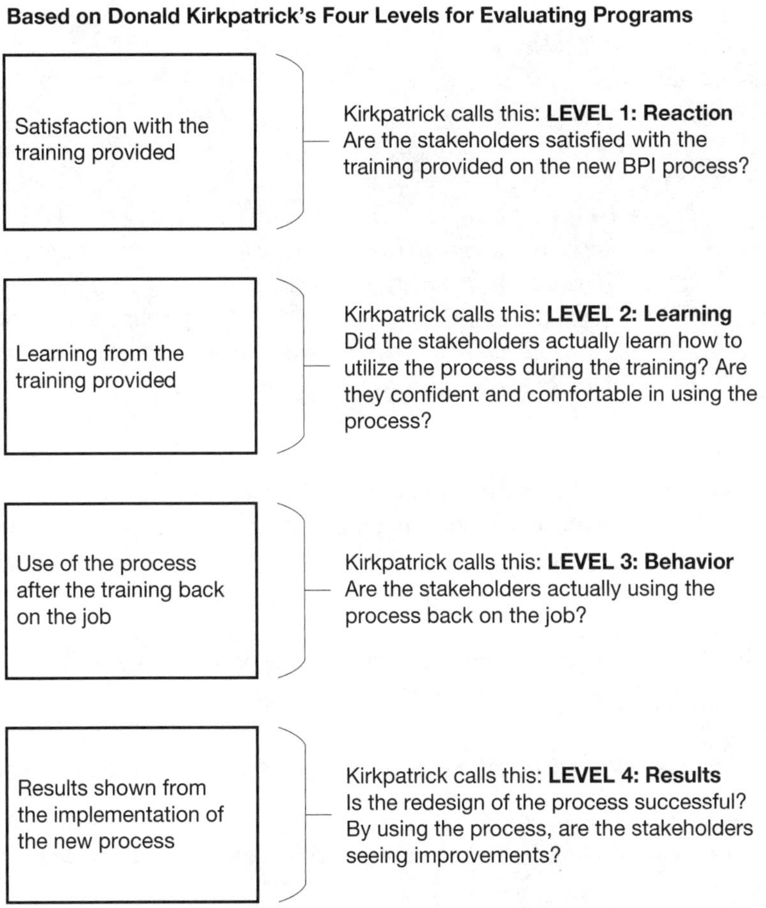

Based on Donald Kirkpatrick's Four Levels for Evaluating Programs

| Satisfaction with the training provided | Kirkpatrick calls this: **LEVEL 1: Reaction** Are the stakeholders satisfied with the training provided on the new BPI process? |

| Learning from the training provided | Kirkpatrick calls this: **LEVEL 2: Learning** Did the stakeholders actually learn how to utilize the process during the training? Are they confident and comfortable in using the process? |

| Use of the process after the training back on the job | Kirkpatrick calls this: **LEVEL 3: Behavior** Are the stakeholders actually using the process back on the job? |

| Results shown from the implementation of the new process | Kirkpatrick calls this: **LEVEL 4: Results** Is the redesign of the process successful? By using the process, are the stakeholders seeing improvements? |

Figure 9.2   Evaluating BPI projects using Kirkpatrick's Levels of Evaluation

the stakeholders are not satisfied with the training provided, it is unlikely that they will utilize the process moving forward, as they will not be comfortable or confident in their ability to change their own behaviors. However, if they are satisfied, but have not used the new process on the job site, then the BPI team needs to look at something other than the training to determine why behavior change has not occurred. Consider this client story.

For a retail client, Gina, one of the authors, while conducting a study of a recent process improvement initiative done in-house, asked all stakeholders after the training on the new process was complete if they were satisfied with the training

(Level 1). All stakeholders noted they were very satisfied. Additionally, during practice, it was obvious they had learned the process and were comfortable using it (Level 2). However, back on the job site, the process was never used (Level 3). It was apparent that training was not the problem, nor a lack of confidence on the part of the stakeholder. This meant that Gina needed to look at what happened back on the job site. What she found in her analysis was that when they went back to their jobs and started to use the process, their manager told them to stick with the old way of working since they had tight deadlines ahead of them. The lesson learned for the client was to better engage the manager early on and provide some training to him on how to oversee and support the new process once the stakeholders got out of training.

In conjunction with the four levels to evaluate the success of the initiative, consider this three-step process, as shown in Figure 9.3, which enables the BPI project team to measure the effectiveness of the newly designed and implemented process. Figure 9.3 also provides how these steps are mapped to the levels shared in Figure 9.2.

Table 9.1 provides some details for each of the steps in Figure 9.3. These steps will be covered in more detail in the balance of the chapter.

Selling the Benefits of Formal Evaluation to Executives

Recall earlier in this chapter the goals accomplished in Phase 6 when an evaluation of the success of the BPI project implementation was completed. These

A Process for Evaluating the BPI Project

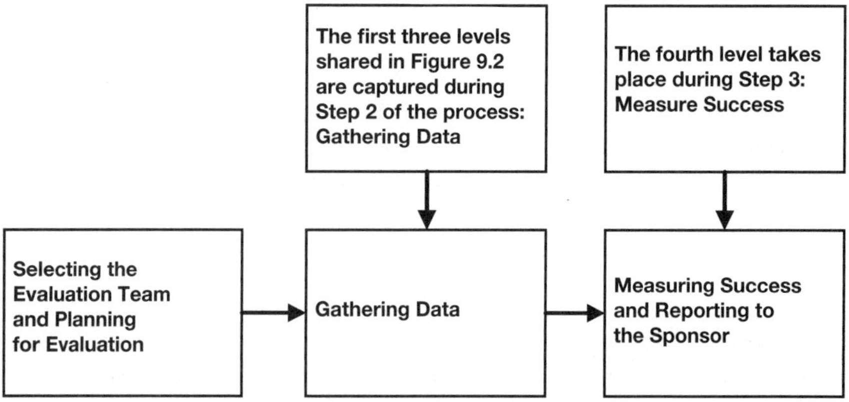

Figure 9.3 Three-step process to evaluate BPI projects

Table 9.1   Description of steps in BPI evaluation process

Step in Evaluation Process	Brief Description
Step 1: Selecting the team and preparing for evaluation	• Determine individuals to comprise evaluation team • Engage stakeholders in evaluation process • Develop evaluation plan
Step 2: Gathering data	• Determine how data will be gathered on the use of the new process • Analyze data received for inconsistencies and patterns
Step 3: Measuring success and reporting to the sponsor	• Evaluate the success of the BPI project implementation • Report on the success to the sponsor and key stakeholders

goals enabled more effective selling of this phase of the project to the sponsor and other key leaders. Evaluation can effectively be an entirely new project that is launched and, therefore, may require the BPI project manager to sell the benefits of a formal evaluation to the executives.

Formal evaluations are not vastly different than capturing and sharing lessons learned. Formal evaluations, besides showing the success of the BPI project implementation, also bring about learning opportunities—such as, what can be done differently the next time around to improve how the new process was rolled out to the organization? Additionally, for more complex BPI initiatives, consider capturing the monetary impact of the new process. For example, let's assume a new product is developed and launched to customers in one-half of the time it used to take because of changes to processes. Previously, a new product that went into development in January did not get launched until mid-October of that year. Sales would occur during November and December, with revenue of $20,000 during those two months. The new processes established and launched a shortened development time. New products that go into development in January, are now launched by mid-May of that year. Sales occur from June through December with revenue of $70,000. This is an increase of revenue to the top line of $50,000—attributable to new processes for development of new products which reduces the time-to-market and therefore makes it possible for sales to occur earlier.

Evaluating these monetary impacts makes a great impression on the executives. These monetary impacts increase the interest and support in BPI projects.

DEVELOPING THE FORMAL EVALUATION PLAN

A formal evaluation plan enables all stakeholders and others involved in the evaluation of the new process to understand *what* will occur *when* and how much time commitment is needed from them to participate in the evaluation. The formal evaluation plan should include the following key information shown in Table 9.2.

Build the formal evaluation plan—specifically components gathered during evaluation meetings and a timeline for reporting back with results—in collaboration with stakeholders, since they are key to the evaluation of the process.

A template for evaluation planning is downloadable from the Web Added Value™ (WAV) Download Resource Center at the publisher's website: www.jrosspub.com/wav (hereafter referred to as the J. Ross website).

PULLING TOGETHER THE EVALUATION TEAM

The evaluation team may include some members of the BPI team, but it is unlikely that every member of the BPI project team will be a member of this

Table 9.2   Evaluation plan components

Component of Plan	Brief Description
Purpose of Evaluation	• Business justification for evaluating the BPI project • Desired, or expected, end results (what equals success)
Stakeholders Involved	• Stakeholders involved in evaluation (process users and process managers)
Data Collecting Methods	• How data on the BPI project implementation and training on the process will be gathered (surveys, observation, small group meetings, etc.)
Evaluation Meetings	• Number of expected meetings as well as estimated dates for gathering data and sharing information with stakeholders (include a kick-off meeting)
Evaluation Team Points of Contact	• Key members of the evaluation team (BPI project team members) and contact information
Budget for Evaluation	• Costs associated with evaluation of the BPI project implementation
Timeline for Reporting on Results	• High-level schedule and milestones

team—nor is it necessary. The evaluation team members should be individuals with a variety of skills and expertise including:

- The ability to engage others and build strong relationships
- Analytical skills
- Strong communication skills
- Ability to interact with all levels of stakeholders
- Experience in performing assessments

Team Roles and Responsibilities in Phase 6

Table 9.3 shows team member roles and responsibilities during evaluation of the BPI project implementation.

The number of individuals in each role is not exact. It really depends on the complexity of the BPI project, how many stakeholders are involved, and whether the stakeholders are remote.

For one project that included 25 stakeholders from four different locations within the United States, four communication leads were included on the evaluation team. Each of the communication leads had responsibility for one location and served as the primary point of contact at that location. They coordinated all schedules for stakeholder meetings and assisted other team members in gathering data on the BPI project implementation.

Table 9.3   Team member roles and responsibilities

Team Member Role/Number of Individuals in Role	Key Responsibilities
BPI Project Manager (1)	• Oversee the evaluation phase of the project • Main point of contact for sponsor/key leaders
Facilitator (1)	• Facilitate meetings with stakeholders (the project manager may fulfill this role if skilled at facilitation)
Communication leads (1-2)	• Develop communication plans for Phase 6 • Point of contact for stakeholders during evaluation phase
Team members (4-6)	• Gathering data from stakeholders using the process and those overseeing the process
Analytical skills: 1-2 team members	• Analyze information gathered
Expertise developing surveys: 1 team member	• Collaborate with evaluation team leader to develop report to share with sponsor/leaders

EVALUATING SUCCESS OF THE PROCESS IMPROVEMENT INITIATIVE

Even during evaluation of the BPI implementation, there will still be stakeholders who require additional *hand holding* to be comfortable with the process. The most successful BPI project implementations provide for ongoing support, training, and coaching on the new process until stakeholders are completely comfortable and confident while using the process. As a best practice, the BPI project team should consider asking stakeholders who are comfortable and confident in using the process to help their colleagues and coworkers to also be comfortable by serving as mentors within the department or division.

The success of the process improvement initiative should be looked at from two standpoints:

- The success associated with getting stakeholders engaged and using the new process upon implementation
- The success in the new process accomplishing the goals that were set out when the BPI project was launched

Communicating the Process for Evaluation

Phase 6 should have been communicated early on in the BPI project, at least from a high-level overview, and then updated in Phase 5. In this phase, that communication should focus on evaluating the process from the two perspectives noted above—the success of getting stakeholders ready for using the new process and whether the new process is accomplishing its goals.

Communication will cover important information for stakeholders including:

- Surveys that will be sent to gather information about the training and other resources provided
- Meetings to be held to understand how effectively the new process is working on the job site
- Evaluation of the new process against metrics set for its success

Also important to mention, would be the points of contact for stakeholders, should questions arise when using the new process.

Using Surveys, Interviews, and Focus Groups

The use of surveys, interviews, and focus groups was discussed in Chapter 5. These same tools are used in the last phase of the BPI project in order to determine the success of the roll out of the process and whether or not the process is achieving its goals.

When trying to determine how successful the stakeholders are in implementing the new process back on the job, the focus should be on whether the training provided, the follow up materials, and other resources and support are sufficient to allow use of the process without oversight—and on ensuring that the stakeholder will not revert back to using the old process.

Figure 9.4 provides a sample of survey questions that may be asked to gauge the effectiveness of preparing the stakeholders for implementation of the new process. A more robust survey is provided for download from the J. Ross website.

Notice that in Figure 9.4 the BPI project team is asking about challenges or barriers to using the process back on the job. Any barriers encountered will need to be addressed to ensure that the process user can perform his/her role in using the process. Barriers are often centered on the following:

- Lack of management support
- Insufficient training on the process
- Old systems in place that make it easy to use the old process

Sample Questions to Gauge Effectiveness of Preparing Stakeholders for BPI Project Implementation

Question Category	Sample Questions
Training	• Was the training of sufficient length to enable learning the process? • Was the training satisfactory (did it give you what you needed and expected)? • Were you able to practice using the process during the training session? • Are you confident that you can utilize the process back on the job?
Additional materials	• Were additional materials, handouts, and access to the portal for information on the process of value after the training session? • What other information would be of value in understanding how to use the process?
Support	• Do you feel you have sufficient access to support in using the process back on the job? • Of the support options provided, which ones are most valuable to you? (This might include the portal, point of contact, follow-up training.)
Using the process	• Have you been able to use the process back on the job? If not, why not? • What challenges or barriers have you encountered in using the process?

Figure 9.4 Sample survey questions

- Lack of training on new systems
- Inability to use the new process (often due to it not being a major responsibility of the stakeholder)

For more robust data, use mainly open-ended questions that inspire the respondent to provide details in the survey response.

Measuring Progress against Metrics

Metrics to measure against were discussed in Chapter 8. Let's expand on that discussion here.

Note that not all metrics can be measured immediately. Some will take longer to measure, especially when more complex processes are involved. For example, if the BPI project involves improving the efficiency of a manufacturing line, it may take running production of products from start to finish at least a few times before efficiencies can be measured. As another example, let's assume the process project was to put procedures in place to reduce the number of accidents on a manufacturing line within a one-year time period. While some measurements can be taken at certain intervals—say 3 months, 6 months, and 9 months—the process evaluation team will wait until a year has passed to see the final results of the process improvement project.

Often what is important to the sponsor and other senior leaders are what are referred to as *hard data* on the process. Hard data is directly attributable to bottom-line results. Hard data is often focused on output from the business (e.g., number of tasks completed by an employee), time involved in development of products and services (e.g., amount of time the manufacturing line is shut down for repairs), cost associated with doing business (e.g., expense associated with selling a product), and the quality of products and services (e.g., number of accidents on a manufacturing line). Figure 9.5 provides a

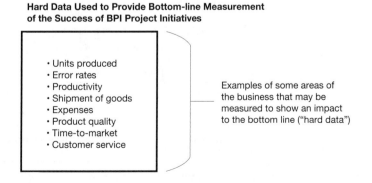

Hard Data Used to Provide Bottom-line Measurement of the Success of BPI Project Initiatives

- Units produced
- Error rates
- Productivity
- Shipment of goods
- Expenses
- Product quality
- Time-to-market
- Customer service

Examples of some areas of the business that may be measured to show an impact to the bottom line ("hard data")

Figure 9.5 Examples of common *hard data* items

partial list of some common hard data items that are impacted by process improvement initiatives.

There are many more areas of the business that could be measured that are impacted by BPI projects. Figure 9.5 is a very small list of hard data categories for measurement.

> *For a biotech client, the authors worked closely with finance to improve a number of processes within the organization that would accomplish the following:*
>
> - *Improve collection of monies from key partners*
> - *Reduce variable costs*
> - *Reduce processing time of FDA applications*
>
> *The reduction in time for processing FDA applications would take longer to measure because they were not prepared yet in the business to submit any applications to the FDA.*

Soft data is also an important measurement of the success of process improvement projects. There is often the misperception that soft data is not measurable. This is not accurate. Nearly everything can be measured. However, soft data may or may not be measured and is usually more focused on the people-side of process improvement initiatives. Examples of soft data items are provided in Figure 9.6.

Certainly these items could be measured to show a bottom-line impact. For example, one of the items in Figure 9.6 is employee retention. Any organization will likely know the cost of losing good employees. This is measured in the time to recruit, interview, hire, and train new employees for the organization and the

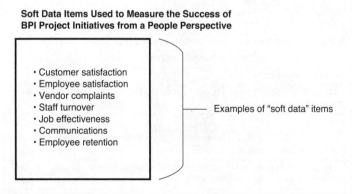

Soft Data Items Used to Measure the Success of BPI Project Initiatives from a People Perspective

- Customer satisfaction
- Employee satisfaction
- Vendor complaints
- Staff turnover
- Job effectiveness
- Communications
- Employee retention

—— Examples of "soft data" items

Figure 9.6   Examples of common *soft data* items

time that passes until they are fully *up to speed* in their role. Dollar amounts can certainly be attributed to each of these areas. For example, it may cost 20% of an employee's salary to hire through an agency, training may be an additional $5,000 per employee, and the salary and fringe benefits of managers pulled from their job to interview potential candidates can be calculated. Employee retention may be attained through focus on hard data measures such as reducing the number of steps associated in completing tasks or reducing equipment downtime.

Surveys, observation, or data gathered from systems or individual stakeholders are some options available to track progress against key metrics or measures of the BPI project.

Reporting to the Sponsor and Key Stakeholders

Throughout the BPI project, as with any project undertaken, the project manager has been reporting on project status. The report to the sponsor and key stakeholders referred to in this section, however, should be focused on the impact and benefits realized from the BPI project. The main question to be answered is: *Did the project achieve its goals as set forth in the project scope?* While there is value in the satisfaction of stakeholders (the process users) with the entire implementation process, what executives are concerned about is the bottom line. Focus the BPI project report on key metrics of importance to the sponsor—the business justification for approving the BPI project in the first place. Figure 9.7 provides an

Outline for Presentation of Results of BPI Project to Sponsor

□	Executive Summary
□	Overview of BPI project and business justification for project
□	Map of "as-is" process with areas of changes highlighted/notated
□	Map of "final" process
□	Implementation plan (especially important if not all components of process have yet been implemented)
□	Stakeholders involved in implementation (by group/department/division)
□	How implementation was achieved (implementation plan from a high level)
□	Overview of metrics measured in roll out of process
□	Past metrics/measures (what was) compared to current metrics/measures achieved (what is)
□	Business impact results
□	Challenges/barriers that may still need to be addressed (retirement of old systems, increased management support)
□	Next steps and wrap up (next steps may include areas of process yet to be implemented and a plan for doing so)

Figure 9.7 Final report outline

outline for a final report to the sponsor and other key stakeholders interested in the outcome of the BPI project.

In addition to providing a written report on the BPI project to the sponsor and key stakeholders, a presentation in either a face-to-face or virtual meeting format will generate a more engaging conversation.

Sometimes, however, the story is not always good and the conversation with the sponsor or other key stakeholders may take a turn for the worse. Manage these conversations carefully by doing your due diligence. Consider, for example, this story from a colleague of the authors.

My supervisor called me and frantically wanted me to step in for another project manager who was on vacation at the time. Apparently our customer, a very large international hotel chain, was demanding immediate resolution to a problem with their phone system. I told my supervisor to send me all the details and I would do what I could. My introduction to the customer was slated for one hour later, so I quickly dug into what the cause of the problem was and discovered that the issue was a flaw with the integration of multiple telecommunications products. Essentially, one product wasn't receiving messages from another product, leading to information not flowing correctly.

The introductory call with the customer started with the CEO and Founder of the very large international hotel chain demanding a fix immediately. I introduced myself and stated that I was taking over in lieu of the other project manager who was on vacation. The CEO then voiced agitation at the fact that the project manager whom I had stepped in for was allowed to even go on vacation, let alone in the midst of the current crisis. I made certain my response was delivered in a very calm and straightforward manner "I have reviewed what has occurred and I believe the issue resides with Solution X not talking to Solution Y. I have requested Resource Z to travel onsite today to correct the issue. Resource Z will arrive at 2 pm Eastern time and begin work on correcting the problem, with an anticipated resolution by 5 pm Eastern time."

The response from the CEO dramatically changed, his tone of voice lowered, and he became focused on a solution rather than complaining about the problem. I also delivered the news in a very measured way, provided clear definition about how it would be resolved and when it would be resolved— leaving no doubt in the CEO's mind that I had done my due diligence prior to our discussion. Make certain that you recognize whom you are talking to and remember that how you deliver your message is often key to a successful result. I learned early in my career as a project manager to never be intimidated by titles or prestige and always deliver a clear message that is results-oriented to whomever is agitated and distressed. Being calm will often have the result of refocusing everyone on a solution to the problem at hand.

The ability for BPI project managers to remain calm in the face of adversity is absolutely essential. Particularly for process improvement initiative stakeholders who may be upset about changes happening around them that likely impact them and how they work. It is necessary for BPI project success for the project manager to have the ability to remain calm, do research, and offer the best possible options.

Managing a Negative Evaluation (Or, Uh Oh, the Project Was Not a Success)

Not all BPI projects will be a success. Certainly go/no-go decisions will be made as the BPI project progresses. Projects may be stopped before completion if it doesn't appear that a change to the process will be impactful or if support cannot be garnered for a BPI initiative. In this section, the focus is on managing reporting on a BPI project that has been implemented but in which the business objectives were not achieved.

One BPI project for a training company never quite achieved its goal. The goal of the project at launch was to reduce operating costs for running in-person training workshops by 40%. The biggest costs associated with running the workshops was in three key areas: venues, food and beverage for students, and "go/no-go" timing for decisions as to whether or not to run the workshop based on attendance. It was difficult for the BPI project manager and his team to get a few of the stakeholders behind the effort—sales felt that changing the venues as well as reducing the food and beverage offered would have a negative impact on sales. Additionally, more time allocated for go/no-go decisions would impact those regular customers who tended to sign up later on for workshops. This would obviously impact sales goals and commissions of sales people. Changes were made to venues and food and beverage, but not significantly enough to achieve the goals of the BPI project. No changes were made to "go/no-go" timing. The operating costs were only reduced by 25%, not the 40% desired by senior executives. While some improvement was seen, the project was still considered less than successful by executives.

When reporting on a BPI project that did not achieve its goals, in whole or in part, be clear as to the reason without putting blame elsewhere. As with any project, the project manager is ultimately responsible for its success or failure. As a best practice, as would be done with any other type of project, regular reporting to the sponsor on risks provides a *heads up* about whether or not a

BPI project will be 100% successful. During the final report on the BPI project initiative, the BPI project manager should ensure that the reason for failure (or a perception of failure) is known and options are provided to executives that would enable improving or correcting the situation.

Ideally, however, before the BPI project manager has to report on a failed BPI project, the following should be considered throughout the BPI project initiative to reduce the risk of failed process improvement projects:

- Red flags should be looked for and managed as they arise. Risk planning and risk management best practices will result in management of the red flags that arise on the project before they impact the success of the initiative.
- Reduce expectations for success early on. Consider again the story of the training company with the goal to reduce operating costs. When the barriers from sales became apparent, the BPI project manager should have informed his sponsor about the challenges and proposed options for either getting past the barriers or reducing expectations on what is success for the BPI project.

WRAP UP OF THE SIX STEPS TO BPI PROJECT SUCCESS

Before the last few chapters of the book are presented, let's wrap up the six steps to BPI project success.

Figure 9.8 provides an overview of the six steps presented in the book so far. Each of these steps builds upon the previous step and requires continuous engagement of stakeholders. As discussed in the beginning of this book, process improvement initiatives are often the most challenging for project managers to lead. They require the ability for project managers to engage others in change—and change is not easy for anyone. Successfully changing a process and getting individuals to utilize that process requires changing their behaviors and their mindset. This requires the project manager and his BPI project team to keep stakeholders involved in the process improvement project. When stakeholders are the ones involved in redesigning the process, they are more apt to buy in to the project and utilize that process. The ability to build consensus is an essential skill in leading BPI initiatives.

Each of these steps will be utilized regardless of the size or complexity of the BPI project. Certainly, more or less time may be spent in each step depending on the BPI project—simple process redesign projects, for example, may combine Steps 2 and 3 by completing the changes to the process in just a few stakeholder

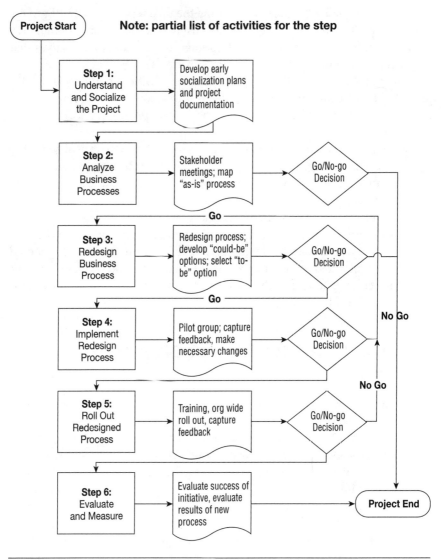

Figure 9.8   Overview of the six steps in the process

meetings; and Steps 4 and 5 may be combined if the process involves just a workgroup or one department, but not the entire organization.

Bottom line—follow these six steps to better manage BPI projects within the organization. A checklist to use for each step in the process is downloadable from the J. Ross website.

In this chapter the authors shared best practices for doing a deeper dive into evaluating the success of the BPI project. The extent to which the success of the BPI project will be evaluated and measured is based on the complexity of the BPI initiative, but also the desires of the executive team. If the sponsor and other key leaders want a detailed evaluation of the project, the best practices provided in this chapter will guide the project manager toward successfully meeting those requirements.

The last few chapters of this book will focus on areas outside of the six steps, but still essential to successfully leading BPI projects. Chapter 10 will provide best practices for project managers who want to influence the organization to adapt a culture of continuous improvement. Chapters 11 and 12 will focus on developing skills in managing stakeholder perceptions of change as well as managing diverse and virtual process improvement teams.

10

CONTINUED EVALUATION BEST PRACTICES

Process improvement initiatives *should be* continuous within an organization. As organizations grow they must change. This means they need to continuously measure, analyze, and refine their processes to ensure they are doing business as effectively and efficiently as possible. Fine-tuning processes provides organizations a competitive advantage in a global marketplace.

Of course, as discussed earlier in this book, too many organizations undertake process improvement initiatives when their proverbial back is up against a wall and they are forced to change. Only the best organizations look to continuously evaluate how they are getting the work done and to improve upon the processes and best practices to remain competitive and on the cutting edge in their industry.

Continuous improvement may not make sense for the entire organization. While manufacturing companies may look to regularly improve how products are developed, an interior design firm may not have a need to regularly evaluate their processes for improvement. It all depends on the work being done within the organization.

This chapter will focus on best practices for continuous evaluation of processes within the organization. While there are many theories and variations on continuous improvement—including Six Sigma, Total Quality Management, Kaizen, and Lean to name just a few—the focus for this book will be on best practices for pushing forward a culture of continuous improvement within the organization.

THE BENEFIT OF A CONTINUOUS IMPROVEMENT CULTURE IN THE ORGANIZATION

Process improvement is a strategy and a tool to help an organization meet its long-term goals and objectives. One key goal for *all* organizations is to meet the demands of their clients—both internal and external. Clients' needs may change due to such things as economic factors, new product introductions, mergers or acquisitions, or expansion or contraction of the business. Continuously reviewing processes for potential improvements and efficiencies enables companies to adapt to their clients' ever-changing needs.

Of course, sometimes continuous improvement has its challenges! An improvement in one process may inadvertently have an adverse effect on other processes. For example, let's assume a company changes its sales order processing. Once that process is improved, it becomes apparent that the improvement in that process has created a backlog in order fulfillment in the manufacturing department. By taking a project management approach to continuous improvement efforts, however, this conflict can be avoided. A business process improvement (BPI) project manager who is leading continuous improvement efforts, or someone who is involved in the efforts as a member of the team, would find the issue and address it during risk planning and the order fulfillment process would have been reviewed as an extension of the sales order process. Alternatively, a decision may have been made not to make changes to the sales order process since doing so would require significant investments in other parts of the company where investments were not possible at the moment.

Figure 10.1 depicts a life cycle for a process improvement initiative. What Figure 10.1 depicts is, effectively, a cyclical environment for continuous improvement. While this may be confused for ongoing operations after deployment of the initiative BPI project, it should, rather, be looked upon as a separate project. Monitoring the process is operational. However, once a need for improvement is recognized, then a project with a defined beginning, a defined end, and with set goals and objectives should be established.

Continuous improvement within an organization makes process improvement initiatives *no big deal* to stakeholders. It becomes the norm within the organization. Stakeholders begin to regularly look for ways to improve the processes around getting the work done and share those ideas with others.

While the book has looked at the launch of process improvement initiatives primarily to drive increased efficiencies and effectiveness, sometimes, when that is the focus we lose sight of other options. For example, sometimes in looking at ways to be more efficient the team is simply tweaking a process that likely should be eliminated. Consider this story.

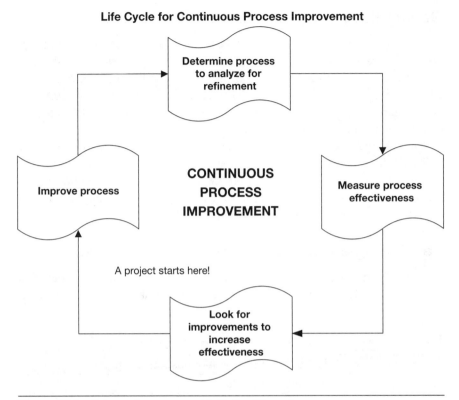

Life Cycle for Continuous Process Improvement

Determine process to analyze for refinement

CONTINUOUS PROCESS IMPROVEMENT

Measure process effectiveness

Improve process

A project starts here!

Look for improvements to increase effectiveness

Figure 10.1   Process improvement initiative life cycle

Alexandria was tasked with leading a Continuous Improvement Team in her organization. One of the processes her team was reviewing was a process that pulled information from a customer relationship management system on a monthly basis that was compiled into a report to share with executives. The process had been in place for the last 3 years, and was initially created when new executives joined the organization and needed to get up to speed on customers of the company. Since that time dashboards were used to deliver information from a variety of systems to the executives' desktops. As part of the review, Alexandria's team met with a number of executives. They learned that the executives never even used the reports and haven't for the last year and a half! Rather than change the process, the process was eliminated. Many hours were freed up for staff to work on other initiatives that were more important and focused on the customer.

Getting Buy-in and Support from Executives

As with any effort desired to be undertaken in an organization, buy-in and support from executives is necessary for an organization to develop a culture of continuous improvement. A focus on the benefits to the organization—from a bottom-line perspective—is essential to achieve this buy-in. Table 10.1 provides a number of bottom-line benefits to developing a culture of continuous improvement within an organization.

The potential impacts noted in Table 10.1 are effectively key performance indicators for an organization. By refining how the work gets done (continuous improvement) the organization can see improvements within the business as well as gains toward achieving long-term strategic goals. To get buy-in and support from executives the focus *must* be on the bottom line.

Developing a Continuous Improvement Culture

Continuous improvement does not have to mean, nor should it mean, that improvements that are undertaken must always be elaborate and large efforts

Table 10.1 Bottom-line impacts for continuous improvement

Benefits of a Culture of Continuous Improvement	
Category	Potential Impacts
Financial	• Increased revenue • Improved profitability • Improved cash flow • Reduced expenses/costs
Customer	• Increased market share • Increased business from customer base • Branch out to other industries • Improved company positioning/branding • Improved competitiveness
Human Resources	• Retention of top talent • Improved problem solving • Improved teamwork
Vendors and Suppliers	• Improved and stronger partnerships • Improved contracting/ability to negotiate better contracts
Products and Services	• Improved inventory management • Better products and services (aligned to customer needs) • Cutting edge products and services • Shorter time-to-market

within the organization. Rather, improvements should be small adjustments, tweaks, or changes that bring about better performance of the process. Continuous improvement efforts are incremental improvements.

As shown in Figure 10.2, continuous improvement cultures engage *all* employees in the business in a positive manner. Since employees are doing the work of the organization, they are usually more effective at determining improvements that can be made within their job functions. In cultures where continuous improvement is valued and supported, employees are frequently offering up ideas and suggestions to improve how the work gets done—which improves how the business supports their customers, drives additional revenue, and increases profitability as well as reduces expenses.

Planning for Continuous Improvement

Project managers can get involved in continuous improvement within the organization by leading continuous improvement teams and using the same best practices that they use to manage projects to push for continuous improvement. Plan to engage others in the benefit of continuous improvement as in any other project—by selling the value to the organization and the individuals within the organization.

Start the effort by reviewing key areas of the business to determine where improvements are possible. Figure 10.3 provides a snapshot of measures related to business processes that may be evaluated for improved performance. Look for potential improvements in these areas of the business.

As seen in Figure 10.3, an area of measurement (cost of production, for example) is evaluated by answering a number of questions to determine where

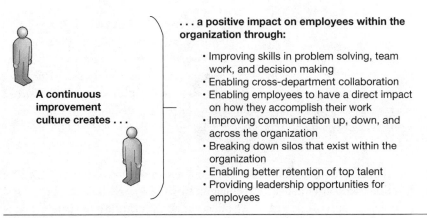

Figure 10.2 A positive impact on employees

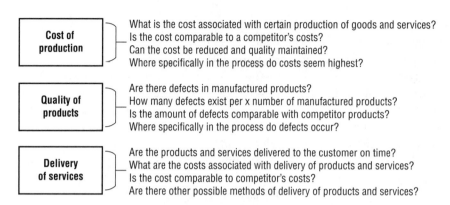

Cost of production — What is the cost associated with certain production of goods and services?
Is the cost comparable to a competitor's costs?
Can the cost be reduced and quality maintained?
Where specifically in the process do costs seem highest?

Quality of products — Are there defects in manufactured products?
How many defects exist per x number of manufactured products?
Is the amount of defects comparable with competitor products?
Where specifically in the process do defects occur?

Delivery of services — Are the products and services delivered to the customer on time?
What are the costs associated with delivery of products and services?
Is the cost comparable to competitor's costs?
Are there other possible methods of delivery of products and services?

Figure 10.3   Examples of business process measures

improvements may exist. In evaluating the cost of production, review all costs associated with producing a product to determine where savings may be realized. However, just reducing the costs of producing a product is not sufficient. The goal is to reduce the cost of producing a product while still maintaining quality or even improving quality of the product.

Three possibilities exist when reviewing processes for improvement:

1. Does the process need to be fixed? Is it broken and causing significant impact on the business?
2. Does the process need to be improved upon? Is it working well overall but needs a few tweaks or adjustments to make it even better?
3. Does a new process need to be created?

The authors added number 3 to the list of possibilities when reviewing processes because they often hear from clients that no processes exist. In fact, rarely have the authors seen a situation where no processes exist at all. The only time that the authors have seen a case where no processes exist is when a company is doing something for the very first time. In all other cases, there are processes. If the work is getting done, there are processes being used—they just are not documented and reside in the heads of those who are doing the work.

When planning for continuous improvement, reach out across the organization to find those who are interested in collaborating to improve business processes. This provides individuals in the organization an opportunity to structure how they will perform their own roles—and that is appealing to anyone.

The Plan-Do-Check-Act (PDCA) Cycle (see Figure 10.4) is another way of looking at processes and determining improvements. The PDCA Cycle is often called the Deming Cycle because it is focused on continuous process improvement.

As is depicted in the figure, PDCA enables continuous improvement in processes by constantly reviewing processes for refinements that increase the effectiveness of the process. Table 10.2 provides a brief explanation of each step in the PDCA Cycle.

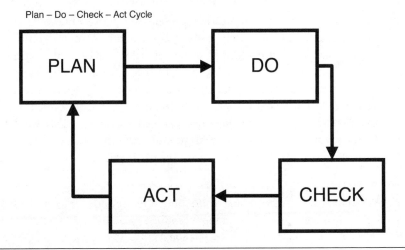

Plan – Do – Check – Act Cycle

Figure 10.4   PDCA cycle

Table 10.2   Description of PDCA cycle steps

Step	Description
Plan	The continuous improvement team identifies an area of the business where problems exist. The team analyzes the problem to determine the root cause and review processes associated with the problem area ("as-is" process).
Do	The continuous improvement team generates a number of potential solutions ("could-be" options). "Could-be" options are narrowed down further based on agreed to criteria and the team selects the best process area, where the most value can be found, to focus improvements ("to-be" option).
Check	A pilot test of the "to-be" process is evaluated to see if it solved the problem. Adjustments are made if necessary and another pilot test is conducted if needed.
Act	The solution ("to-be" process) is implemented more widely. The team moves to the next area of evaluation, looking for other areas of potential improvement.

The PDCA Cycle is one of the more popular tools used by continuous process improvement teams. When used to evaluate processes within the business it facilitates focus that improves effectiveness and efficiency and helps the business to achieve goals and objectives.

USING CROSS-FUNCTIONAL CONTINUOUS IMPROVEMENT TEAMS

Continuous improvement teams must represent the entire organization—all workgroups, departments, divisions, and locations. Team members come from finance, operations, marketing, human resources, sales, and other departments. Team members should also come from a variety of educational, experience, and skill backgrounds—from individual contributor roles up to leadership roles. Some cross-functional teams will also include individuals from outside of the organization—such as suppliers, vendors, or even customers. This would be especially important if a focus of the continuous improvement team is to review processes that impact individuals outside of the organization.

For one client, a cross-functional continuous improvement team included long-term customers as well as shipping vendors. These external individuals were on the team for a few months while the team undertook a review of the processes concerning fulfilling and shipping customer orders. It was felt that the perspective of both the customer and the shipping vendor would be of value in the evaluation of the current processes.

Cross-functional teams are commonly self-directed teams. They rely on the expertise and input from a variety of individuals throughout the organization to accomplish their tasks.

Cross-functional continuous improvement teams provide tremendous benefits to the organization because they bring together individuals with a variety of ideas, perspectives, and opinions. This diversity initiates better solutions to problems and increased creativity and innovation overall.

Enabling Cross-functional Team Success

As with any team, the individual leading the cross-functional continuous improvement team must allow time for team members to get to know each other. Refer to Chapter 3 where we discussed the benefits and values to encourage team building.

In particular, for the cross-functional continuous improvement team, time spent understanding the experiences and background of each team member provides a strong foundation when it comes to assigning roles and responsibilities on the team. Individuals serving on cross-functional teams are required to accomplish their regular day-to-day responsibilities as well as the work of the cross-functional teams. To that end, providing these teams with support and resources that are needed is essential to their success. Support might come in the form of providing space to meet, a budget for food and beverages for meetings, and access to senior leaders within the organization for guidance.

Leadership is sometimes a challenge with cross-functional continuous improvement teams, as the purpose of the team is to be self-directed as they collaborate to reach their goals. Therefore, clear processes and procedures should be developed on how decisions will be made, how conflicts will be resolved, and how information will be shared between team members.

One cross-functional continuous improvement team was established to work over a year's time, reviewing key business processes for increased efficiencies. The team took turns sharing the leadership role with a member of the team being the "leader" for two months at a time. Additionally, decision-making processes were established that enabled each team member to take the lead on decision making, depending on their expertise.

To ensure that the cross-functional continuous improvement team can be successful in accomplishing their initiatives, executives should ensure that the rest of the organization is aware of the team's existence and their mission. Make sure that everyone knows that the team will need information from others throughout the organization to properly perform their function and, therefore, assistance should be provided in the form of responding to surveys, answering questions, and providing documentation as requested.

GETTING EMPLOYEES ENGAGED IN CONTINUOUS IMPROVEMENT

Getting employees engaged in continuous improvement can be done through focusing on the benefits to the *individual* more than the benefits to the organization. Benefits to individuals involved in continuous-improvement teams include:

- Increasing collaboration and teamwork with others
- Learning new skills and continuing to build knowledge
- Being seen as a leader within the organization
- Determining how the work should be accomplished in the organization
- Making an impact on the bottom line
- Helping the organization achieve long-term strategic goals
- Deepening the understanding of the organization and how it all fits together

When these benefits are the focus of the conversation with employees, they are more apt to be engaged and therefore willing to participate on continuous-improvement teams.

Continuous Improvement as a Component of Professional Development

Serving on a continuous improvement team is, essentially, a professional development opportunity for employees. Consider the bulleted list presented that covered the benefits to the individual while serving on such teams. Those benefits are all professional development opportunities—especially within smaller organizations where there are limited career paths for employees. Those employees are basically in their roles until employees above them leave their organizations or are promoted; and those individuals may not be able to move up until employees above them leave! When service on continuous improvement teams is linked to opportunities for professional and personal growth, organizations that may otherwise not have opportunities for employees will find that retention of top talent is increased.

For a marketing and public relations client with 300 employees, Gina, one of the authors, accomplished significant changes within the organization by reviewing and refining processes through the use of cross-functional continuous improvement teams. Team members, representing all functional areas and with a variety of experiences, were tasked with evaluating a variety of processes and developing plans to improve processes where it made sense to do so. What was the benefit to the employees? They were able to develop a variety of new skills, have new experiences, and were able to make a positive, bottom-line impact on the organization.

While a project manager may not single-handedly be able to create a culture of continuous improvement within his organization, he or she can certainly influence a movement in that direction. By actively looking for areas where improvement may be possible—even a small incremental improvement in a process—the project manager can then make a business case to the executives. Focus on what's important to the executives—the bottom line. Refer back to Table 10.1 which provides a number of benefits associated with having a culture of continuous improvement in a variety of areas within the business.

11

THE PEOPLE-SIDE OF CHANGE MANAGEMENT

Most project managers focus on change from the perspective of managing changes to the business process improvement (BPI) project. These changes might include expanding the scope based on additional findings during documentation of the *as-is* process or adjusting the schedule to accommodate a larger group of stakeholders from which information is needed. Rarely, however, do project managers consider the impact of change *on the people*.

The ability to manage change is *not solely* from the perspective of changes required of the project (think *project change management*) but also, and *more importantly*, people's perceptions of change. The BPI project manager who can understand how change impacts others and why some individuals can *go along* with change while others cannot will be far more effective and successful in managing BPI projects.

This chapter will provide a base foundation for understanding people and change. It will also provide a few key best practices for engaging people through change-focused projects such as BPI initiatives.

UNDERSTANDING PERCEPTIONS OF CHANGE

Every business goes through change; it is necessary and provides organizations with opportunities for growth, improved competition, and innovation. Sounds like the reason to undertake BPI projects, doesn't it? Change is an emotional experience and is frequently a roller coaster ride of emotions as the change is being implemented. Consider BPI projects—they are about changing the way in which individuals in the organization get work done. If one of the stakeholders of a BPI project has been using the process for a number of years and, in fact, was the primary designer of that process, imagine how he feels when the process will be changed. It is an emotional experience!

Simply because a process has been changed and is a better way of getting a task completed, doesn't mean stakeholders will utilize that process. There needs to be a behavioral component to BPI projects—stakeholders must start doing work differently than they did in the past.

Amanda's supervisor just notified her that the department was undertaking a process improvement project to change how data would be entered into the Customer Relationship Manager (CRM) system. Amanda's supervisor wanted her to be involved with the BPI project by acting as the point of contact between the BPI project team and the department. Amanda was excited about the responsibility but realized that this project means that her coworkers—many of whom had been working within the department, doing the process the same way year after year—would have to change how they work. They would have to behave differently—changing how they work to fit with the new process. Amanda also knew that because her coworkers had been working with the process for such a long time, that change would not come easy. They were comfortable. This is a simple fact of human nature.

What Impacts How People Perceive Change

There are many factors that impact how stakeholders perceive change. Table 11.1 provides a number of factors that may impact how stakeholders will react to the BPI project.

Later on in this chapter, we'll discuss how to effectively utilize and deploy change management teams. Change management teams will arrange for more effective management and engagement of *individual* stakeholders who may feel negatively about the BPI project. Other factors in addition to the ones listed in Table 11.1 that will impact the perception of the BPI project include:

- The belief that *if it isn't broke, don't fix it*
- Too much going on in the organization that the individual simply cannot focus on one more thing
- Significant perceived risks with changing the process
- Lack of understanding about why the BPI project has been launched

Table 11.1   Factors that impact stakeholder's perceptions

Factors that May Impact Perception of BPI Project	Expected Reaction to Change (positive or negative)
New skills that will be required to perform the tasks associated with the new process	Either positive (if interested in building new skills/motivated) or negative (if happy with the status quo).
Fear of the unknown	Negative—not understanding what the BPI project means for the individual is worrisome to them.
Personal history around past BPI initiatives	Either positive (if past initiatives have been successful and benefited the individual) or negative (if past initiatives have caused layoffs or significant changes in the job).
What else is going on outside the workplace	Either positive (if all else is going well personally in the individual's life, he may be more receptive to change) or negative (if the individual's personal life is in turmoil, a BPI project will not be welcome).

The ability to engage stakeholders in change, and to understand their perceptions around change and why those perceptions exist, is essential to getting stakeholders to actually use the new process.

DEVELOPING THE *PEOPLE* CHANGE MANAGEMENT PLAN

The *people* change management plan should be focused on how stakeholders will be engaged in the BPI project. It includes a number of documents that will comprise the plan:

- A stakeholder assessment template that captures information about the stakeholder group impacted by the BPI project.
- A communication plan that focuses on what is needed from stakeholders for a successful BPI project as well as how the BPI project team will communicate with these stakeholders.
- A stakeholder meeting/conversation preparation template that can be used in the early planning stages that includes common questions asked by stakeholders. This template helps with planning responses

to stakeholders' questions and concerns to enable them to adapt more quickly to the BPI project.

These documents will prepare the BPI project team for how much, or how little, the stakeholders will need to be engaged *early on* in the BPI project. The more positive the stakeholders are, the less time will be needed to make them comfortable and confident about the BPI project. But don't mistake this for meaning that stakeholders do not need to be engaged. Even those who are positive and champions of the BPI initiative will still need to be provided information and kept updated on the project to remain engaged and committed.

All of these templates are available via download from the Web Added Value™ (WAV) Download Resource Center at the publisher's website: www.jrosspub.com/wav (hereafter referred to as the J. Ross website). Figures 11.1, 11.2, and 11.3 provide a snapshot of each template.

Figure 11.1 provides a snapshot of a stakeholder assessment template that can be used to develop the *people* change management plan.

Stakeholder Group	How are they impacted by the BPI project?	How critical to the success of the BPI project are they? (low, med, high)	How much effort is required to change how they work? (low, med, high)	What are their expected or known concerns?
Marketing	Need to be involved in review and change of processes for capturing client data	High	Medium	Comfortable with current processes Upcoming new product releases effecting workload
Sales	Will need to change how they utilize the system when out in the field	Medium	Medium	Often on the road and difficult to connect with Trying to meet end of year revenue goals and may not support BPI project

Figure 11.1 Snapshot of stakeholder assessment

In Figure 11.1, two groups are impacted by the BPI project—marketing and sales. Both groups have other projects in which they are involved, or need to be involved, that will impact their ability and desire to support the BPI project. The next example, Figure 11.2, will utilize a communication plan template to show how one of these groups may be managed.

In Figure 11.2, concerns of the marketing group—and specifically the analysts in the group—are focused on having used the current process for a number of years and, thus, being comfortable with it. The assumption can be made, therefore, that they will be hesitant to change. While communications about the process could have been conducted via e-mail or a larger group format (such as sales and marketing combined), in this case, the initial communication will be through a face-to-face meeting. This will enable the BPI project team to build a stronger relationship with the marketing analysts and begin to address their concerns, which will increase their comfort level and participation in the BPI project.

Figure 11.3 is a stakeholder meeting/conversation preparation template that might be used early on during BPI project planning to answer stakeholder questions and address concerns.

As the BPI project team prepares for the project by understanding the reason behind it (business case for the project) as well as the impact it will have within the organization, this template (see Figure 11.3) can be utilized to write expected questions and concerns along with appropriate responses. This helps

Stakeholder Group (or individuals within the group)	Impact from change	Concerns they may have	What is needed from them	How the team will communicate with them
Marketing (analyst role)	Will need to change how data is entered into the CRM system	Involved in other initiatives On average analysts have been using the process for a number of years and are comfortable with it	Assistance in mapping "as-is" process Testing of new process prior to full roll out	Initial face-to-face meeting to discuss the BPI project and address concerns and request their assistance Follow-up e-mails about progress and to schedule testing for new "to-be" process

Figure 11.2   Snapshot of a communication plan

Question/concern	Response to address the question/concern with stakeholders
What do we expect will be different when a refined or updated process is implemented?	• Time now spent entering information will be able to be allocated to more strategicinitiatives within marketing. • New technology is being launched which includes an updated CRM system. This system is tied to other systems which will enable "pulling" information and thereby reducing the amount of data to be manually entered (as is done now).
What impact will this BPI project have on current roles and responsibilities?	• Roles and responsibilities for marketing analysts will reflect new responsibilities more tied to strategic initiatives within marketing. Updated job descriptions are being worked on my marketing leadership.
What will be provided to stakeholders to be comfortable using the new process?	• Advanced training on the new CRM system and the new process for entering data. • The ability to be involved in the design of the "to-be" process. • Pilot testing of the process before full roll out. • Brief "how-to" webinars that will review the process and how to enter data (supporting training).

Figure 11.3 Snapshot of stakeholder meeting/conversation preparation

to ensure that all stakeholders are getting the same information, regardless of who they are communicating with on the BPI project team.

A template with more complete questions and concerns that commonly arise on BPI projects is included in the downloadable files from the J. Ross website.

Evaluating the Impact of Change and Ensuring an Understanding of the Need for Change

As discussed earlier in this chapter and previously in the book, it is essential that the BPI project team understands the need for the BPI project and is able to communicate that need from a high-level (organizational) perspective, as well as a division and department perspective and an individual-contributor perspective.

Stakeholder engagement in the BPI project is increased when the following is known by stakeholders:

- The vision for the BPI project—why the change is necessary now
- The impact that the change will have on each individual stakeholder
- That everything has been considered about the BPI project—such as, skills needed to work with the new process, training on this new process, and some time to *try out* the new process

Early meetings with stakeholders who will be involved in the BPI project should be focused on discussions around those bulleted items.

In working with a retail organization going through significant change that was impacting many of their business processes, stakeholders noted in an all-staff meeting that they were concerned that processes were being changed at the same time that the organization was closing its books for the year and sales was trying to bring in more revenue. The BPI project team was able to communicate that these concerns had already been addressed at the leadership level and it was determined that new processes for finance would roll out in February, after closing of the books in January and sales would roll out in January after ending the year in December.

Engaging Employees in Change and Getting Them Prepared for Change

At a pharmaceutical company that was going through significant change that would impact many of their business processes across the organization, Gina, one of the authors, held a number of divisional meetings with various stakeholders focused on one question to ponder and brainstorm: "We see many changes coming our way. If we got in front of those changes, what would that look like?" This simple question allowed the stakeholders of the upcoming BPI project to consider the project from a positive, future opportunity perspective—which was certainly a significant change.

Figure 11.4 provides a simple model for preparing for change, mapped to each phase of the six-step approach to managing BPI projects.

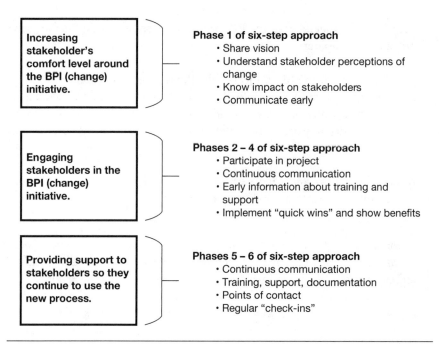

Figure 11.4   A model for preparing for change

To prepare stakeholders for upcoming BPI initiatives that will impact how they work, get them engaged early on by looking at the project from a positive perspective. Best practices for engaging stakeholders have been shared in previous chapters. The story shared by the authors focuses on the *what could be* rather than what the stakeholders perceive they may be losing. *What could be* is a more positive outlook.

Information is power. The more information about the BPI project that the team can share, the more comfortable and confident the stakeholders will be, as they will feel that they have some control over their situation. This is why getting stakeholders involved in discussions concerning processes—mapping out *as-is* processes, designing *could-be* processes and providing information and input to finalize *to-be* processes—is so essential. This enables stakeholders to feel in control and will, therefore, support and champion the BPI project.

One of the best ways to sell BPI projects that require significant change is to sell problems rather than solutions. Once stakeholders understand the problem that needs to be solved through a BPI project, they can then be engaged in contributing to finding a solution to that problem.

Using Change Management Teams

Change management teams bring about many of the same benefits as other subteams discussed in previous chapters of this book. Along with a number of other benefits, some of those benefits include:

- Points of contact for stakeholders being impacted by change from the BPI project
- Helping stakeholders get past personal obstacles that are impacting their ability to change
- Sharing information about the BPI project and how stakeholders will be supported through the change

Change management teams should have a number of skills that make them effective when working closely with stakeholders who need to be *brought along* to champion the BPI project. These skills include:

- The ability to build strong relationships with stakeholders
- Understanding of the organization as a whole and why this change must happen
- Understanding the impact of the change on the individual
- The ability to communicate effectively throughout the organization
- Excellent listening skills (how are stakeholders *really* feeling about the change that will occur because of the BPI project?)
- The ability to empathize with others
- Experience going through BPI projects that required significant change (complex BPI initiatives)

These are not dissimilar skills to what is required of BPI project teams and sub-teams in general for them to be effective in implementing BPI projects.

The authors would suggest that individuals who have been through complex BPI project initiatives from a stakeholder perspective make some of the best change management team members. Not only do they want those who have been through successful BPI projects, but also individuals who have been through less than successful BPI projects. This will cultivate increased empathy for stakeholders on the current BPI project and a better understanding of why stakeholders may not be comfortable about the upcoming changes that the BPI project will necessitate.

COMMUNICATING EFFECTIVELY—EARLY ON AND OFTEN

Every BPI project, as with any other project, should require regular and frequent communications with stakeholders—as stakeholders *will* drive the success or failure of the project. However, BPI projects that will necessitate significant change by stakeholders due to dramatically different or new processes must be given special consideration in communications.

The BPI project manager might task the change management team with getting stakeholders engaged in the BPI project by holding regular meetings with stakeholders to listen to and understand their concerns and then bringing that intelligence back to the BPI project team. The change management team effectively plays the role of the bridge between the BPI project team and stakeholders impacted by the BPI project.

Figure 11.5 provides a checklist to use when checking in with stakeholders about the BPI project and especially during times when the stakeholders are actively going through change associated with the project.

FOLLOWING UP WITH THOSE IMPACTED BY CHANGE

Once the BPI project is launched, communication with those impacted must continue. Failure to continue to engage those stakeholders who have been most impacted by change due to the BPI project will, in many cases, increase the chances that they will revert back to the old way of doing things (using the as-is process). Change is not a one-time event that, when implemented, is complete. It is a continuous process that requires persistence and patience to pay off. Change management teams that stay together to support the change after the BPI project has been implemented by the core BPI team will keep the stakeholders moving forward with the change. Additionally, the role of following up with

Yes	No	Question to consider...
☐	☐	Are communications effective and sufficient to keep stakeholders updated on the BPI project and upcoming changes associated with the project?
☐	☐	Do stakeholders understand how they have to change, and why they have to change, to support the new process being implemented by the BPI project?
☐	☐	Do stakeholders feel that their opinions, ideas, concerns, and suggestions are being considered?
☐	☐	Is there sufficient dialog happening within the various departments engaged in the BPI initiative that shows that they are engaged in the project?
☐	☐	Have those who are most impacted (potentially adversely) by the BPI project been communicated with individually or in smaller groups to ensure their needs are being met and concerns are being addressed?

Figure 11.5　Checklist: checking in with stakeholders

those stakeholders who are impacted by the BPI project can be fulfilled by the continuous process improvement team.

The length of time in which stakeholders should be kept engaged through follow-up conversations will vary depending on the complexity of the BPI project and the amount of change that project requires of individual stakeholders.

For a company that provides training products, the continuous process improvement team—working collaboratively with a change management team—kept checking in with stakeholders after BPI project implementation for a 6-month period. Initially check-ins happened via small group meetings and then, over time, moved to checking in via the Q&A section on the company intranet portal.

This chapter focused on the *people-side* of change. The people-side of change enables increased success in BPI project implementations. When the BPI project team focuses on the stakeholders and how the change associated with the BPI project will impact each stakeholder, they are more likely to keep them engaged with the initiative. When stakeholders are engaged, they are motivated to change and support the project. In order to be comfortable with the change, stakeholders must understand *why* the change is happening and *why* it matters to them. If the BPI project team cannot answer these questions—they need to find the answers. This all goes back to understanding the business case for the BPI project. When the business case is understood, and shared with stakeholders, then there is increased support and involvement in the BPI project.

MANAGING A VIRTUAL AND DIVERSE PROCESS IMPROVEMENT PROJECT TEAM

In today's world nearly *every* business process improvement (BPI) project team is comprised of virtual and diverse members. Team members may be coming from clear across the country, around the world, or even in another office only a few states away. Stakeholders—an extension of the team—will likely come from a variety of locations when the process improvement project is more complex and spans a number of divisions within a larger organization.

Virtual team members and virtual stakeholders add complexity to the BPI project because the challenges that the BPI project manager faces will increase. If you add in global teams, challenges may include cultural differences, language barriers, varying business practices, technology infrastructure, and time zone differences. In order to be successful at managing his team and achieving the goals of the project, the project manager will need to overcome all of these challenges.

The ability to manage virtual and diverse BPI project teams and stakeholders is another necessary skill for today's project manager. Before the BPI project is kicked off, the project manager will need to have a variety of processes and procedures in place in order to effectively manage the team. Some of these necessary processes, such as for solving problems and resolving conflicts, were discussed in earlier chapters.

This chapter will provide a variety of best practices for keeping virtual BPI teams moving forward through the many challenges they will encounter as well as on how to take advantage of the diversity of virtual project teams.

UNDERSTANDING AND APPRECIATING DIVERSITY

Allen's project team for the financial process improvement initiative had just launched. It consisted of employees from offices within the United States—primarily in the Midwest and on the West Coast. While introducing himself to the team members via phone before the first team meeting, he soon realized he had a very diverse team on this project! He learned the following about his team: team members' ethnic backgrounds were very diverse and included Sofia who was born in Italy and came to the United States at the age of 20; Ralf who was born in the United States but spent much of his childhood in Germany before returning to the States to go to college; and Demetrios, born and raised in the U.S. but with very close ties to his family in Greece.

Simply because the BPI project team is located within the United States doesn't mean diversity is not a concern for the project manager. The United States has had an increasing change of demographics through continuous incorporation of new immigrants and a shifting in race percentages which increases the need to understand, value, and appreciate the diversity that is all around us, every day.

While this book is not about cultural diversity, the authors would like to share common barriers to diversity that can impact the ability of a diverse BPI project team to accomplish its goals and the ability of the project manager to effectively lead a diverse team. Table 12.1 provides four common barriers and a brief description of each.

Project managers can begin to appreciate and embrace cultural diversity on their project teams when they better understand their own barriers and learn how to break through those barriers. When they do this, they can assist their team members in doing the same by including team-building activities that show the value of diversity on the BPI project team.

Jeremiah was having difficulty working with one of his team members who wanted to take on more responsibility that would effectively give him a leadership role. Jeremiah believed that for the team member to take on a leadership role on the team, he had to have a college degree—and Samuel did not

Table 12.1   Four common barriers

Barrier to Accepting Cultural Diversity	Brief Description of the Barrier
Ethnocentrism	Ethnocentrism refers to an individual's assumption that their way of thinking, working, and acting is superior to all others. People who are ethnocentric measure every-one else against what they believe is right, normal, or expected behaviors.
Stereotyping	Stereotyping are unverified and oversimplified general-izations about a particular group of people. Stereotypes are developed and learned through association with our family and friends.
Prejudice	Prejudice is an inflexible judgment of an individual or group of individuals based on limited and insufficient knowledge of their cultures and values. Stereotyping feeds into prejudices as does information individuals are exposed to in their early years from family, friends, and neighbors.
Discrimination	Discrimination results from our prejudices. It is the unequal treatment of individuals based on any number of factors, including heavy accents, piercings they may have, and how they dress.

have a degree. Jeremiah felt that having a college degree was an important indicator of someone's intelligence and was obviously proud of the degree he had obtained. In his opinion, Samuel would not be able to take on any responsibilities that would put him in a leadership role, if he did not have a degree. Jeremiah's barrier to accepting and working effectively with Samuel was based on Jeremiah's stereotype that if someone does not have a college degree, they cannot take on leadership responsibilities.

The Challenge of a Variety of Cultural Identities on the Team

The more diverse in cultural identities the project team is, the more likely that challenges will arise in how individuals work together as a team. BPI project managers leading culturally diverse teams need to ensure that cliques do not form among *like* team members.

Depending on individual team members' cultural backgrounds, challenges will arise in a number of areas, including:

- How comfortable team members are in participating in problem-solving and decision-making meetings.

Some team members, depending on their cultural background and upbringing, are more comfortable with having others in a formal leadership role making decisions that they will then implement—they are not comfortable with, nor do they plan on, participating in decision making, since they are not leaders in the organization.

- How comfortable team members are dealing with uncertainty or ambiguity.

Some team members feel that they must have detailed information and a clear vision for the project in which they are participating—ambiguity, for them, simply brings more risk than they are comfortable with.

- How much communication team members want/expect on the project.

Some team members want very detailed, significant amounts of documentation—all historical background, recaps of conversations on the topic, team members' opinions, and other such details. This is especially important if they are expected to evaluate data prior to participating in decision making. For others, however, only the facts are required and the information provided should be as minimal as possible—everyone's ideas and suggestions are not as relevant as cold, hard facts.

- The motivation of team members to contribute to the project.

Every individual is motivated by something different. Let's relate that to BPI project teams through the following mini case study.

Dana has been assigned to engage a number of stakeholders in the BPI project. It is expected that she will reach out to a list of stakeholders who are not happy with the planned process improvement initiative because they feel that this is not the time to change the way work is being accomplished and there is already too much going on in the organization. These stakeholders are senior to Dana.

Dana was assigned the task during a recent team kick-off meeting. She was participating virtually, since she is located across the country. Dana didn't accept or decline the assignment, she said nothing.

Let's skip ahead. Two weeks have passed and Dana still has not taken any action toward completing her task. There is another virtual team meeting scheduled and Dana is expected to report on progress. She is unsure what to do.

There are a number of issues that have caused this situation. First, the BPI project manager never took the initiative to get to know the individuals who comprise the team. Dana was assigned this task *prior* to the project manager having any knowledge about who Dana is and how Dana works. Second, Dana is an introvert. She tends to be very quiet, doesn't build relationships easily, and is shy. She has no idea how to approach this task. Third, Dana believes that junior employees should not be trying to engage with and change the minds of more senior-level employees.

There are two factors in particular that hinder Dana from achieving the goal:

1. The goal is not feasible to Dana; she believes that it is unlikely she can achieve the goal. Not because the goal is too big to achieve, but rather, because she doesn't have the skills to do so.
2. She doesn't want to achieve the goal. Not because she is a lazy team member, but because to achieve it, she would have to step outside her comfort zone and engage with stakeholders who are above her in the corporate hierarchy.

The smart BPI project manager takes the time to get to know his team and the individual members, as well as their preferences for working with and communicating with others. With this knowledge, the project manager is more likely to get a group of individuals up and running and functioning as a team much quicker—which means the work of the BPI project can begin to be accomplished much sooner. By getting to know BPI project team members, the project manager understands what tasks are more aligned to the skills, behaviors, and knowledge of each team member as well as those tasks that each team member is comfortable accomplishing. Certainly people-focused project managers will spend time helping team members expand their comfort zone and take on tasks that are more challenging for them; but this is done in collaboration with the team member and through providing the team member the support needed to accomplish the task.

Downloadable from the Web Added Value™ (WAV) Download Resource Center at the publisher's website: www.jrosspub.com/wav (hereafter referred to as the J. Ross website) are a few assessments and questionnaires that BPI project managers can use to gauge their understanding of their diverse team members and to help them in getting team members to work together effectively.

The Value of Diverse Process Improvement Teams

In Chapter 3 the value of diversity in skills, experience, and qualifications in BPI project teams was discussed. Here, the focus will be on diversity in cultural backgrounds, or how people interact with others, and how they approach working on a team, sharing ideas, and thinking through problems.

In addition to benefits around different perspectives bringing increased creativity and innovation on the project team, the value of diverse process improvement teams is also evident in:

- The creation of products and services that meet the needs of a diverse group of stakeholders—which increases profitability when the BPI project team is comprised of members from those geographic locations where products or services will be launched.
- The ability to open up new markets for products and services more successfully because of *inside* information—understand the needs, wants, and expectations of the end consumer better because the BPI project team members include individuals who represent that end-consumer general profile.

A manufacturer of household products had expanded into China and built a new manufacturing plant. The CEO launched a project to develop processes and procedures, based on what was working successfully at two other manufacturing plants—one in the United States and one in Germany. The project team assigned was expected to get the plant up and running in China within nine months. The project team, however, had team members that came only from the United States—which was where the headquarters of the organization were located—not one team member came from China. It would be difficult, if not impossible, for the project manager who was leading this business process design project to determine what would work in China. What works in plants in the United States and Germany was not necessarily going to be successful in China.

The successful BPI project manager seeks out cultural diversity in his team members in order to not just increase the success of a BPI project but also to go above and beyond the expectations set out by the sponsor. Consider the story of the manufacturer expanding into China. Even if it was not possible to include team members from China on the team, the business process design team should have a few resources in China to tap into to understand the culture and how business gets done. This would better enable the team to design processes that work effectively within China.

Factors That Impact the Success of Virtual and Diverse Process Improvement Teams

A colleague of the authors tells this story: "I was engaged as a project manager for a large global program to create a new interactive voice response application for a large wireless provider. Interactive voice response systems are utilized by large companies to buffer call center agents from being flooded with calls. Essentially you dial what is typically a toll-free number and receive prompts to guide you through a call flow. Something like, 'press 1 for accounts payable; press 2 for billing questions; etc.' The application being built was a custom interactive voice response system with speech recognition, and all of the work was being done by software developers in Argentina and Brazil, whom I had never worked with before. Additionally, the virtual team was working in an Agile Scrum methodology to enable rapid iterations of the product, which were incrementally reviewed by the project sponsor before being released.

All was going well and I was using instant messenger to communicate with the software developers in Argentina and Brazil on a daily basis. Rather than have an in-person daily stand-up call, as preferred when working in an Agile Scrum method, I would pose questions to all the developers via instant messenger about their progress. About a week into the program, our first deliverable was getting closer to delivery, and I believed all was on track. Each day in that week, my questions posed to each developer via instant messenger resembled something like, 'How is module three development going?' with a response of, 'Good' or 'Okay.' At the end of the week, I happily started my early morning with the firm belief that all was 'good' and 'okay' and that the first deliverable would be met on time. The project sponsor from the customer was equally excited given I had communicated a green-light 'all is a go' status the entire week.

The compiled code delivery arrived and I reviewed the product against the deliverables. Nothing was complete! Horrified, (especially since I had to deliver our initial prototype to the project sponsor) I frantically called the Lead Developer in Brazil and asked why I was misled, to which he responded, 'You didn't ask if the tasks were done. You asked how it was going, to which they responded 'good' and 'okay.' I had made the critical error of not bridging the language gap with my virtual team members and modifying my approach accordingly. Needless to say, I had egg on my face with our first deliverable to the project sponsor, but afterward, I successfully delivered each subsequent one. I learned to always assess whether 'good' and 'okay' means 'done' with whatever virtual delivery team I am working with and I now avoid being exposed to the results of miscommunication."

The success of virtual process improvement teams, especially those that may be global in nature, are impacted by a number of factors, including those shown in Table 12.2.

Perhaps, even more importantly, the success of virtual process improvement teams relies on the project manager having the ability to communicate effectively, in a way that works for all team members. This does not happen naturally and requires specific focus on setting up a variety of ways for team members to communicate effectively about the project and with each other.

Virtual teams are often challenged by effective communications. Without the ability to communicate effectively, the team cannot effectively fulfill their responsibilities on the team—and the potential for issues to arise on the project increases. Even more challenging is when the virtual BPI project team is a global one. Communications for such teams are often inconsistent due to either a lack of appropriate technologies or expectations of communication among individuals. Working in collaboration with virtual BPI project team members to develop appropriate and available channels for communication on the project is essential early on in project planning. As a best practice, when communicating with virtual team members across cultural boundaries, consider the following:

- Do cultural differences exist between the team members that will impact the communications?
- Given differences that may exist, what is the best way, or ways, to communicate the message?
- What feedback is being received from team members—both verbal and nonverbal—that is impacting how they receive the message?

Craft communications based on the responses to the questions above.

Table 12.2 Factors that impact virtual process improvement team success

Factors that Impact Success of Global Business Process Improvement Teams	
• Varying policies and procedures in place at the individual's "home" office	• Lack of access to collaboration tools and technology to effectively communicate
• Misunderstanding of the various cultures represented on the project team	• Lack of effective team leadership
• Lack of understanding how one's role and responsibilities fit into the project team overall	• Discomfort working with individuals from different cultures

SUCCESSFUL VIRTUAL AND DIVERSE PROCESS IMPROVEMENT TEAMS

For the balance of this chapter the discussion will focus on a number of ways to enable success on virtual and culturally diverse process improvement teams. While BPI teams that are co-located can more easily adapt to each other and, therefore, be effective as a team in a short time period, much more attention needs to be paid to geographically dispersed BPI project teams. It is much easier for virtual team members to feel less than committed to the project or ignore the impact on other team members when they don't complete tasks simply because they are not face-to-face.

To resolve this problem, team-developed documentation on working together is often effective. Such team-based documents establish a way for team members to understand the expectations of working as a member of the BPI project team. When developed collaboratively with the team, these documents set the tone for how the team will work together to accomplish the goals of the project. These documents are additional to the usual project management documentation and are specifically focused on the team.

Using Team Charters

A team charter provides the BPI project team with an understanding around the purpose and high-level goals of the process improvement project. For example, the purpose of the project may be to decrease the number of days from when an order is received to when it is shipped to the customer. The goal for this project may be to reduce the time to ship from the current goal of five days from receipt of order to shipping within two and one-half days of receipt of order.

Also included in the team charter is information about:

- The composition of the team (who is on the team and contact information, including time zone)
- How the team will operate (ground rules, processes for working together, communications between team members)
- How team performance will be assessed
- Major milestones the team needs to achieve

While much of this information can certainly be found in other project documentation, it is valuable to have it in one document that is developed in collaboration with the team.

A downloadable team charter template as well as a sample file is available on the J. Ross website.

Team Norms and Operating Agreements

Team norms were discussed in Chapter 3 and included the areas that might be covered during the team kick-off meeting to help the team get off on the right track. The J. Ross website provides a downloadable team norms and operating agreement template as well as a sample file. A team norms and operating agreement should be developed in collaboration with the team during the kick-off meeting.

While such an agreement is of value for every BPI project, it is especially valuable when the BPI project team is a virtual one. Similar to the team charter, the team norms and operating agreement provides details for the team members as to how they have agreed to work together to support the BPI project initiatives and to support each other.

Table 12.3 provides a list of the areas to be covered in a team norms and operating agreement. All of this information to be captured in the team norms and operating agreement have been covered throughout this book. This template is just an easy way of keeping the information on how the team members will work together in one document for easy reference.

Ensuring a Clear Vision of the Process Improvement Project

Many of the authors' clients often kick off a process improvement initiative without having a clear vision for what they are trying to achieve. Yes, there is always the goal to be more efficient in some particular area or do a better job for the customer—but what does that mean? Team members working on a BPI project must have a clear vision of what they are trying to accomplish. When that is provided, they are much more likely to come up with creative and innovative solutions to the problem they are trying to address. And, when implemented, the project is far more likely to meet the needs of the stakeholder because it was clear from the start what the project was trying to accomplish when it was launched within the organization.

Having a clear vision enables the project team to understand what they are trying to achieve. This makes it easier to set goals on the team to achieve the overall objectives of the BPI project. But the vision goes beyond the vision for the project. The best BPI project managers also collaborate with the team to set a vision for how the team will work together—what processes, procedures, and

Table 12.3 Areas to be covered in a team norm and operating agreement

Areas of importance to include in a team norms and operating agreement to increase the effectiveness of the BPI project team include...	
• Operating norms	• Meeting guidelines
• Communication guidelines	• Decision-making processes
• Problem-solving processes	• Conflict resolution approach
• Team collaboration approach	• How the team will support each other

approaches toward getting the work of the project accomplished will be taken by each team member.

Ensuring Effective Communication Channels for Virtual Teams

Effective communication and communication channels have been discussed throughout this book, in most cases focused on communications with stakeholders. Some complexity is added to communications when teams are not just virtual, but also globally distributed. While each BPI project team should have an understanding of how and when they will communicate with each other, in many cases for co-located teams this is an easier task. Co-located teams are likely to get together for regular team meetings and team members can easily stop by a colleague's desk or office to ask a question, pass on work, or problem solve an issue. Collaboration is easier for co-located teams. All this can be done on virtual BPI project teams also but requires many more processes to ensure effectiveness in communication and to enable collaboration. Virtual teams rely on technology to be effective in collaborating to achieve goals. Access to technology, however, will vary from country to country, even within the same company from one location to another.

Working collaboratively, the BPI project team should determine how they will communicate, when they will communicate, and what they will communicate. Figure 12.1 provides one example of a communication path for a BPI project team. This particular path is focused on how one team member will pass work to another, who is involved in the *path*, and the channels used to pass work along.

Developing such communications paths—either graphical or simply in a table—provides team members with a better understanding of how work will flow from one team member to another. Keep this information, as well as other team documentation in one location on the BPI project portal so it is easily accessible by all team members.

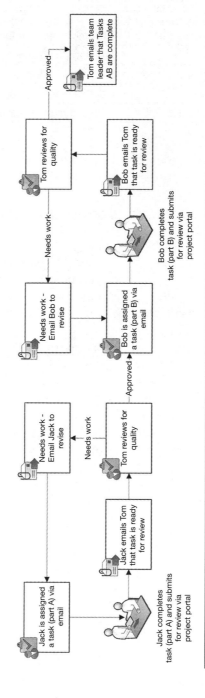

Figure 12.1   Example communication plan

UTILIZING DIVERSE SUB-TEAMS TO ACHIEVE GREATER SUCCESS

In addition to diversity in core BPI project team members, diversity in sub-teams is an excellent way to engage and provide attention to stakeholders in global locations. Stakeholders in global locations may be more comfortable communicating in their own language about a process or may simply prefer to talk to individuals who work within their office or understand their culture. By providing these stakeholders access to sub-team members that speak their language and understand them from a cultural perspective, as well as understand how they work, the BPI project core team is more likely to get the information they need.

> *Tom's core BPI project team was at a disadvantage—they were all from the United States. Stakeholders were from the United States and from Germany. In fact, more than half of the stakeholders were from Germany. His team had been trying to work with the Munich and Dusseldorf offices to document the current process and understand their challenges, but they were having difficulty doing so. All the stakeholders spoke English, so language wasn't the problem. They just didn't seem to be able to get what they needed and the meetings with stakeholders to gather information were not going well. In speaking to a colleague who had worked with the German offices on a previous BPI project, Tom learned that using sub-teams to gather the information from the employees worked out very well. They were very responsive to talking with people from their own office. Tom pulled together a sub-team of employees from both Munich and Dusseldorf who had been involved in BPI projects in the past. Within 3 days they were able to capture the information needed and had some great ideas for a few "quick wins" for the project!*

BPI projects benefit well from the deployment of sub-teams overall. Sub-teams may be teams who are comprised of process mappers, analysts, subject matter experts, and any number of individuals whose involvement in the project generates increased success of the initiative. Diverse sub-teams are certainly of value when team members need to stay involved after implementation to provide support as needed, additional training, or just mentor employees using the new process.

While, certainly, challenges exist with any team, there always seem to be more challenges with virtual teams with culturally diverse members. The savvy BPI project manager gets ahead of the challenges by being proactive and preparing ahead of time *before* the team officially begins work on the project. This is done through preparing for a team kick-off meeting where time is spent socializing with each other to build relationships among team members and collaborating on processes, procedures, and approaches to working together. While there are many challenges working with virtual, culturally diverse teams, the rewards are far greater!

SUMMARY

All projects require best practices, processes, and procedures to be followed in order to enable success of the project; BPI projects, however, require special attention above and beyond the basics. Certainly the same best practices that project managers apply to their current projects will be utilized on BPI projects. However, the most successful BPI project managers move beyond what is normally done to manage projects by adding a focus on the stakeholder.

BPI projects are all about change. If the focus is *not* on the stakeholder— the person impacted by the BPI project and the one who has to change for the project to be a success—the BPI project cannot be successful. After all, only the stakeholder can truly change their behavior and their way of working for the BPI project to be successful. Implementing a good process that meets the objectives set forth at the start of the BPI project can only be successful overall if the stakeholder will utilize that process.

Throughout this book, a variety of best practices have been provided on how to effectively manage BPI projects. This includes best practices for:

- Ensuring a complete understanding of why the BPI project is being launched—what problem is the project trying to solve.
- Socializing the BPI project at the very start to get stakeholders engaged and excited about the project.
- Working with key stakeholders (process users and process owners) to document the current *as-is* process, evaluate *could-be* options to refine or redesign the process, and design a final *to-be* process for roll out.
- Working collaboratively with stakeholders to find gaps between the current *as-is* process and the goals of the BPI project to achieve a final *to-be* process.

- Using a variety of sub-teams to assist through various phases of the project—primarily by providing support for stakeholders and assisting in keeping the project moving forward.
- Resolving conflicts and problems that arise on the team through a collaborative approach.
- Providing a variety of channels for communication between team members and between the BPI project team and stakeholders.
- Engaging stakeholders in being members of a pilot group to test the *to-be* process in a *real-world* situation.
- Keeping stakeholders engaged throughout the BPI project life cycle in a variety of ways.
- Evaluating the BPI project and measuring success—were the goals of the BPI project achieved?

Also included would be those *people-focused* skills necessary for BPI project managers to be effective when leading BPI projects.

Regardless of the reader's level of skill in project management and business process improvement, this book will have provided the reader with a number of best practices to use in the performance of his/her own job. When BPI projects are looked at from the stakeholder's point of view—the individual who is most impacted when a BPI project is undertaken—the BPI project team will do a far better job of keeping stakeholders engaged and committed to the project. Remember, without the stakeholder there is no BPI project success.

Refer to the downloadable surveys, assessments, tools, and templates available via download from the J. Ross Publishing website. These documents will facilitate more effective management of the reader's next BPI project.

Thank you for reading!

INDEX